Collection Editor: Jennifer Grünwald
Assistant Editor: Sarah Brunstad
Associate Managing Editor: Alex Starbuck
Editor, Special Projects: Mark D. Beazley
Senior Editor, Special Projects: Jeff Youngquist
SVP Print, Sales & Marketing: David Gabriel

Editor in Chief: Axel Alonso
Chief Creative Officer: Joe Quesada
Publisher: Dan Buckley
Executive Producer: Alan Fine

SPIDER-WOMAN VOL. 2: NEW DUDS. Contains material originally published in magazine form as SPIDER-WOMAN #5-10. First printing 2016. ISBN# 978-0-7851-5459-4. Published by MARVEL WORLDWIDE, IN a subsidiary of MARVEL ENTERTAINMENT, LLC. OFFICE OF PUBLICATION: 135 West 50th Street, New York, NY 10020. Copyright © 2016 MARVEL No similarity between any of the names, characters, persons, and/ institutions in this magazine with those of any living or dead person or institution is intended, and any such similarity which may exist is purely coincidental. **Printed in Canada.** ALAN FINE, President, Marvel Entertainment DAN BUCKLEY, President, TV, Publishing and Brand Management; JOE QUESADA, Chief Creative Officer; TOM BREVOORT, SVP of Publishing; DAVID BOGART, SVP of Operations & Procurement, Publishing; C.B. CEBULSK VP of International Development & Brand Management; DAVID GABRIEL, SVP Print, Sales & Marketing; JIM O'KEEFE, VP of Operations & Logistics; DAN CARR, Executive Director of Publishing Technology; SUSAN CRESI Editorial Operations Manager; ALEX MORALES, Publishing Operations Manager; STAN LEE, Chairman Emeritus. For information regarding advertising in Marvel Comics or on Marvel.com, please contact Jonatha Rheingold, VP of Custom Solutions & Ad Sales, at jrheingold@marvel.com. For Marvel subscription inquiries, please call 800-217-9158. **Manufactured between 12/4/2015 and 1/11/2016 by SOLISCO PRINTER SCOTT, QC, CANADA.**

10 9 8 7 6 5 4 3 2 1

SPIDER·WOMAN

NEW DUDS

WRITER
DENNIS HOPELESS

ISSUES #5-9
PENCILER
JAVIER RODRIGUEZ

INKER
ALVARO LOPEZ

COLORISTS
JAVIER RODRIGUEZ (5-6) & MUNTSA VICENTE (#7-9)

ISSUE #10
ARTIST
NATACHA BUSTOS

COLOR ARTIST
VERO GANDINI

LETTERER
VC'S TRAVIS LANHAM

COVER ART
JAVIER RODRIGUEZ

EDITOR
DEVIN LEWIS

SENIOR EDITOR
NICK LOWE

PREVIOUSLY

As a child, Jessica Drew fell ill with a fatal disease. To save her life, her scientist father injected her with a serum of spider blood. The injection worked, but it also gave her unbelievable spider-like powers. With this power, Jessica became Spider-Woman!

After teaming up with other Spider-Men and Women to take down the villainous Inheritors, Jessica returned to the Earth she knew, ready for a change. She quit the Avengers in order to reconnect with the normal world — and what does a new mission call for? An all-new costume!

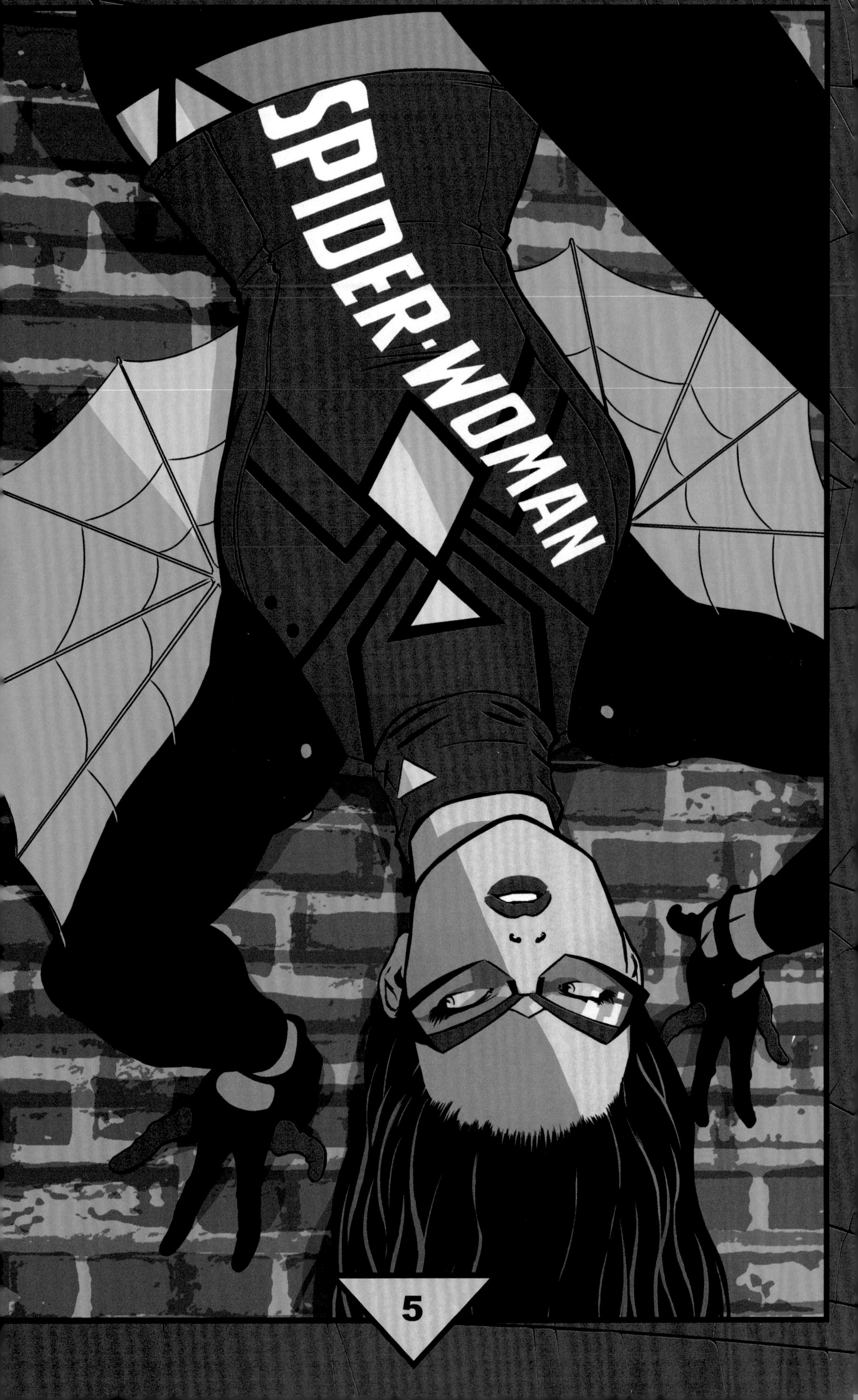
SPIDER-WOMAN
5

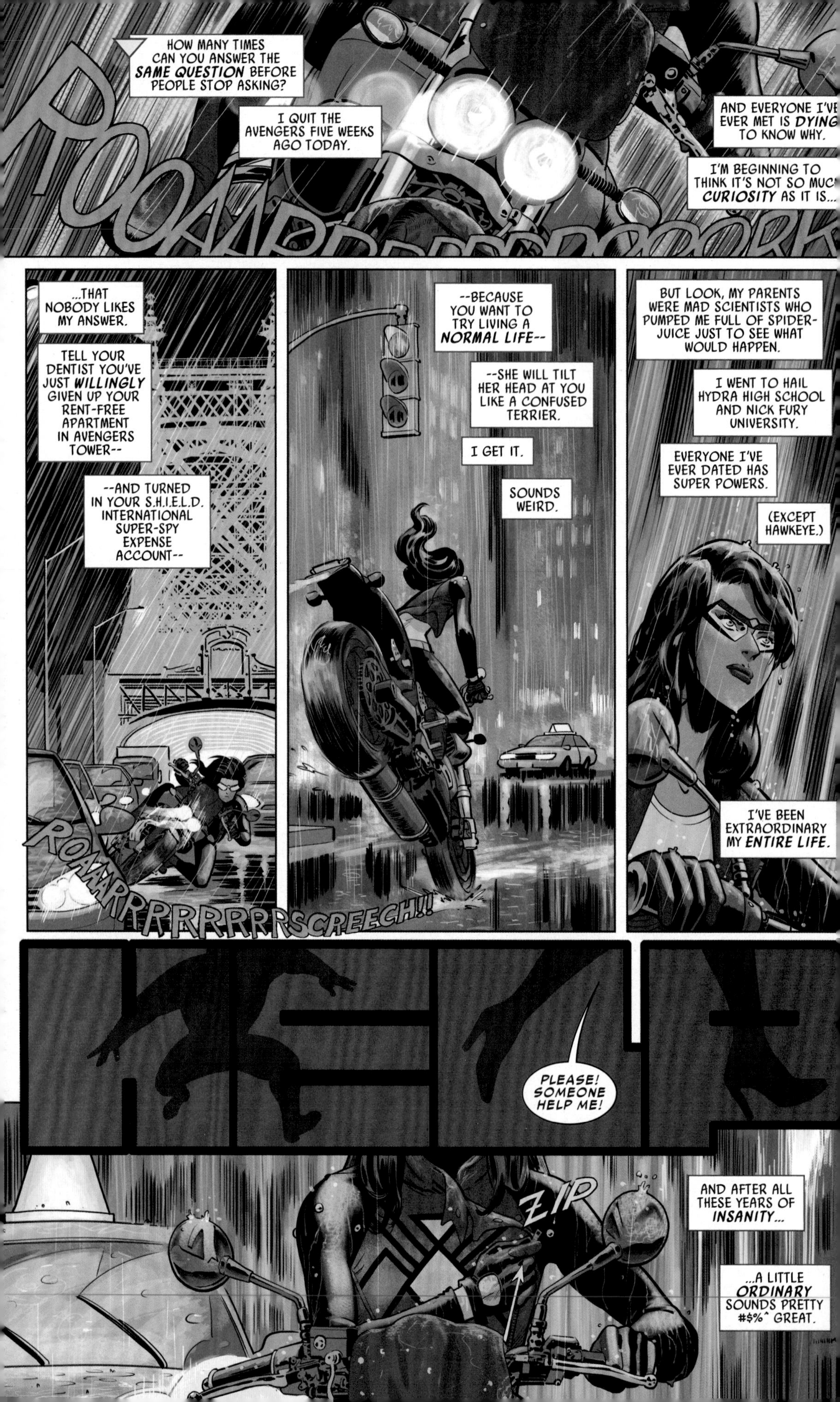

HOW MANY TIMES CAN YOU ANSWER THE SAME QUESTION BEFORE PEOPLE STOP ASKING?
I QUIT THE AVENGERS FIVE WEEKS AGO TODAY.
AND EVERYONE I'VE EVER MET IS DYING TO KNOW WHY.
I'M BEGINNING TO THINK IT'S NOT SO MUCH CURIOSITY AS IT IS...
ROOAARRRRRRRROOOORK
...THAT NOBODY LIKES MY ANSWER.
TELL YOUR DENTIST YOU'VE JUST WILLINGLY GIVEN UP YOUR RENT-FREE APARTMENT IN AVENGERS TOWER--
--AND TURNED IN YOUR S.H.I.E.L.D. INTERNATIONAL SUPER-SPY EXPENSE ACCOUNT--
ROAAARRRRRRRRRSCREECH!!
--BECAUSE YOU WANT TO TRY LIVING A NORMAL LIFE--
--SHE WILL TILT HER HEAD AT YOU LIKE A CONFUSED TERRIER.
I GET IT.
SOUNDS WEIRD.
BUT LOOK, MY PARENTS WERE MAD SCIENTISTS WHO PUMPED ME FULL OF SPIDER-JUICE JUST TO SEE WHAT WOULD HAPPEN.
I WENT TO HAIL HYDRA HIGH SCHOOL AND NICK FURY UNIVERSITY.
EVERYONE I'VE EVER DATED HAS SUPER POWERS.
(EXCEPT HAWKEYE.)
I'VE BEEN EXTRAORDINARY MY ENTIRE LIFE.
HELP
PLEASE! SOMEONE HELP ME!
ZIP
AND AFTER ALL THESE YEARS OF INSANITY...
...A LITTLE ORDINARY SOUNDS PRETTY #$%^ GREAT.

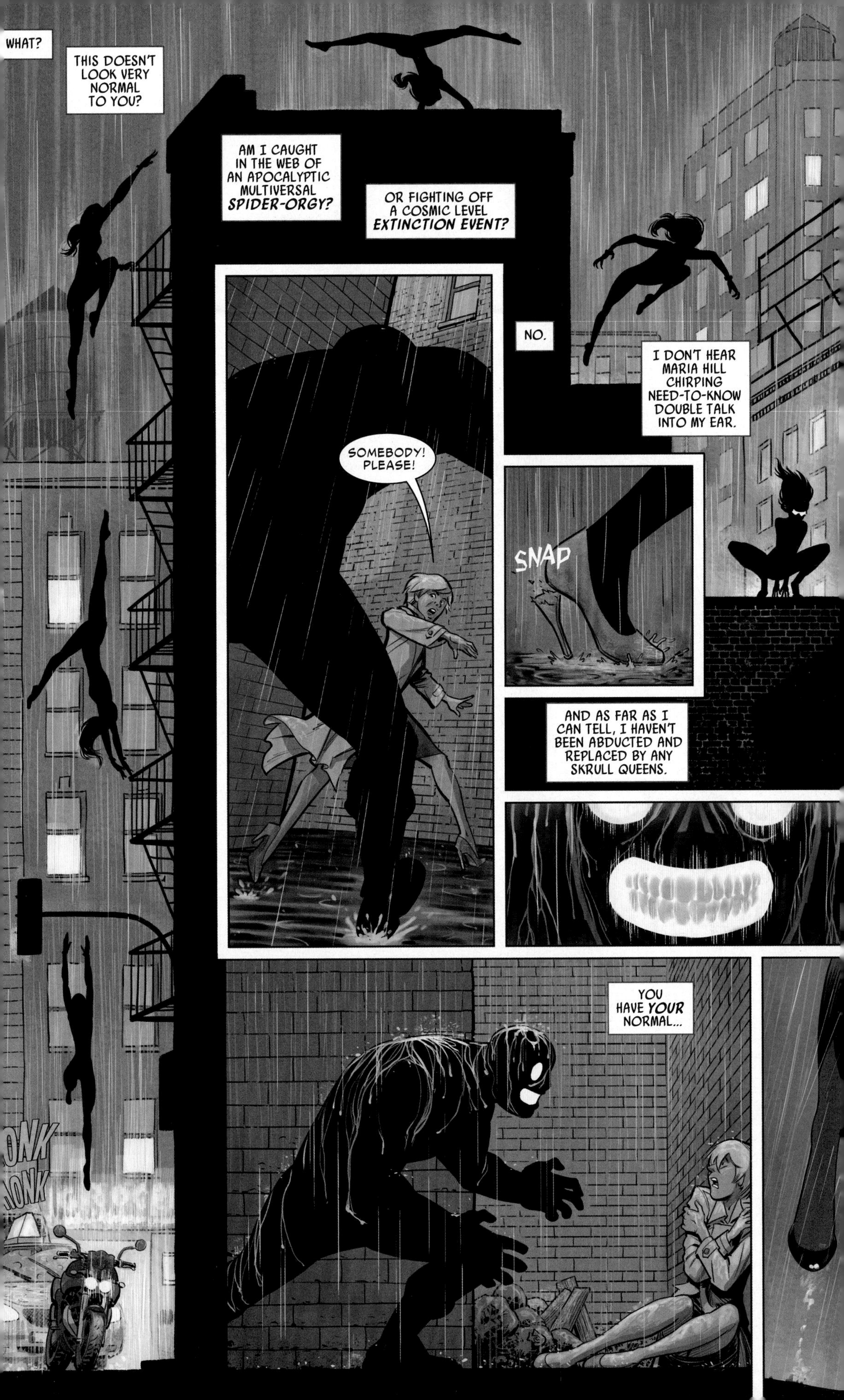
WHAT?
THIS DOESN'T LOOK VERY NORMAL TO YOU?
AM I CAUGHT IN THE WEB OF AN APOCALYPTIC MULTIVERSAL SPIDER-ORGY?
OR FIGHTING OFF A COSMIC LEVEL EXTINCTION EVENT?
NO.
I DON'T HEAR MARIA HILL CHIRPING NEED-TO-KNOW DOUBLE TALK INTO MY EAR.
SOMEBODY! PLEASE!
SNAP
AND AS FAR AS I CAN TELL, I HAVEN'T BEEN ABDUCTED AND REPLACED BY ANY SKRULL QUEENS.
YOU HAVE YOUR NORMAL...

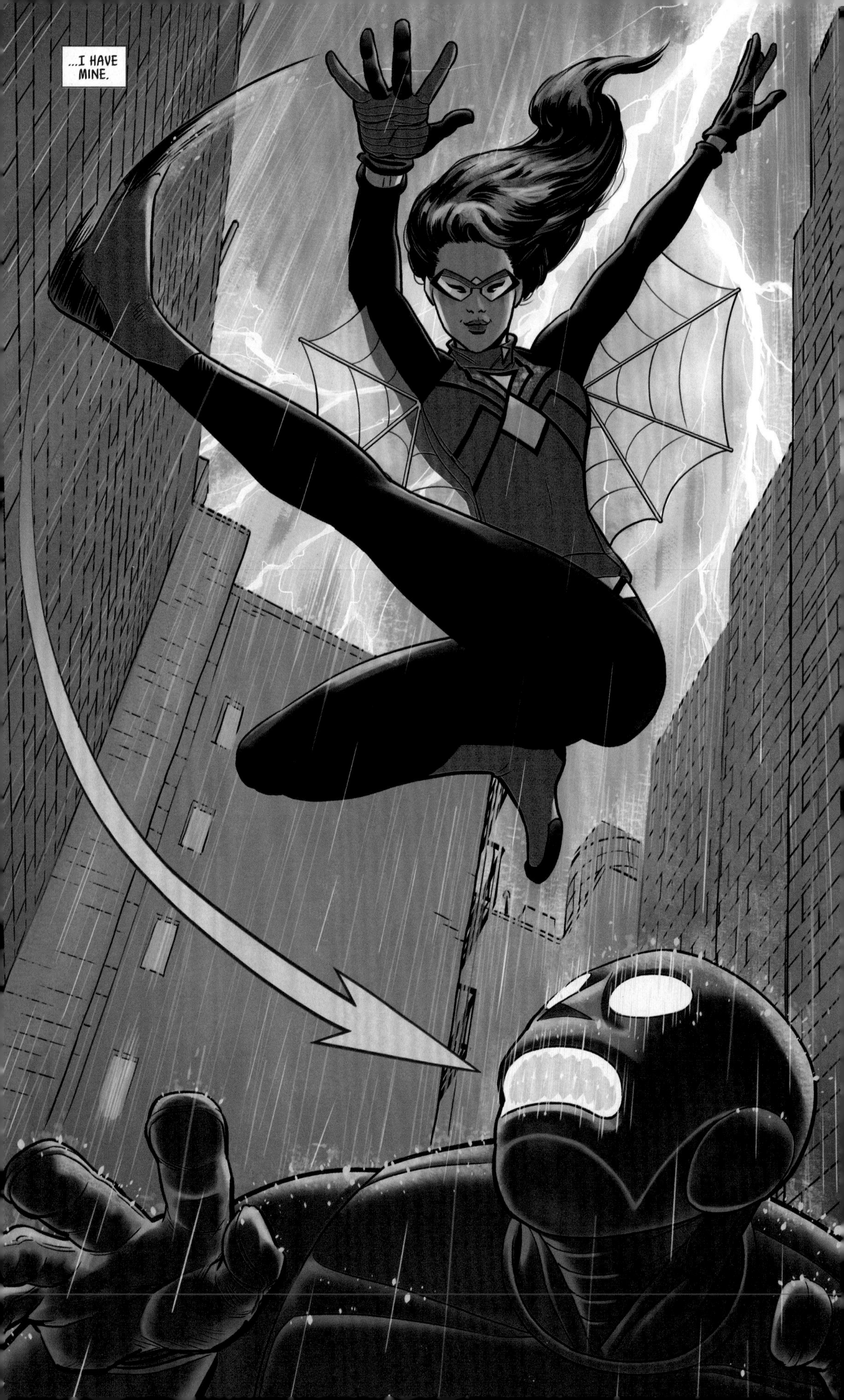
...I HAVE
MINE.

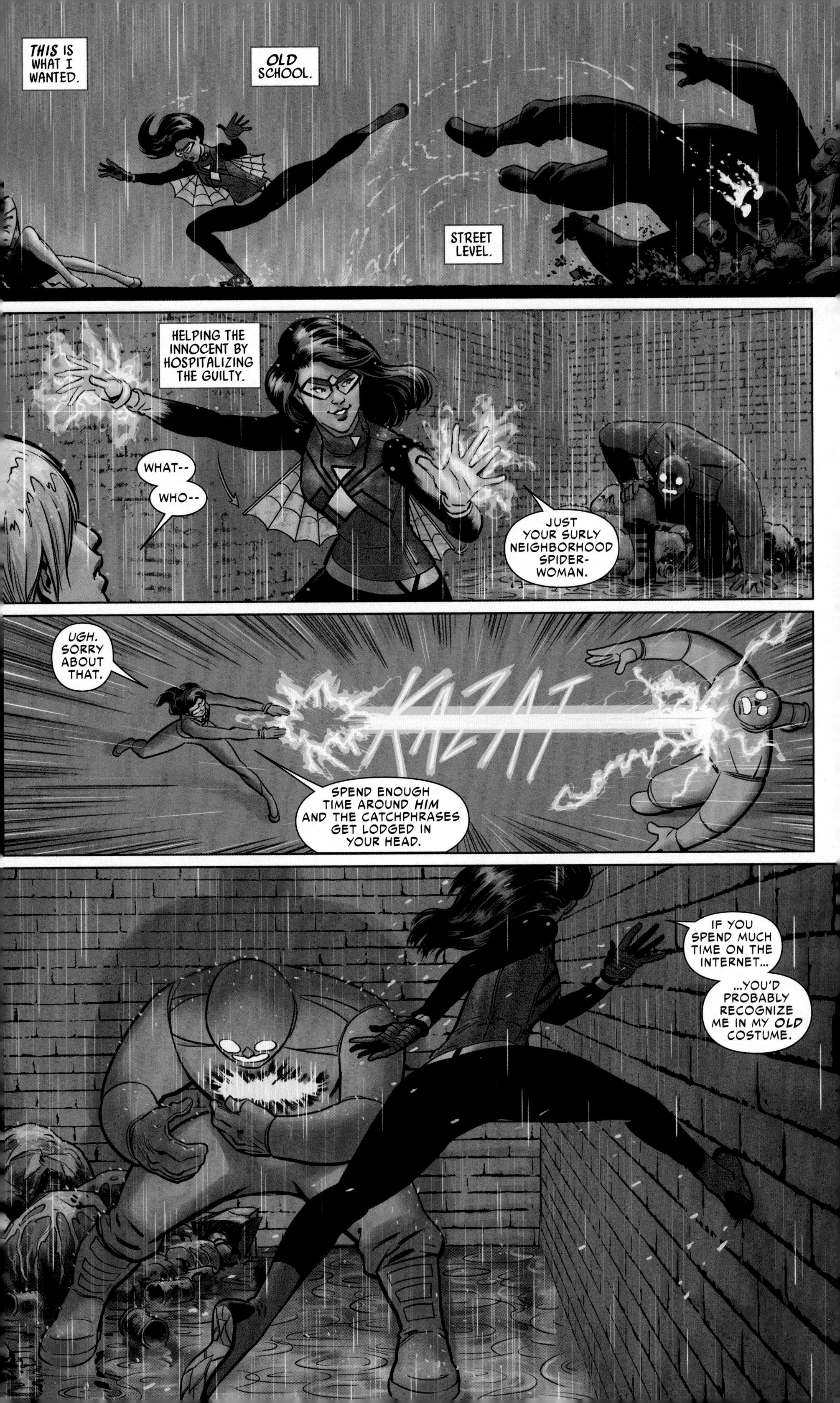
THIS IS WHAT I WANTED.
OLD SCHOOL.
STREET LEVEL.
HELPING THE INNOCENT BY HOSPITALIZING THE GUILTY.
WHAT--
WHO--
JUST YOUR SURLY NEIGHBORHOOD SPIDER-WOMAN.
UGH. SORRY ABOUT THAT.
KAZAT
SPEND ENOUGH TIME AROUND HIM AND THE CATCHPHRASES GET LODGED IN YOUR HEAD.
IF YOU SPEND MUCH TIME ON THE INTERNET...
...YOU'D PROBABLY RECOGNIZE ME IN MY OLD COSTUME.

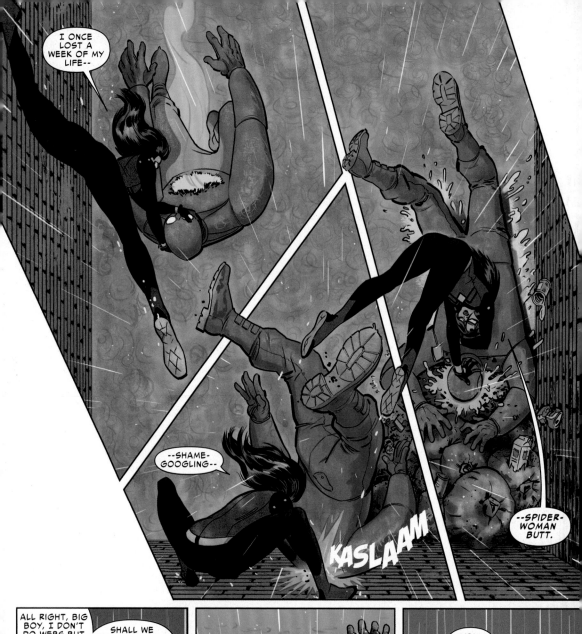

I ONCE LOST A WEEK OF MY LIFE--

--SHAME-GOOGLING--

--SPIDER-WOMAN BUTT.

KASLAAM

ALL RIGHT, BIG BOY, I DON'T DO WEBS BUT I'VE GOT A LOAD OF ZIP TIES HERE--

SHALL WE TRY OUR HANDS AT THE OL' STRAP A BADDIE TO THE STREETLIGHT AND--

POLICE

--PHONE THE... ...POLICE?

YOU CAN PROBABLY SKIP THE PHONE CALL--

KA-CHUK

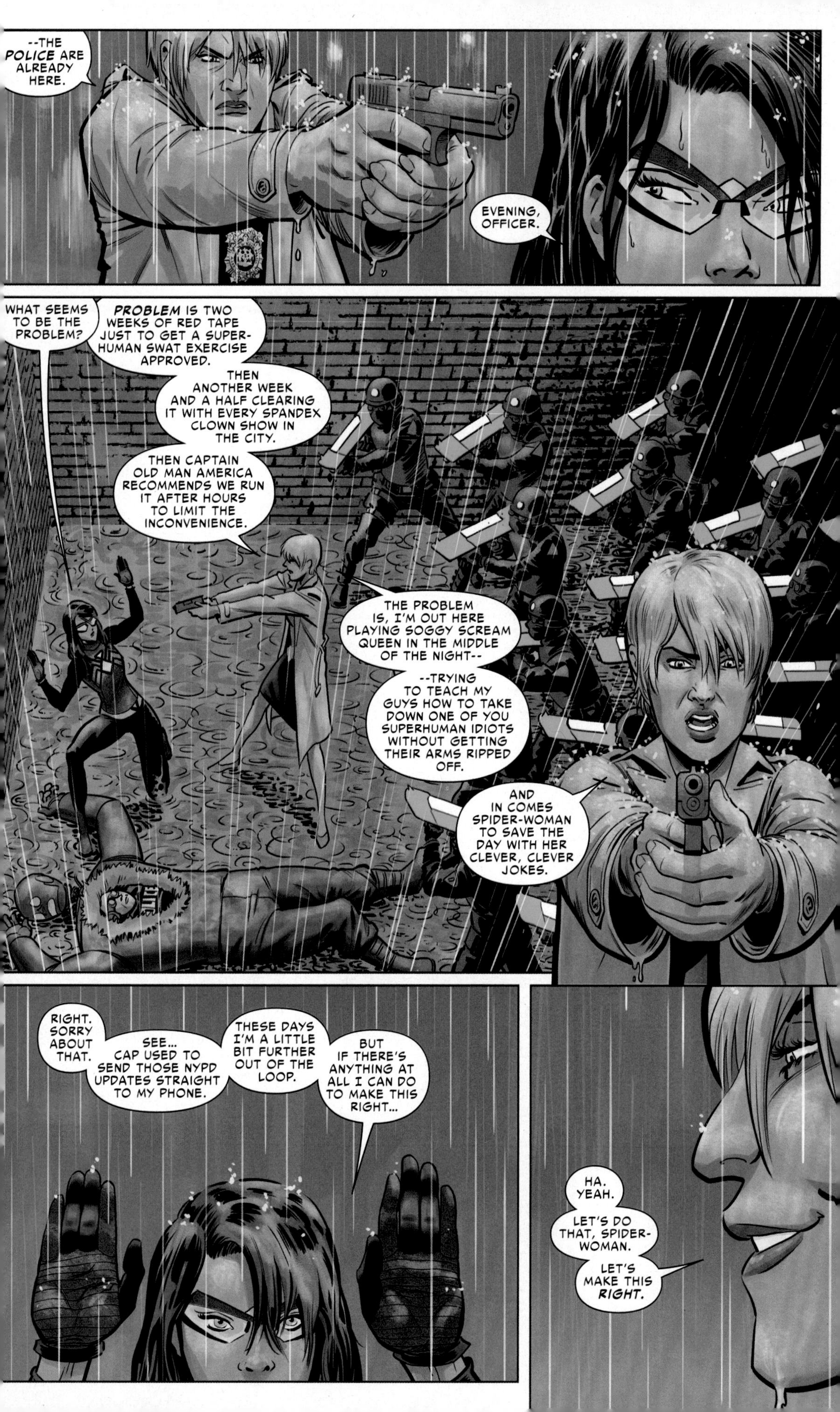

--THE *POLICE* ARE ALREADY HERE.
EVENING, OFFICER.
WHAT SEEMS TO BE THE PROBLEM?
PROBLEM IS TWO WEEKS OF RED TAPE JUST TO GET A SUPER-HUMAN SWAT EXERCISE APPROVED.
THEN ANOTHER WEEK AND A HALF CLEARING IT WITH EVERY SPANDEX CLOWN SHOW IN THE CITY.
THEN CAPTAIN OLD MAN AMERICA RECOMMENDS WE RUN IT AFTER HOURS TO LIMIT THE INCONVENIENCE.
THE PROBLEM IS, I'M OUT HERE PLAYING SOGGY SCREAM QUEEN IN THE MIDDLE OF THE NIGHT--
--TRYING TO TEACH MY GUYS HOW TO TAKE DOWN ONE OF YOU SUPERHUMAN IDIOTS WITHOUT GETTING THEIR ARMS RIPPED OFF.
AND IN COMES SPIDER-WOMAN TO SAVE THE DAY WITH HER CLEVER, CLEVER JOKES.
RIGHT. SORRY ABOUT THAT.
SEE... CAP USED TO SEND THOSE NYPD UPDATES STRAIGHT TO MY PHONE.
THESE DAYS I'M A LITTLE BIT FURTHER OUT OF THE LOOP.
BUT IF THERE'S ANYTHING AT ALL I CAN DO TO MAKE THIS RIGHT...
HA. YEAH.
LET'S DO THAT, SPIDER-WOMAN.
LET'S MAKE THIS *RIGHT*.

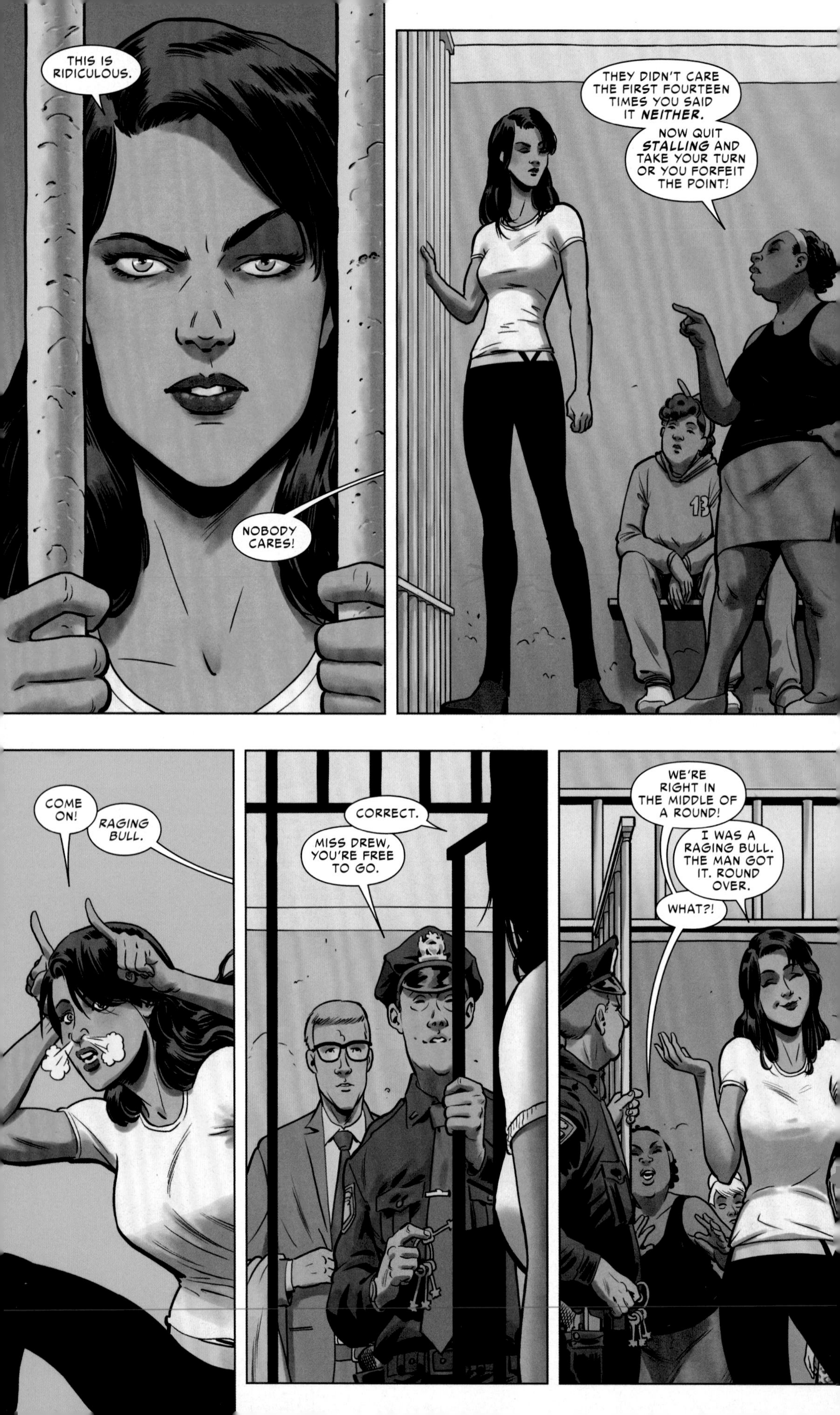
THIS IS RIDICULOUS.
NOBODY CARES!
THEY DIDN'T CARE THE FIRST FOURTEEN TIMES YOU SAID IT NEITHER.
NOW QUIT STALLING AND TAKE YOUR TURN OR YOU FORFEIT THE POINT!
COME ON!
RAGING BULL.
CORRECT.
MISS DREW, YOU'RE FREE TO GO.
WE'RE RIGHT IN THE MIDDLE OF A ROUND!
I WAS A RAGING BULL. THE MAN GOT IT. ROUND OVER.
WHAT?!

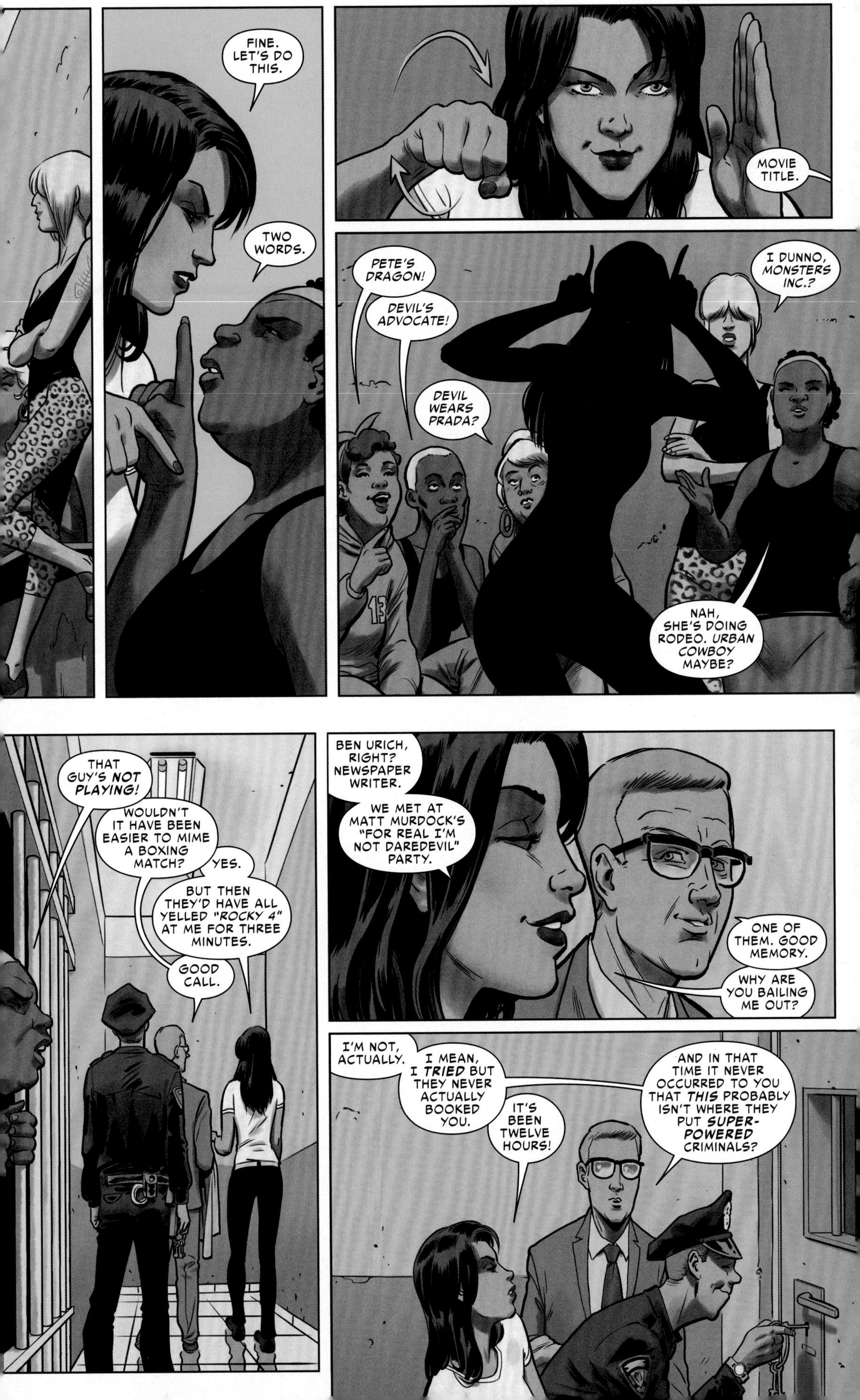
FINE. LET'S DO THIS.
TWO WORDS.
MOVIE TITLE.
PETE'S DRAGON!
DEVIL'S ADVOCATE!
DEVIL WEARS PRADA?
I DUNNO, MONSTERS INC.?
NAH, SHE'S DOING RODEO. URBAN COWBOY MAYBE?
THAT GUY'S NOT PLAYING!
WOULDN'T IT HAVE BEEN EASIER TO MIME A BOXING MATCH?
YES.
BUT THEN THEY'D HAVE ALL YELLED "ROCKY 4" AT ME FOR THREE MINUTES.
GOOD CALL.
BEN URICH, RIGHT? NEWSPAPER WRITER.
WE MET AT MATT MURDOCK'S "FOR REAL I'M NOT DAREDEVIL" PARTY.
ONE OF THEM. GOOD MEMORY.
WHY ARE YOU BAILING ME OUT?
I'M NOT, ACTUALLY.
I MEAN, I TRIED BUT THEY NEVER ACTUALLY BOOKED YOU.
IT'S BEEN TWELVE HOURS!
AND IN THAT TIME IT NEVER OCCURRED TO YOU THAT THIS PROBABLY ISN'T WHERE THEY PUT SUPER-POWERED CRIMINALS?

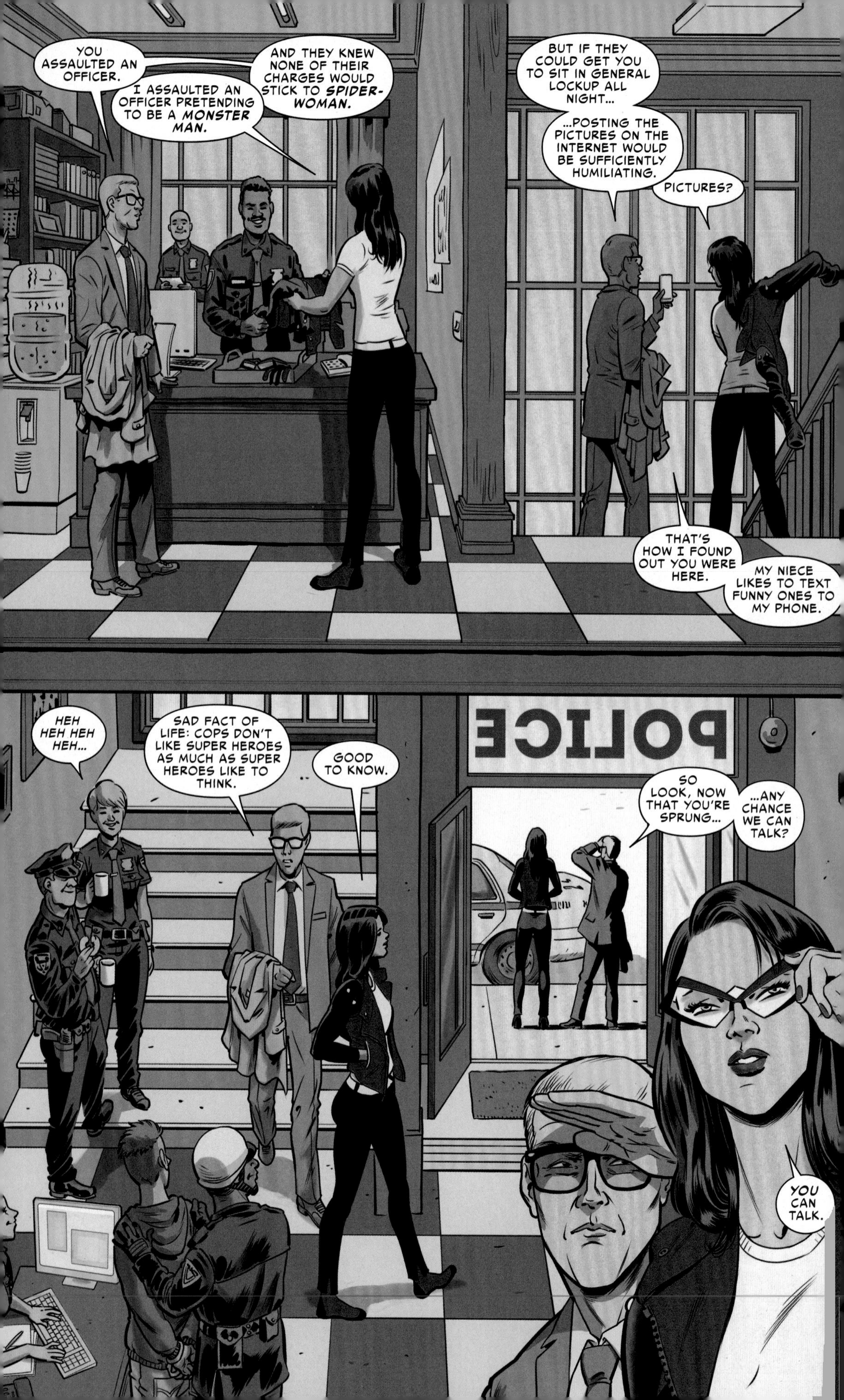
YOU ASSAULTED AN OFFICER.
I ASSAULTED AN OFFICER PRETENDING TO BE A MONSTER MAN.
AND THEY KNEW NONE OF THEIR CHARGES WOULD STICK TO SPIDER-WOMAN.
BUT IF THEY COULD GET YOU TO SIT IN GENERAL LOCKUP ALL NIGHT...
...POSTING THE PICTURES ON THE INTERNET WOULD BE SUFFICIENTLY HUMILIATING.
PICTURES?
THAT'S HOW I FOUND OUT YOU WERE HERE.
MY NIECE LIKES TO TEXT FUNNY ONES TO MY PHONE.
HEH HEH HEH HEH...
SAD FACT OF LIFE: COPS DON'T LIKE SUPER HEROES AS MUCH AS SUPER HEROES LIKE TO THINK.
GOOD TO KNOW.
POLICE
SO LOOK, NOW THAT YOU'RE SPRUNG...
...ANY CHANCE WE CAN TALK?
YOU CAN TALK.

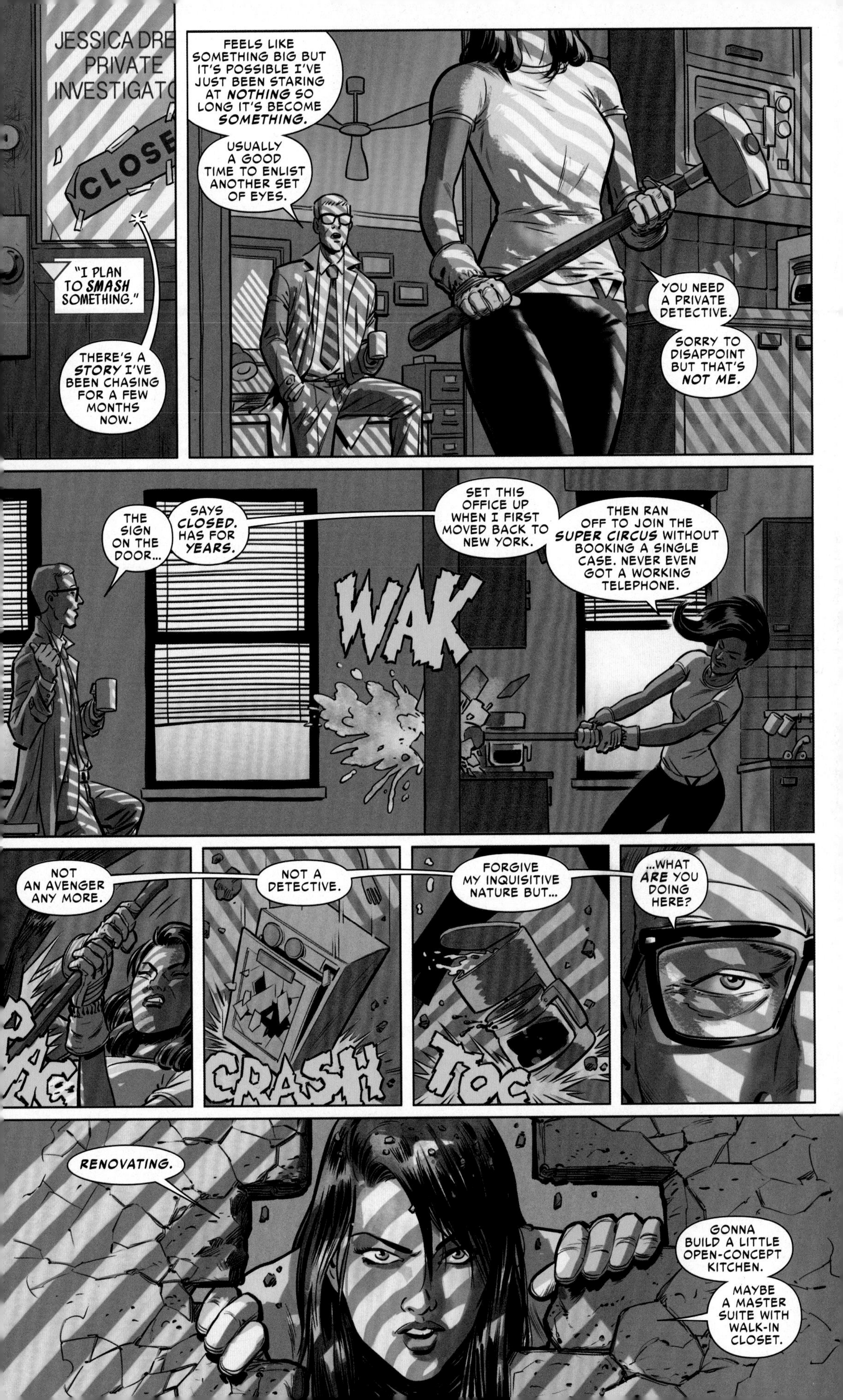

JESSICA DRE
PRIVATE
INVESTIGATO
CLOSE
"I PLAN TO SMASH SOMETHING."
THERE'S A STORY I'VE BEEN CHASING FOR A FEW MONTHS NOW.
FEELS LIKE SOMETHING BIG BUT IT'S POSSIBLE I'VE JUST BEEN STARING AT NOTHING SO LONG IT'S BECOME SOMETHING.
USUALLY A GOOD TIME TO ENLIST ANOTHER SET OF EYES.
YOU NEED A PRIVATE DETECTIVE.
SORRY TO DISAPPOINT BUT THAT'S NOT ME.
THE SIGN ON THE DOOR...
SAYS CLOSED. HAS FOR YEARS.
SET THIS OFFICE UP WHEN I FIRST MOVED BACK TO NEW YORK.
THEN RAN OFF TO JOIN THE SUPER CIRCUS WITHOUT BOOKING A SINGLE CASE. NEVER EVEN GOT A WORKING TELEPHONE.
WAK
NOT AN AVENGER ANY MORE.
NOT A DETECTIVE.
CRASH
FORGIVE MY INQUISITIVE NATURE BUT...
TOC
...WHAT ARE YOU DOING HERE?
RENOVATING.
GONNA BUILD A LITTLE OPEN-CONCEPT KITCHEN.
MAYBE A MASTER SUITE WITH WALK-IN CLOSET.

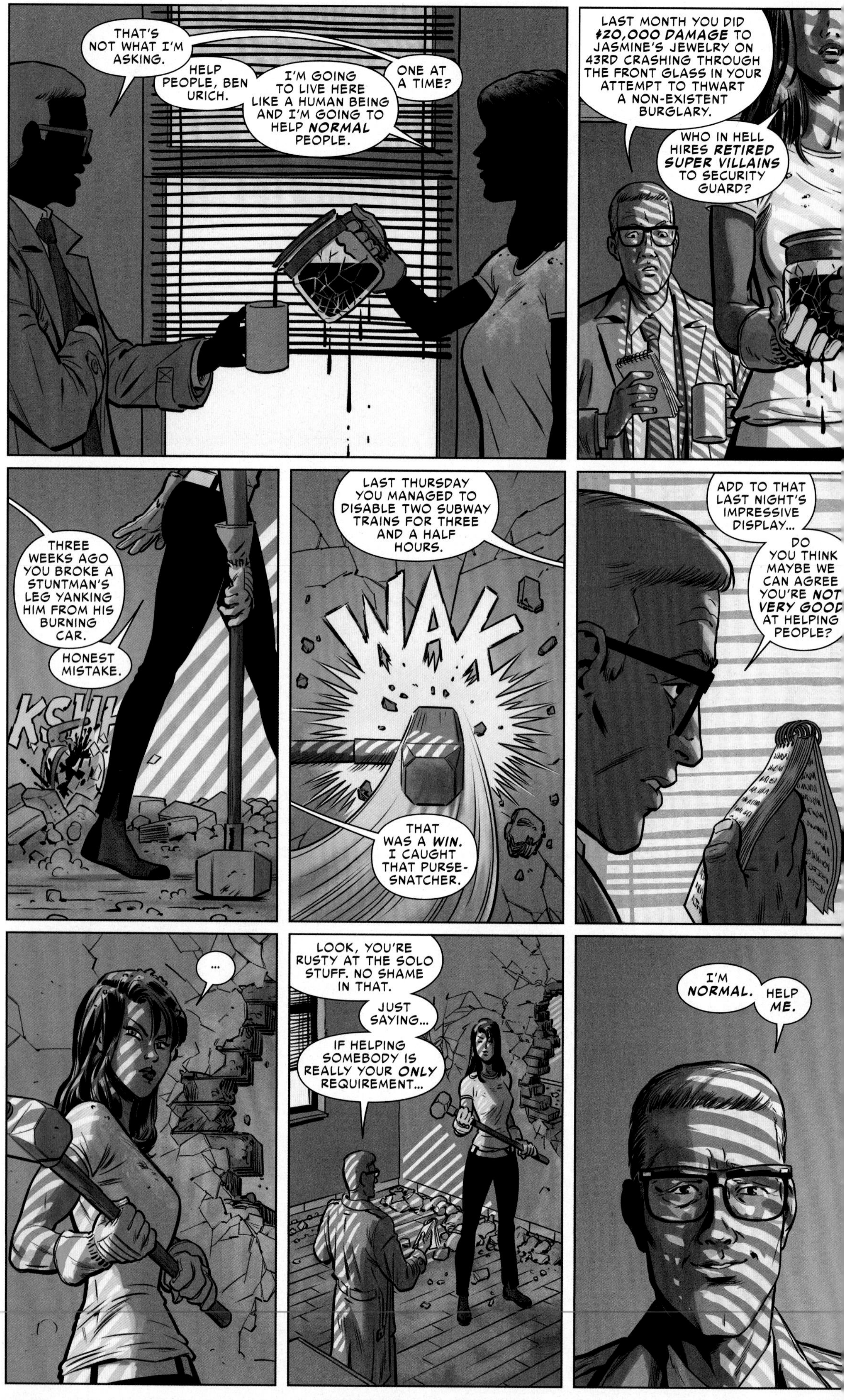
THAT'S NOT WHAT I'M ASKING.
HELP PEOPLE, BEN URICH.
I'M GOING TO LIVE HERE LIKE A HUMAN BEING AND I'M GOING TO HELP NORMAL PEOPLE.
ONE AT A TIME?
LAST MONTH YOU DID $20,000 DAMAGE TO JASMINE'S JEWELRY ON 43RD CRASHING THROUGH THE FRONT GLASS IN YOUR ATTEMPT TO THWART A NON-EXISTENT BURGLARY.
WHO IN HELL HIRES RETIRED SUPER VILLAINS TO SECURITY GUARD?
THREE WEEKS AGO YOU BROKE A STUNTMAN'S LEG YANKING HIM FROM HIS BURNING CAR.
HONEST MISTAKE.
KSHH
LAST THURSDAY YOU MANAGED TO DISABLE TWO SUBWAY TRAINS FOR THREE AND A HALF HOURS.
WAK
THAT WAS A WIN. I CAUGHT THAT PURSE-SNATCHER.
ADD TO THAT LAST NIGHT'S IMPRESSIVE DISPLAY...
DO YOU THINK MAYBE WE CAN AGREE YOU'RE NOT VERY GOOD AT HELPING PEOPLE?
...
LOOK, YOU'RE RUSTY AT THE SOLO STUFF. NO SHAME IN THAT.
JUST SAYING...
IF HELPING SOMEBODY IS REALLY YOUR ONLY REQUIREMENT...
I'M NORMAL.
HELP ME.

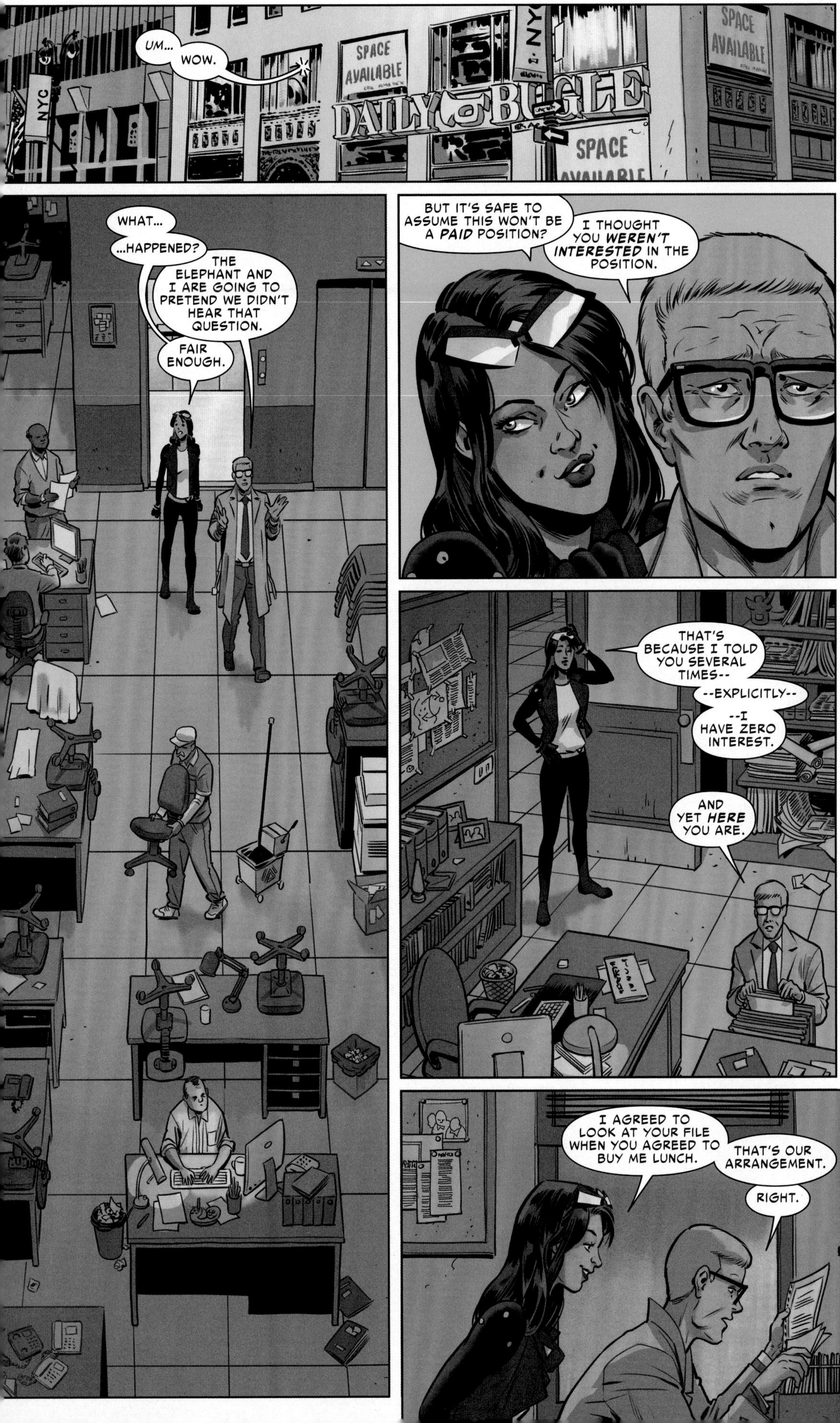

UM...
WOW.
SPACE AVAILABLE
DAILY BUGLE
SPACE AVAILABLE
SPACE
NYC
WHAT...
...HAPPENED?
THE ELEPHANT AND I ARE GOING TO PRETEND WE DIDN'T HEAR THAT QUESTION.
FAIR ENOUGH.
BUT IT'S SAFE TO ASSUME THIS WON'T BE A *PAID* POSITION?
I THOUGHT YOU ***WEREN'T INTERESTED*** IN THE POSITION.
THAT'S BECAUSE I TOLD YOU SEVERAL TIMES--
--EXPLICITLY--
--I HAVE ZERO INTEREST.
AND YET ***HERE*** YOU ARE.
I AGREED TO LOOK AT YOUR FILE WHEN YOU AGREED TO BUY ME LUNCH.
THAT'S OUR ARRANGEMENT.
RIGHT.

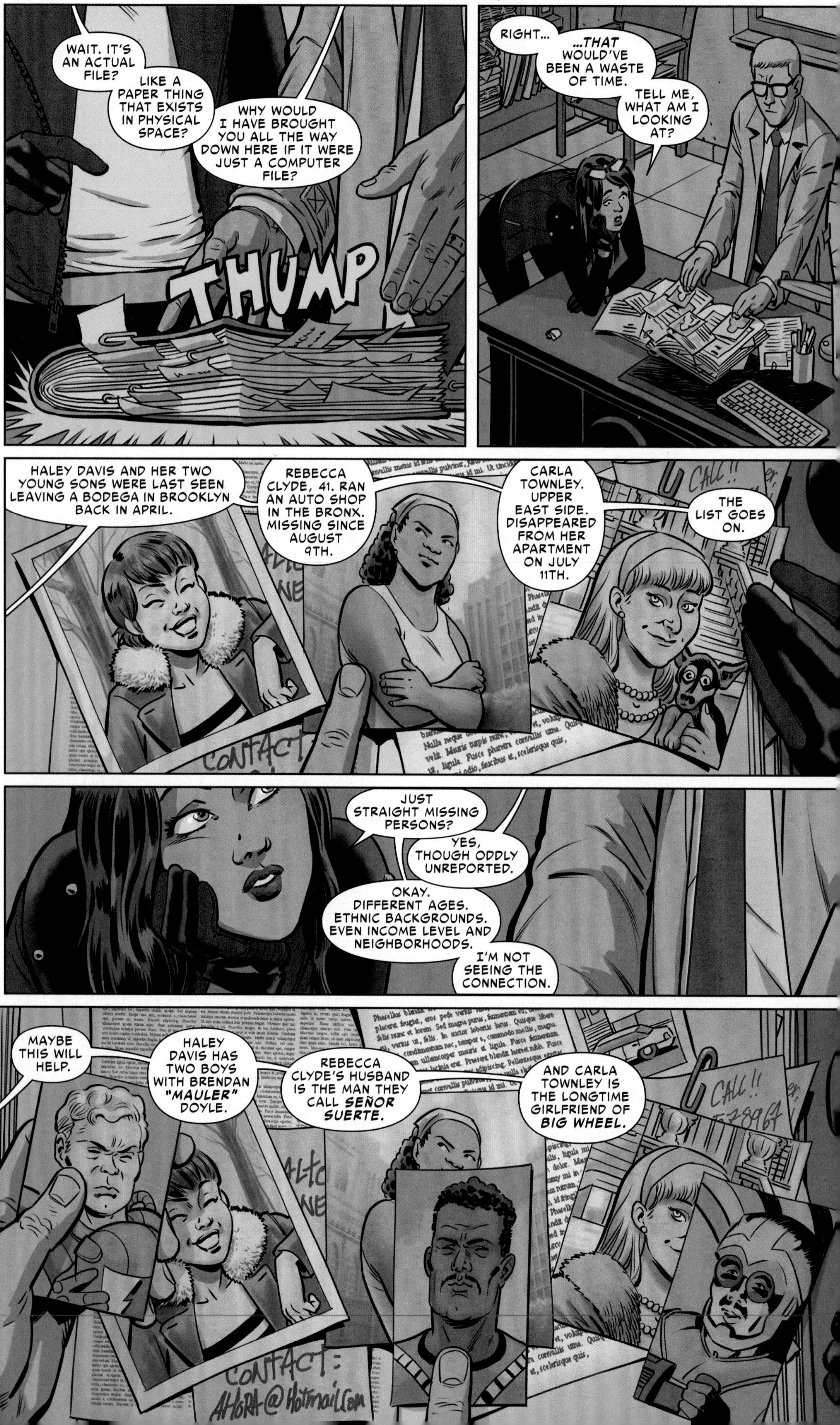
WAIT. IT'S AN ACTUAL FILE?
LIKE A PAPER THING THAT EXISTS IN PHYSICAL SPACE?
WHY WOULD I HAVE BROUGHT YOU ALL THE WAY DOWN HERE IF IT WERE JUST A COMPUTER FILE?
THUMP
RIGHT...
...THAT WOULD'VE BEEN A WASTE OF TIME.
TELL ME, WHAT AM I LOOKING AT?
HALEY DAVIS AND HER TWO YOUNG SONS WERE LAST SEEN LEAVING A BODEGA IN BROOKLYN BACK IN APRIL.
REBECCA CLYDE, 41. RAN AN AUTO SHOP IN THE BRONX. MISSING SINCE AUGUST 9TH.
CARLA TOWNLEY. UPPER EAST SIDE. DISAPPEARED FROM HER APARTMENT ON JULY 11TH.
THE LIST GOES ON.
CALL!!
CONTACT
JUST STRAIGHT MISSING PERSONS?
YES, THOUGH ODDLY UNREPORTED.
OKAY. DIFFERENT AGES. ETHNIC BACKGROUNDS. EVEN INCOME LEVEL AND NEIGHBORHOODS.
I'M NOT SEEING THE CONNECTION.
MAYBE THIS WILL HELP.
HALEY DAVIS HAS TWO BOYS WITH BRENDAN "MAULER" DOYLE.
REBECCA CLYDE'S HUSBAND IS THE MAN THEY CALL SEÑOR SUERTE.
AND CARLA TOWNLEY IS THE LONGTIME GIRLFRIEND OF BIG WHEEL.
CALL!!
CONTACT:
AHORA@Hotmail.com

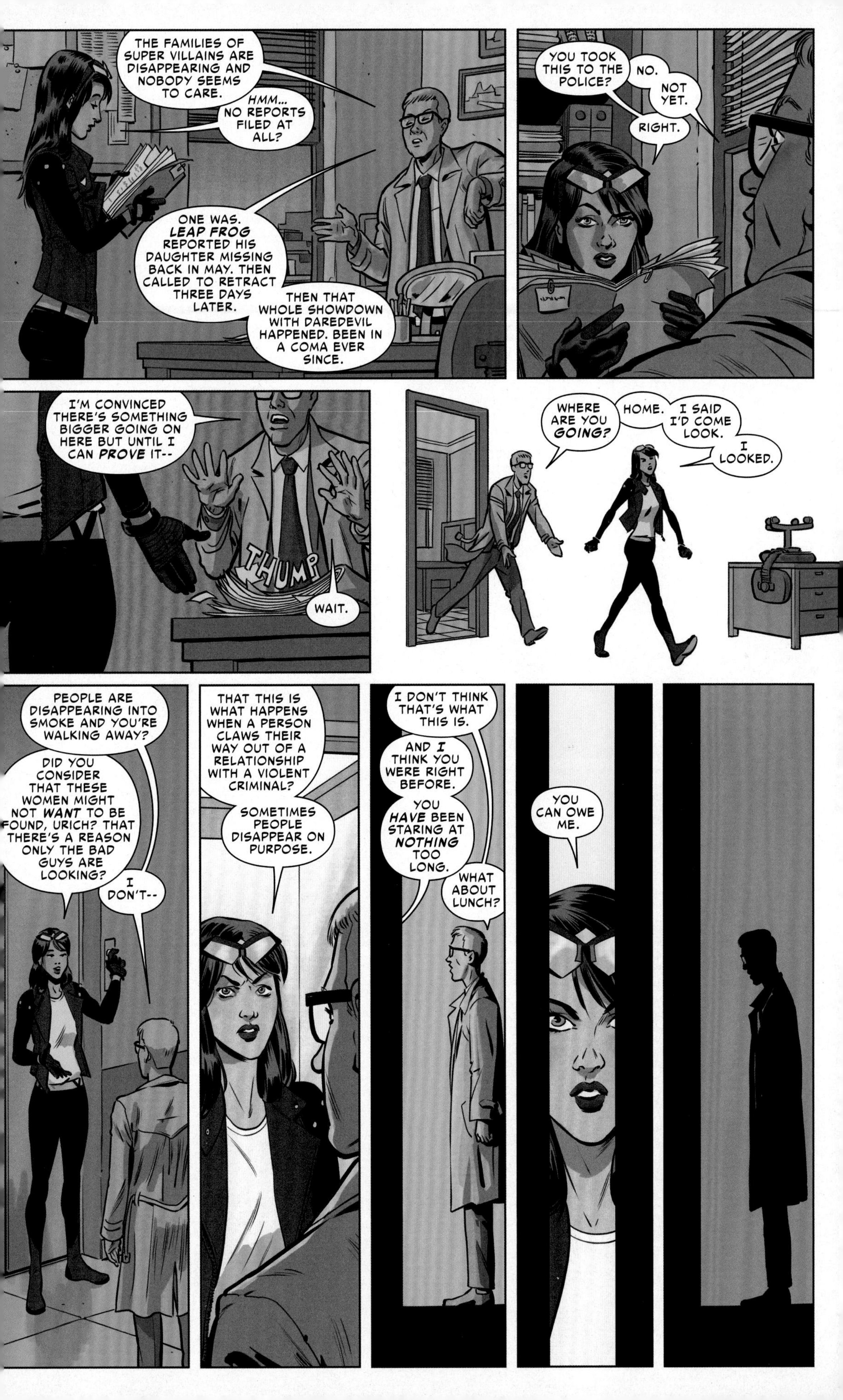

THE FAMILIES OF SUPER VILLAINS ARE DISAPPEARING AND NOBODY SEEMS TO CARE.
HMM... NO REPORTS FILED AT ALL?
ONE WAS. LEAP FROG REPORTED HIS DAUGHTER MISSING BACK IN MAY. THEN CALLED TO RETRACT THREE DAYS LATER.
THEN THAT WHOLE SHOWDOWN WITH DAREDEVIL HAPPENED. BEEN IN A COMA EVER SINCE.
YOU TOOK THIS TO THE POLICE?
NO.
NOT YET.
RIGHT.
I'M CONVINCED THERE'S SOMETHING BIGGER GOING ON HERE BUT UNTIL I CAN PROVE IT--
THUMP
WAIT.
WHERE ARE YOU GOING?
HOME.
I SAID I'D COME LOOK.
I LOOKED.
PEOPLE ARE DISAPPEARING INTO SMOKE AND YOU'RE WALKING AWAY?
DID YOU CONSIDER THAT THESE WOMEN MIGHT NOT WANT TO BE FOUND, URICH? THAT THERE'S A REASON ONLY THE BAD GUYS ARE LOOKING?
I DON'T--
THAT THIS IS WHAT HAPPENS WHEN A PERSON CLAWS THEIR WAY OUT OF A RELATIONSHIP WITH A VIOLENT CRIMINAL?
SOMETIMES PEOPLE DISAPPEAR ON PURPOSE.
I DON'T THINK THAT'S WHAT THIS IS.
AND I THINK YOU WERE RIGHT BEFORE.
YOU HAVE BEEN STARING AT NOTHING TOO LONG.
WHAT ABOUT LUNCH?
YOU CAN OWE ME.

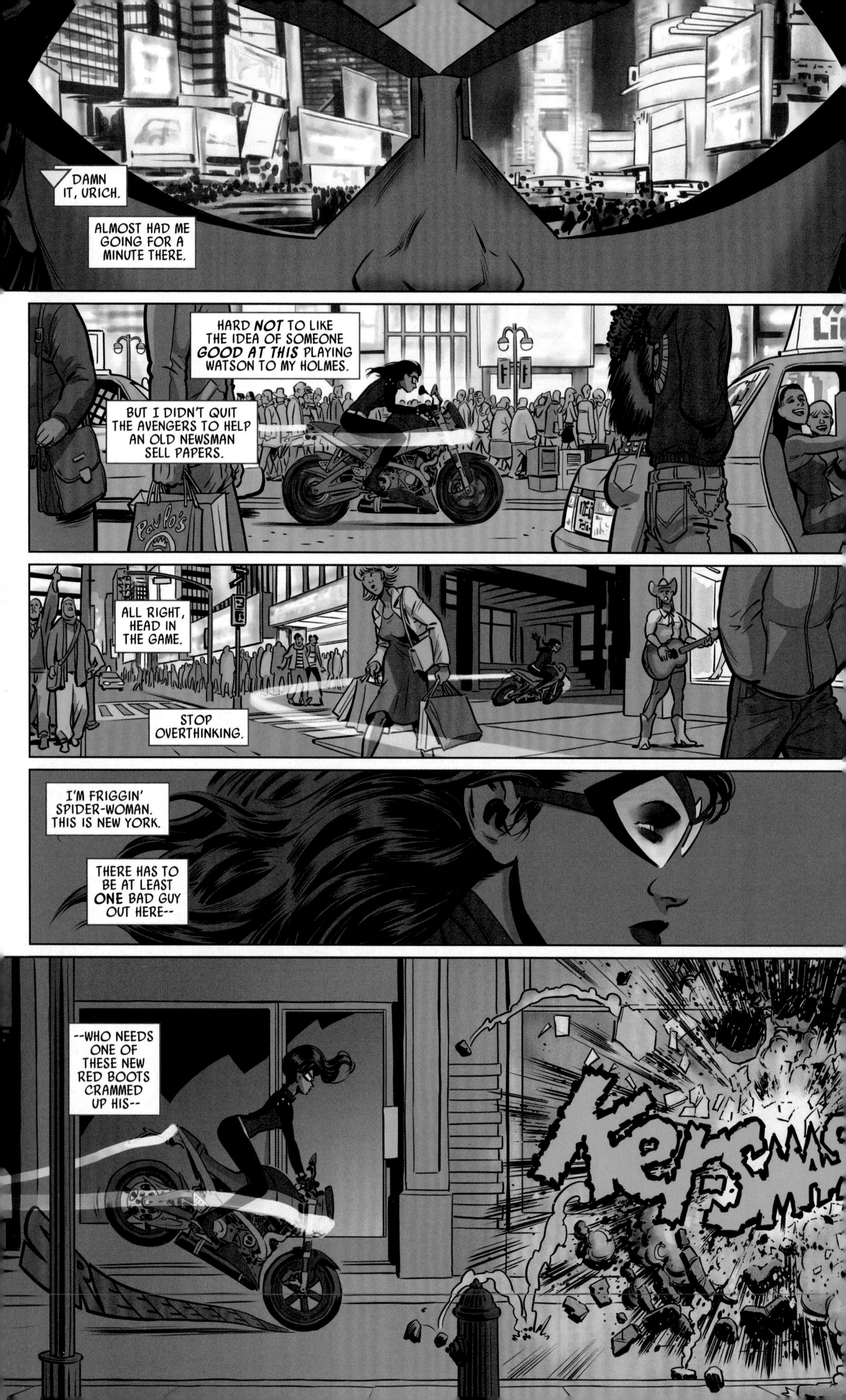
DAMN IT, URICH.
ALMOST HAD ME GOING FOR A MINUTE THERE--
HARD NOT TO LIKE THE IDEA OF SOMEONE GOOD AT THIS PLAYING WATSON TO MY HOLMES.
BUT I DIDN'T QUIT THE AVENGERS TO HELP AN OLD NEWSMAN SELL PAPERS.
ALL RIGHT, HEAD IN THE GAME.
STOP OVERTHINKING.
I'M FRIGGIN' SPIDER-WOMAN. THIS IS NEW YORK.
THERE HAS TO BE AT LEAST ONE BAD GUY OUT HERE--
--WHO NEEDS ONE OF THESE NEW RED BOOTS CRAMMED UP HIS--

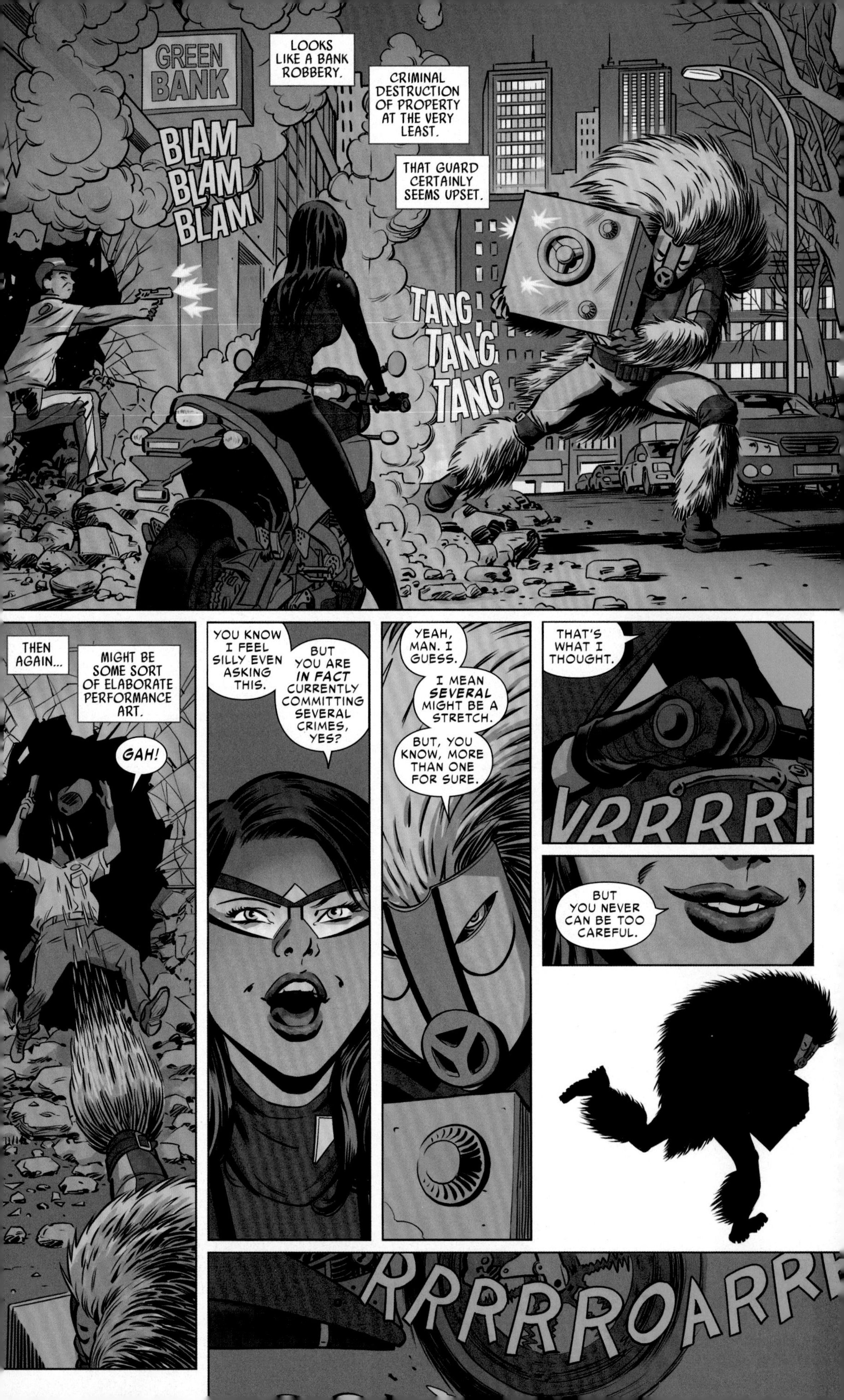
GREEN BANK
LOOKS LIKE A BANK ROBBERY.
CRIMINAL DESTRUCTION OF PROPERTY AT THE VERY LEAST.
THAT GUARD CERTAINLY SEEMS UPSET.
BLAM BLAM BLAM
TANG TANG TANG
THEN AGAIN...
MIGHT BE SOME SORT OF ELABORATE PERFORMANCE ART.
GAH!
YOU KNOW I FEEL SILLY EVEN ASKING THIS.
BUT YOU ARE *IN FACT* CURRENTLY COMMITTING SEVERAL CRIMES, YES?
YEAH, MAN. I GUESS.
I MEAN ***SEVERAL*** MIGHT BE A STRETCH.
BUT, YOU KNOW, MORE THAN ONE FOR SURE.
THAT'S WHAT I THOUGHT.
VRRRRR
BUT YOU NEVER CAN BE TOO CAREFUL.
RRRRROARRR

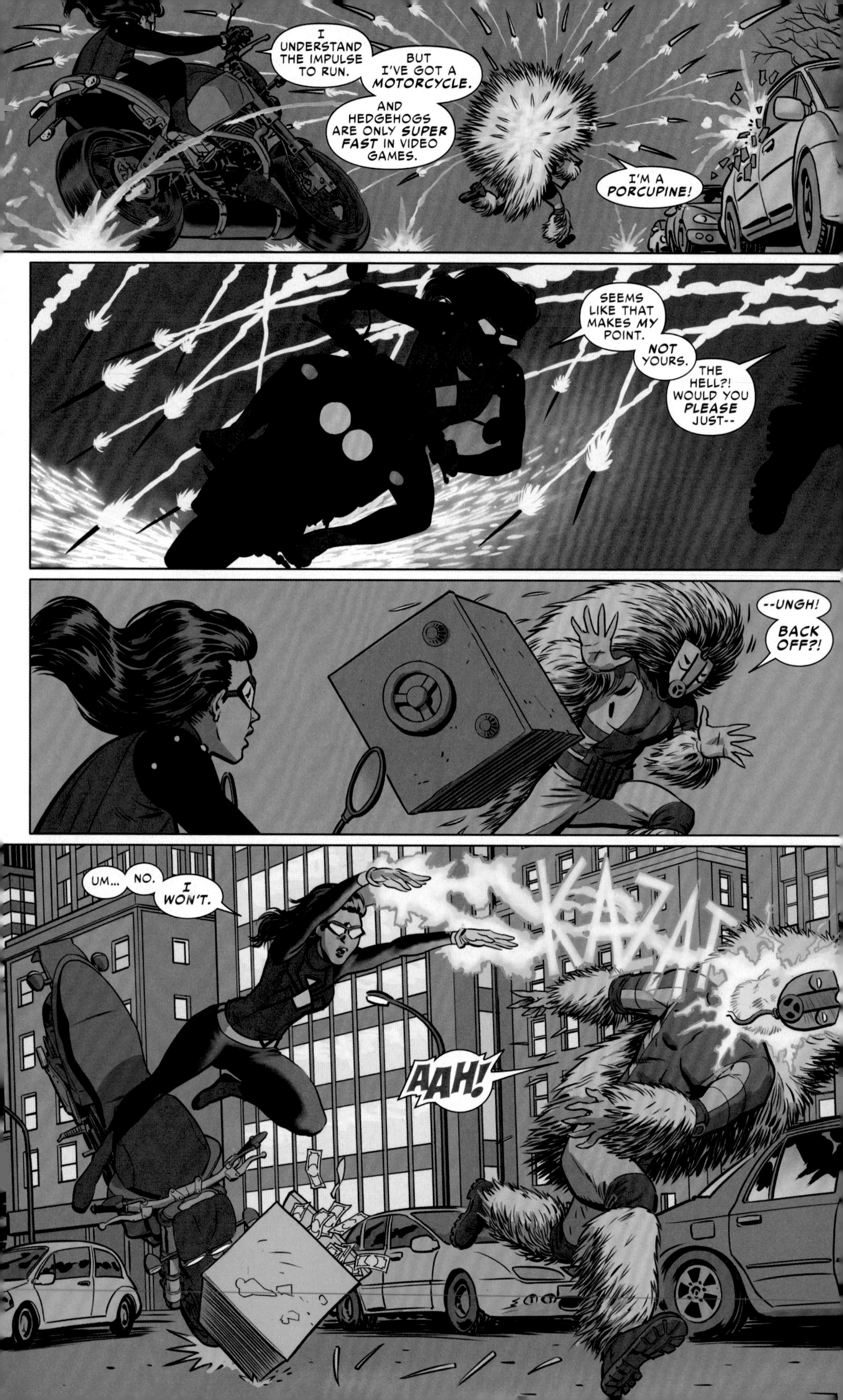
I UNDERSTAND THE IMPULSE TO RUN.
BUT I'VE GOT A MOTORCYCLE.
AND HEDGEHOGS ARE ONLY SUPER FAST IN VIDEO GAMES.
I'M A PORCUPINE!
SEEMS LIKE THAT MAKES MY POINT.
NOT YOURS.
THE HELL?! WOULD YOU PLEASE JUST--
--UNGH!
BACK OFF?!
UM... NO.
I WON'T.
KAZAT!
AAH!

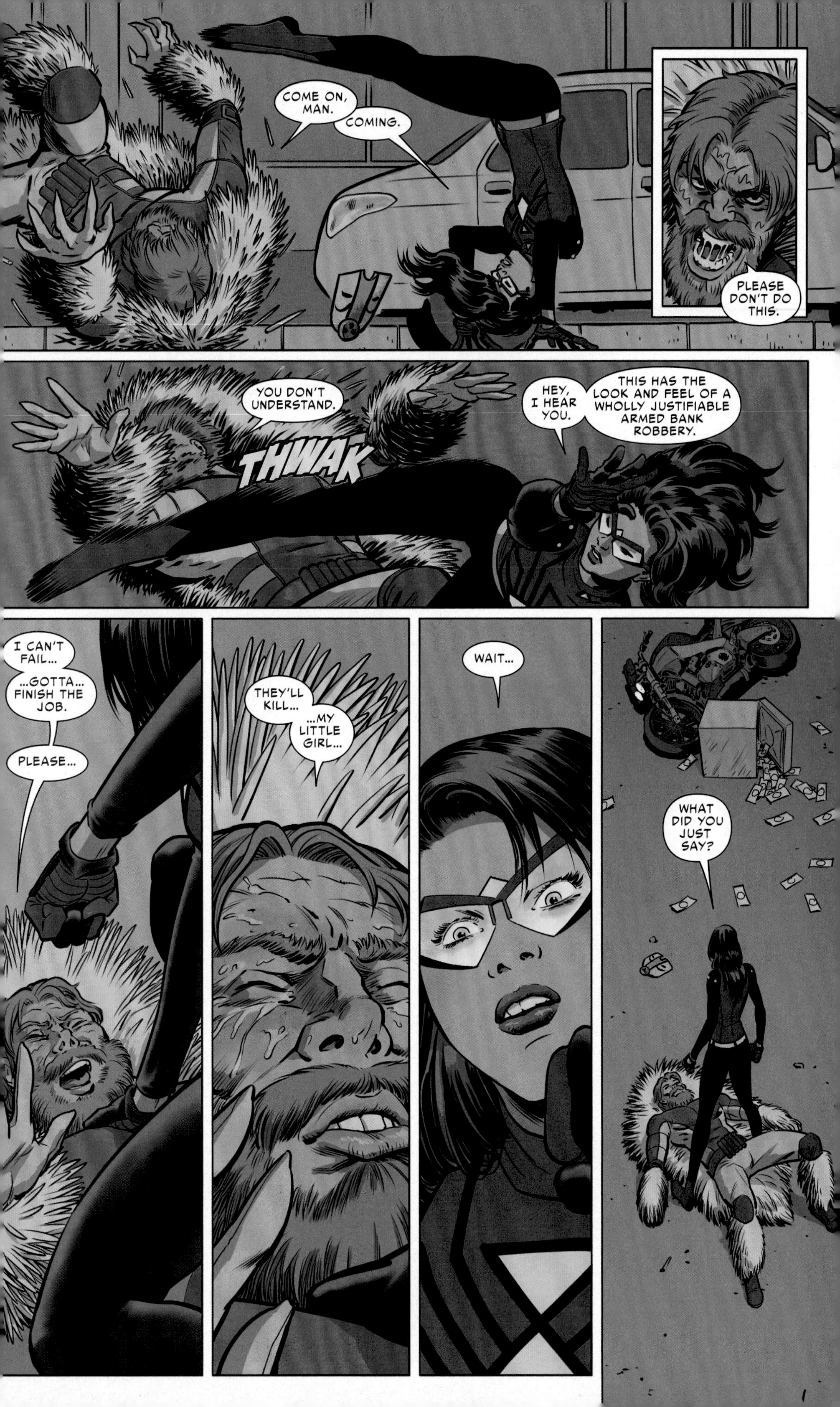
COME ON, MAN.
COMING.
PLEASE DON'T DO THIS.
YOU DON'T UNDERSTAND.
THWAK
HEY, I HEAR YOU.
THIS HAS THE LOOK AND FEEL OF A WHOLLY JUSTIFIABLE ARMED BANK ROBBERY.
I CAN'T FAIL...
...GOTTA... FINISH THE JOB.
PLEASE...
THEY'LL KILL...
...MY LITTLE GIRL...
WAIT...
WHAT DID YOU JUST SAY?

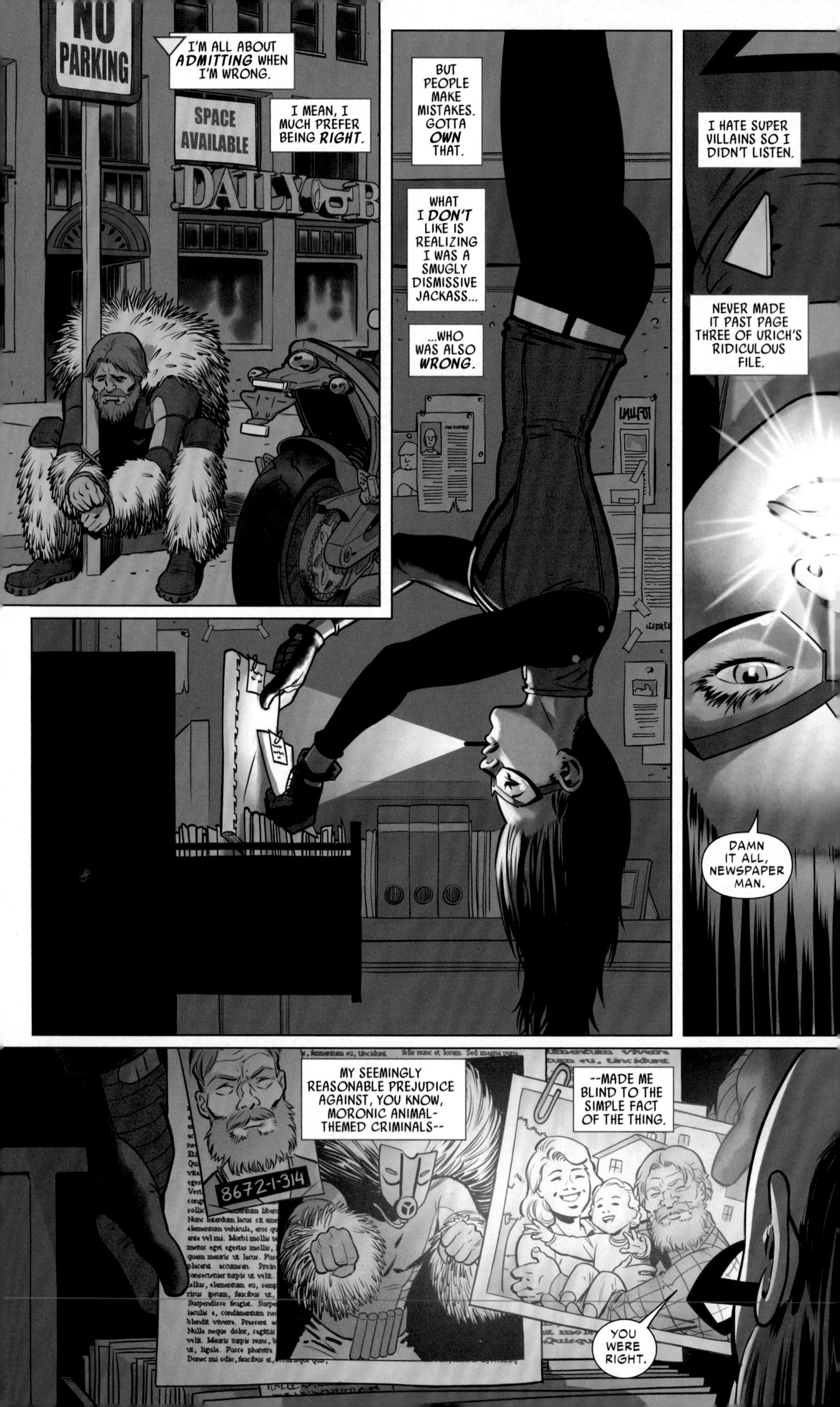
NO PARKING
SPACE AVAILABLE
I'M ALL ABOUT ADMITTING WHEN I'M WRONG.
I MEAN, I MUCH PREFER BEING RIGHT.
BUT PEOPLE MAKE MISTAKES. GOTTA OWN THAT.
WHAT I DON'T LIKE IS REALIZING I WAS A SMUGLY DISMISSIVE JACKASS...
...WHO WAS ALSO WRONG.
I HATE SUPER VILLAINS SO I DIDN'T LISTEN.
NEVER MADE IT PAST PAGE THREE OF URICH'S RIDICULOUS FILE.
DAMN IT ALL, NEWSPAPER MAN.
MY SEEMINGLY REASONABLE PREJUDICE AGAINST, YOU KNOW, MORONIC ANIMAL-THEMED CRIMINALS--
--MADE ME BLIND TO THE SIMPLE FACT OF THE THING.
8672-1-314
YOU WERE RIGHT.

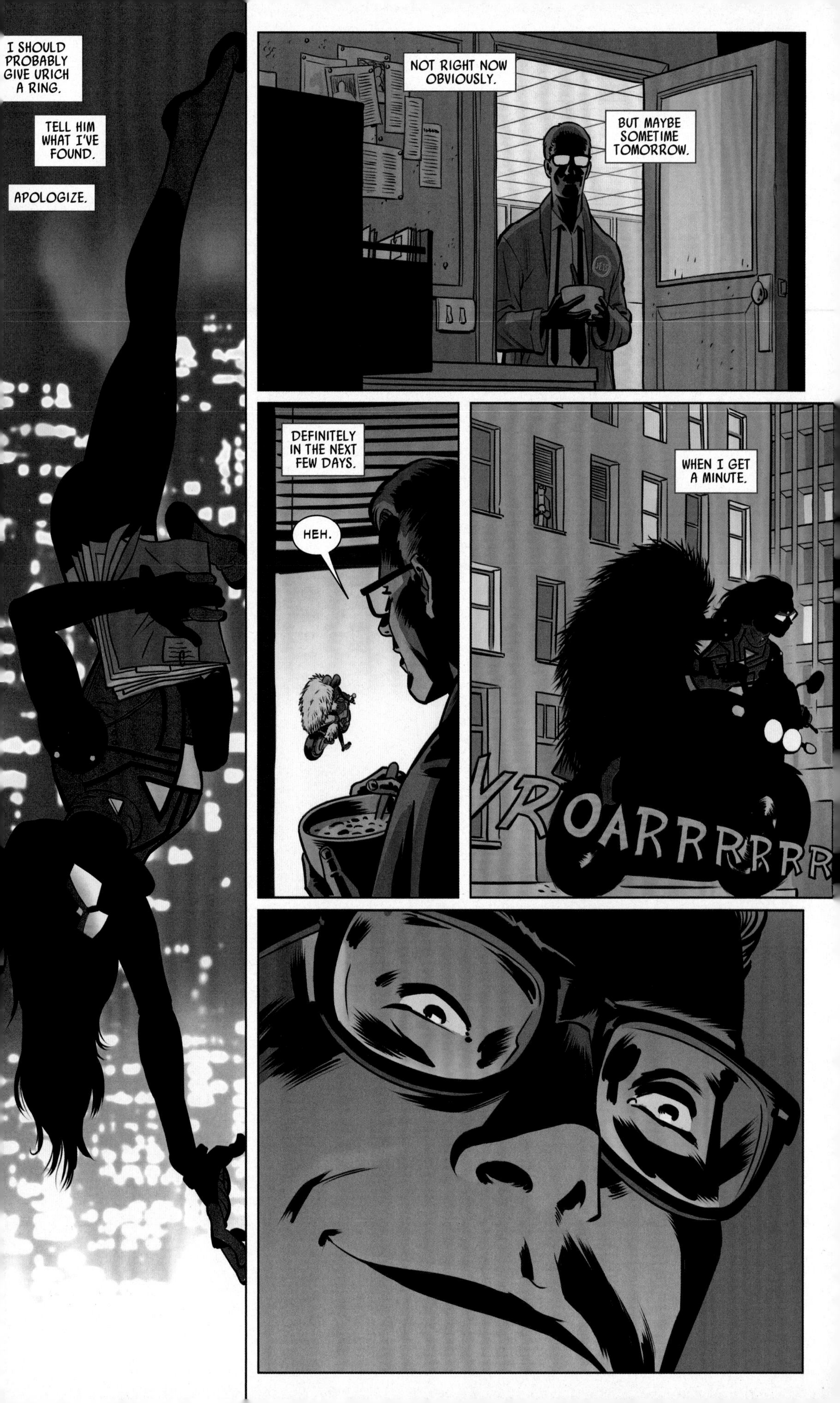
I SHOULD PROBABLY GIVE URICH A RING.
TELL HIM WHAT I'VE FOUND.
APOLOGIZE.
NOT RIGHT NOW OBVIOUSLY.
BUT MAYBE SOMETIME TOMORROW.
DEFINITELY IN THE NEXT FEW DAYS.
HEH.
WHEN I GET A MINUTE.
VROARRRRRR

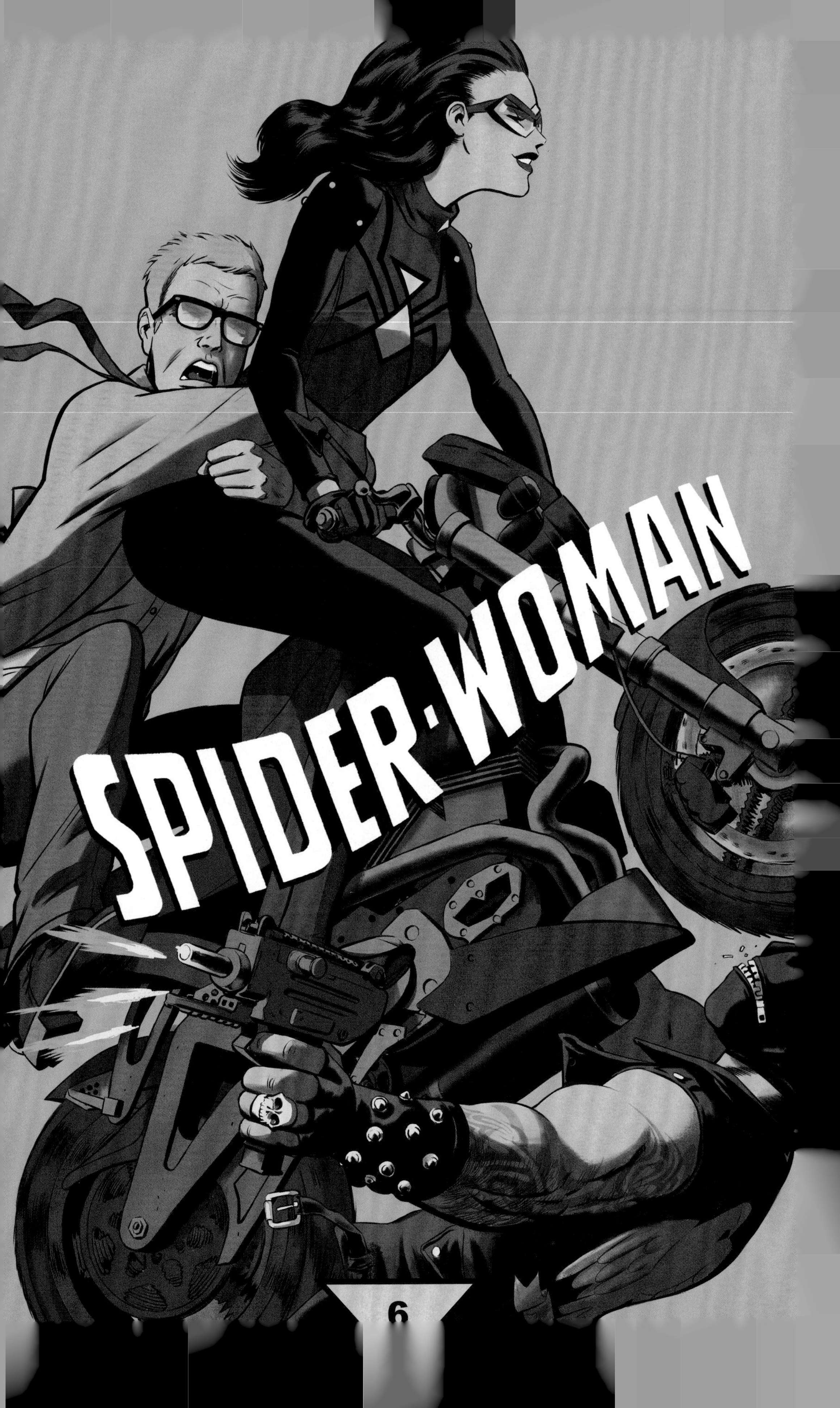
SPIDER-WOMAN
6

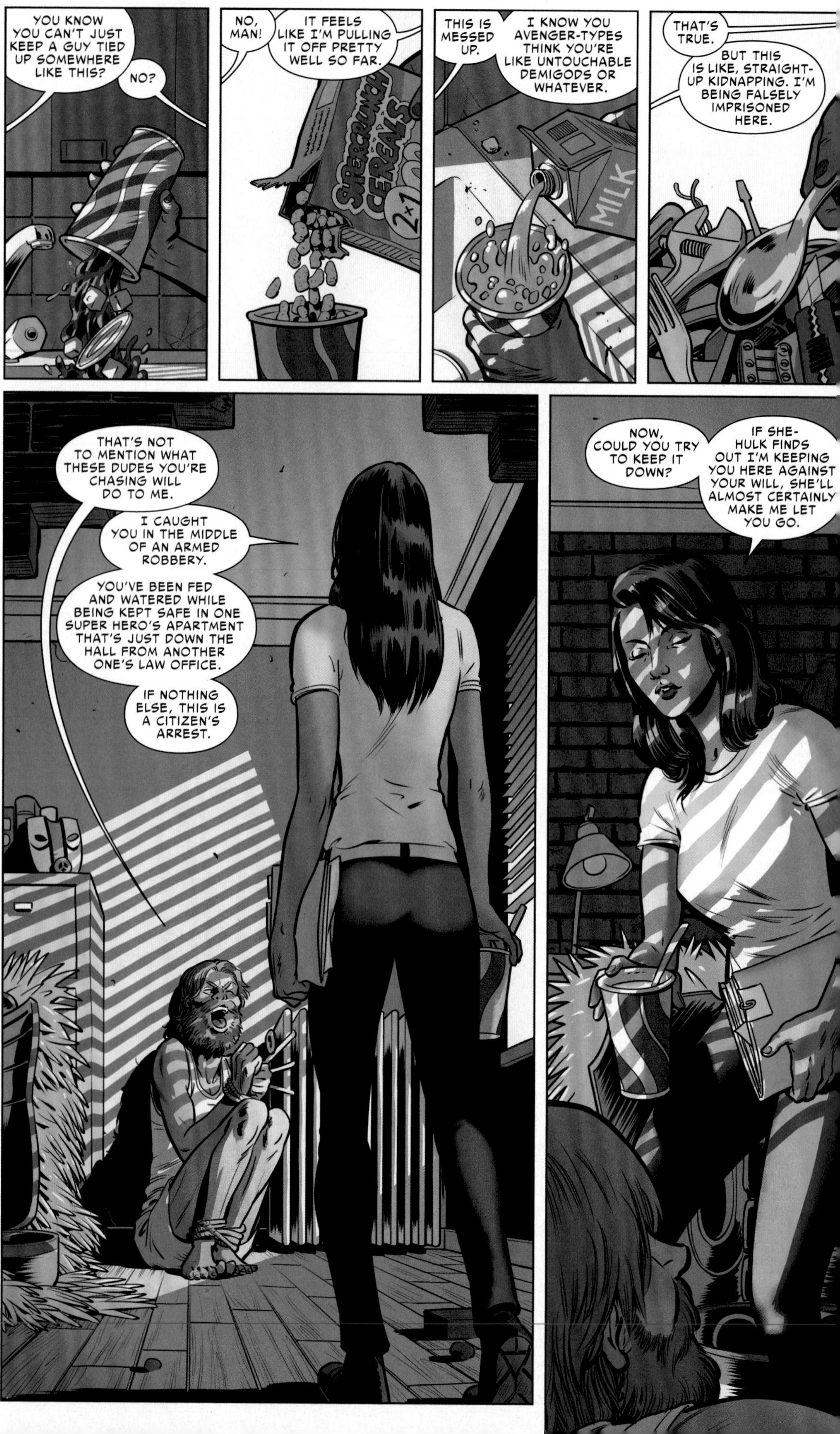

YOU KNOW YOU CAN'T JUST KEEP A GUY TIED UP SOMEWHERE LIKE THIS?
NO?
NO, MAN!
IT FEELS LIKE I'M PULLING IT OFF PRETTY WELL SO FAR.
SUPERCRUNCH CEREALS
2×1
THIS IS MESSED UP.
I KNOW YOU AVENGER-TYPES THINK YOU'RE LIKE UNTOUCHABLE DEMIGODS OR WHATEVER.
MILK
THAT'S TRUE.
BUT THIS IS LIKE, STRAIGHT-UP KIDNAPPING. I'M BEING FALSELY IMPRISONED HERE.
THAT'S NOT TO MENTION WHAT THESE DUDES YOU'RE CHASING WILL DO TO ME.
I CAUGHT YOU IN THE MIDDLE OF AN ARMED ROBBERY.
YOU'VE BEEN FED AND WATERED WHILE BEING KEPT SAFE IN ONE SUPER HERO'S APARTMENT THAT'S JUST DOWN THE HALL FROM ANOTHER ONE'S LAW OFFICE.
IF NOTHING ELSE, THIS IS A CITIZEN'S ARREST.
NOW, COULD YOU TRY TO KEEP IT DOWN?
IF SHE-HULK FINDS OUT I'M KEEPING YOU HERE AGAINST YOUR WILL, SHE'LL ALMOST CERTAINLY MAKE ME LET YOU GO.

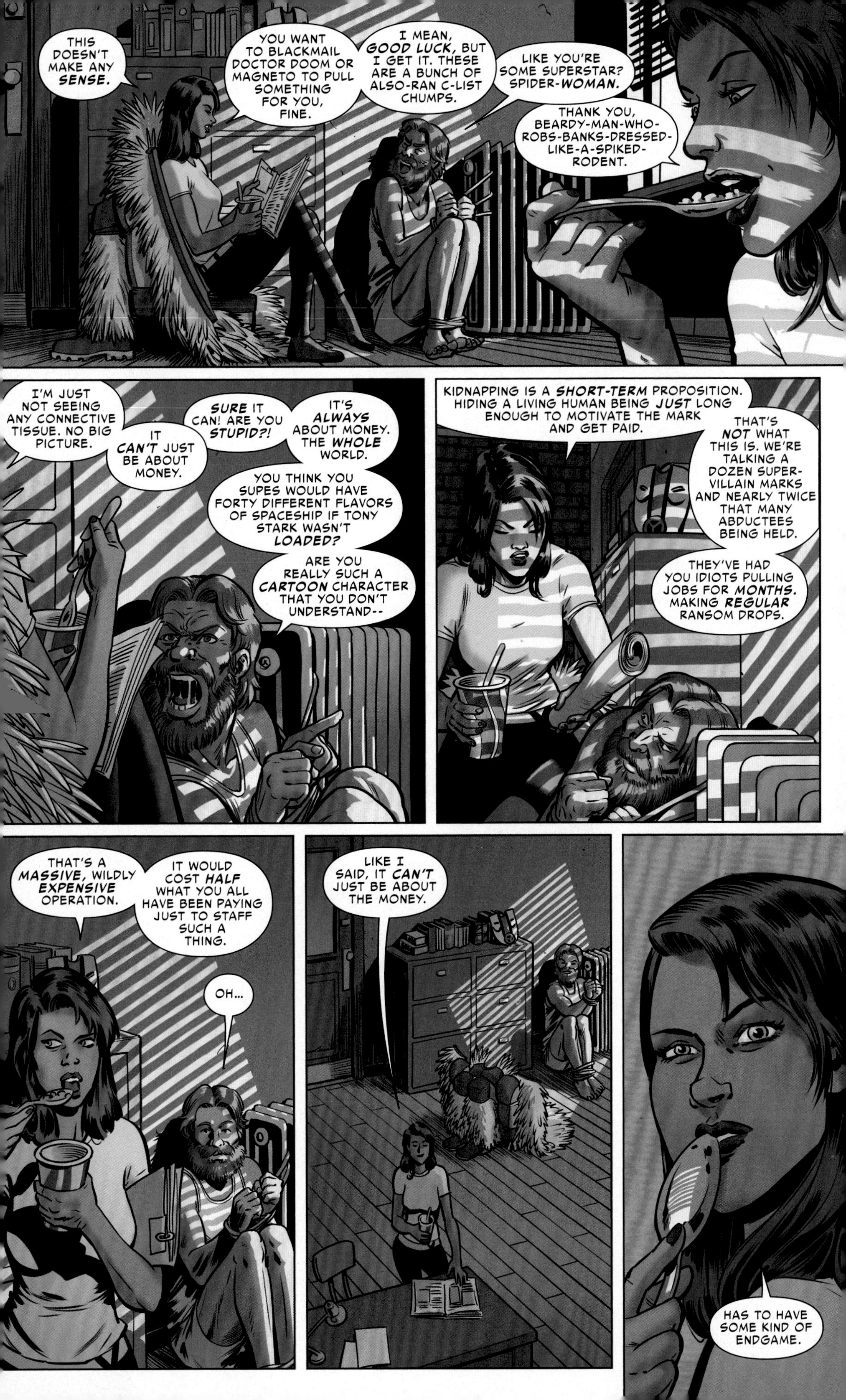
THIS DOESN'T MAKE ANY **SENSE.**
YOU WANT TO BLACKMAIL DOCTOR DOOM OR MAGNETO TO PULL SOMETHING FOR YOU, FINE.
I MEAN, **GOOD LUCK,** BUT I GET IT. THESE ARE A BUNCH OF ALSO-RAN C-LIST CHUMPS.
LIKE YOU'RE SOME SUPERSTAR? SPIDER-**WOMAN.**
THANK YOU, BEARDY-MAN-WHO-ROBS-BANKS-DRESSED-LIKE-A-SPIKED-RODENT.
I'M JUST NOT SEEING ANY CONNECTIVE TISSUE. NO BIG PICTURE.
IT **CAN'T** JUST BE ABOUT MONEY.
SURE IT CAN! ARE YOU **STUPID?!**
IT'S **ALWAYS** ABOUT MONEY. THE **WHOLE** WORLD.
YOU THINK YOU SUPES WOULD HAVE FORTY DIFFERENT FLAVORS OF SPACESHIP IF TONY STARK WASN'T **LOADED?**
ARE YOU REALLY SUCH A **CARTOON** CHARACTER THAT YOU DON'T UNDERSTAND--
KIDNAPPING IS A **SHORT-TERM** PROPOSITION. HIDING A LIVING HUMAN BEING **JUST** LONG ENOUGH TO MOTIVATE THE MARK AND GET PAID.
THAT'S **NOT** WHAT THIS IS. WE'RE TALKING A DOZEN SUPER-VILLAIN MARKS AND NEARLY TWICE THAT MANY ABDUCTEES BEING HELD.
THEY'VE HAD YOU IDIOTS PULLING JOBS FOR **MONTHS.** MAKING **REGULAR** RANSOM DROPS.
THAT'S A **MASSIVE,** WILDLY **EXPENSIVE** OPERATION.
IT WOULD COST **HALF** WHAT YOU ALL HAVE BEEN PAYING JUST TO STAFF SUCH A THING.
OH...
LIKE I SAID, IT **CAN'T** JUST BE ABOUT THE MONEY.
HAS TO HAVE SOME KIND OF ENDGAME.

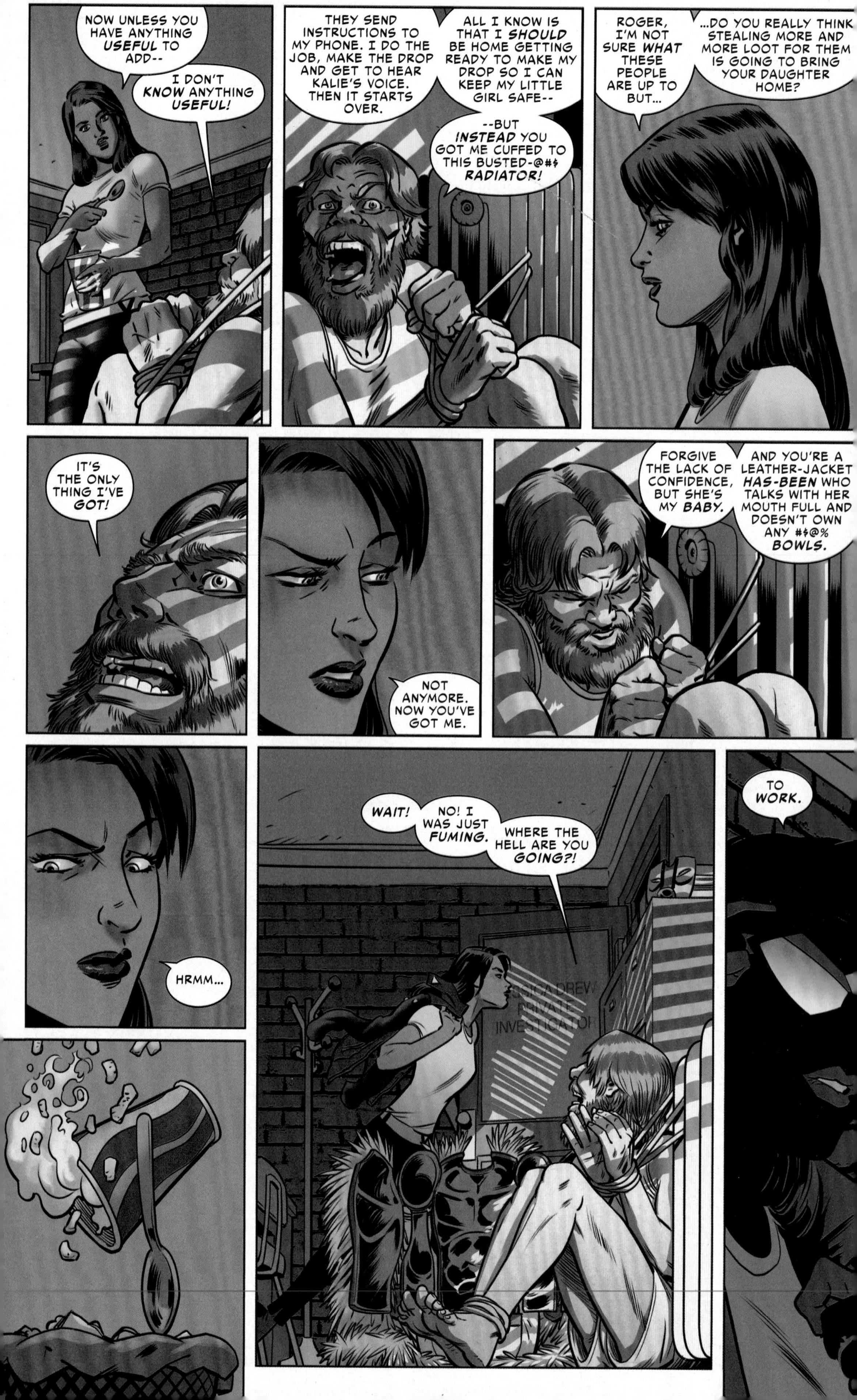
NOW UNLESS YOU HAVE ANYTHING USEFUL TO ADD--
I DON'T KNOW ANYTHING USEFUL!
THEY SEND INSTRUCTIONS TO MY PHONE. I DO THE JOB, MAKE THE DROP AND GET TO HEAR KALIE'S VOICE. THEN IT STARTS OVER.
ALL I KNOW IS THAT I SHOULD BE HOME GETTING READY TO MAKE MY DROP SO I CAN KEEP MY LITTLE GIRL SAFE--
--BUT INSTEAD YOU GOT ME CUFFED TO THIS BUSTED-@#$ RADIATOR!
ROGER, I'M NOT SURE WHAT THESE PEOPLE ARE UP TO BUT...
...DO YOU REALLY THINK STEALING MORE AND MORE LOOT FOR THEM IS GOING TO BRING YOUR DAUGHTER HOME?
IT'S THE ONLY THING I'VE GOT!
NOT ANYMORE. NOW YOU'VE GOT ME.
FORGIVE THE LACK OF CONFIDENCE, BUT SHE'S MY BABY.
AND YOU'RE A LEATHER-JACKET HAS-BEEN WHO TALKS WITH HER MOUTH FULL AND DOESN'T OWN ANY #$@% BOWLS.
HRMM...
WAIT!
NO! I WAS JUST FUMING.
WHERE THE HELL ARE YOU GOING?!
TO WORK.

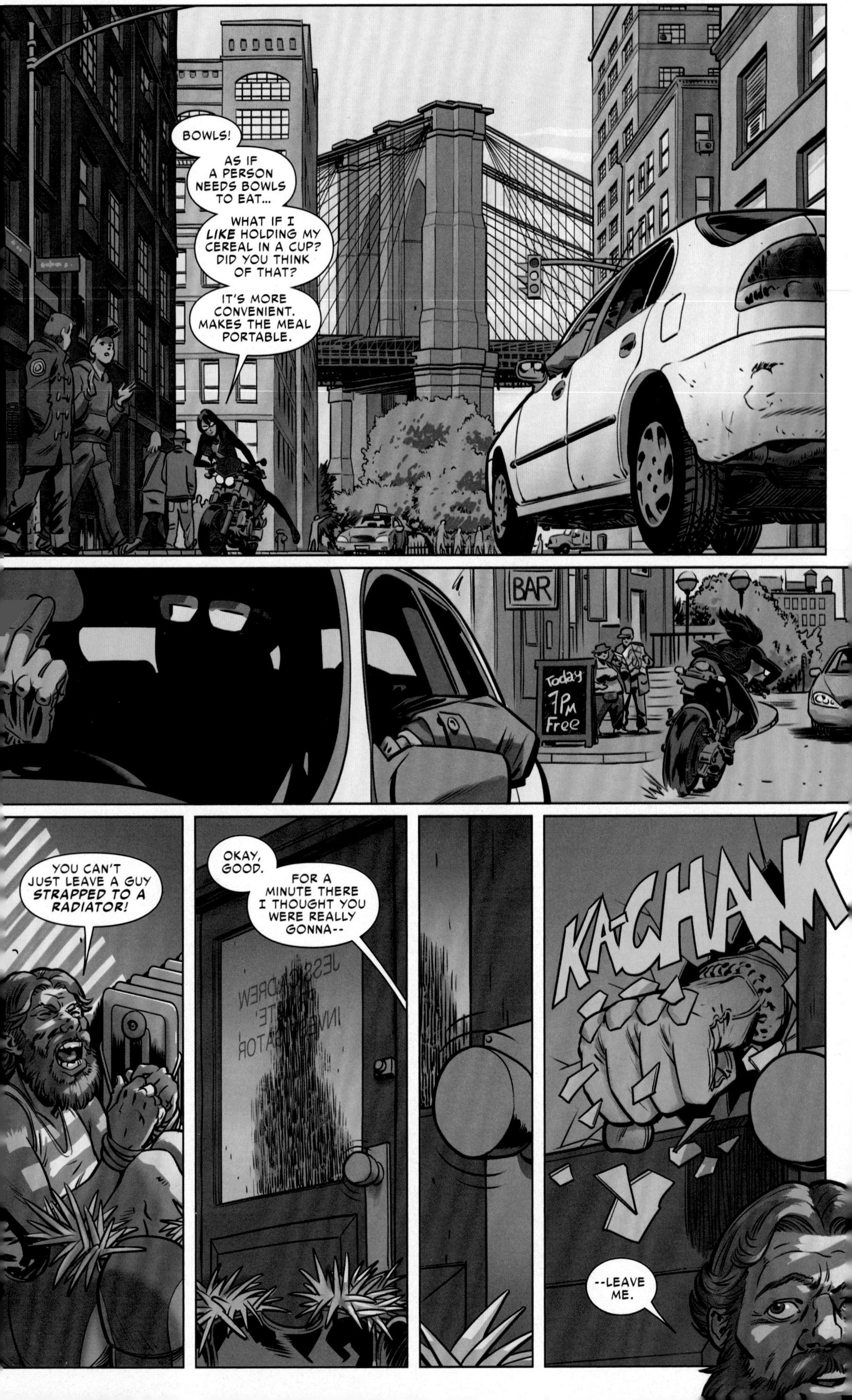

BOWLS!
AS IF A PERSON NEEDS BOWLS TO EAT...
WHAT IF I *LIKE* HOLDING MY CEREAL IN A CUP? DID YOU THINK OF THAT?
IT'S MORE CONVENIENT. MAKES THE MEAL PORTABLE.
BAR
Today 7PM Free
YOU CAN'T JUST LEAVE A GUY *STRAPPED TO A RADIATOR!*
OKAY, GOOD.
FOR A MINUTE THERE I THOUGHT YOU WERE REALLY GONNA--
KA-CHANK
--LEAVE ME.

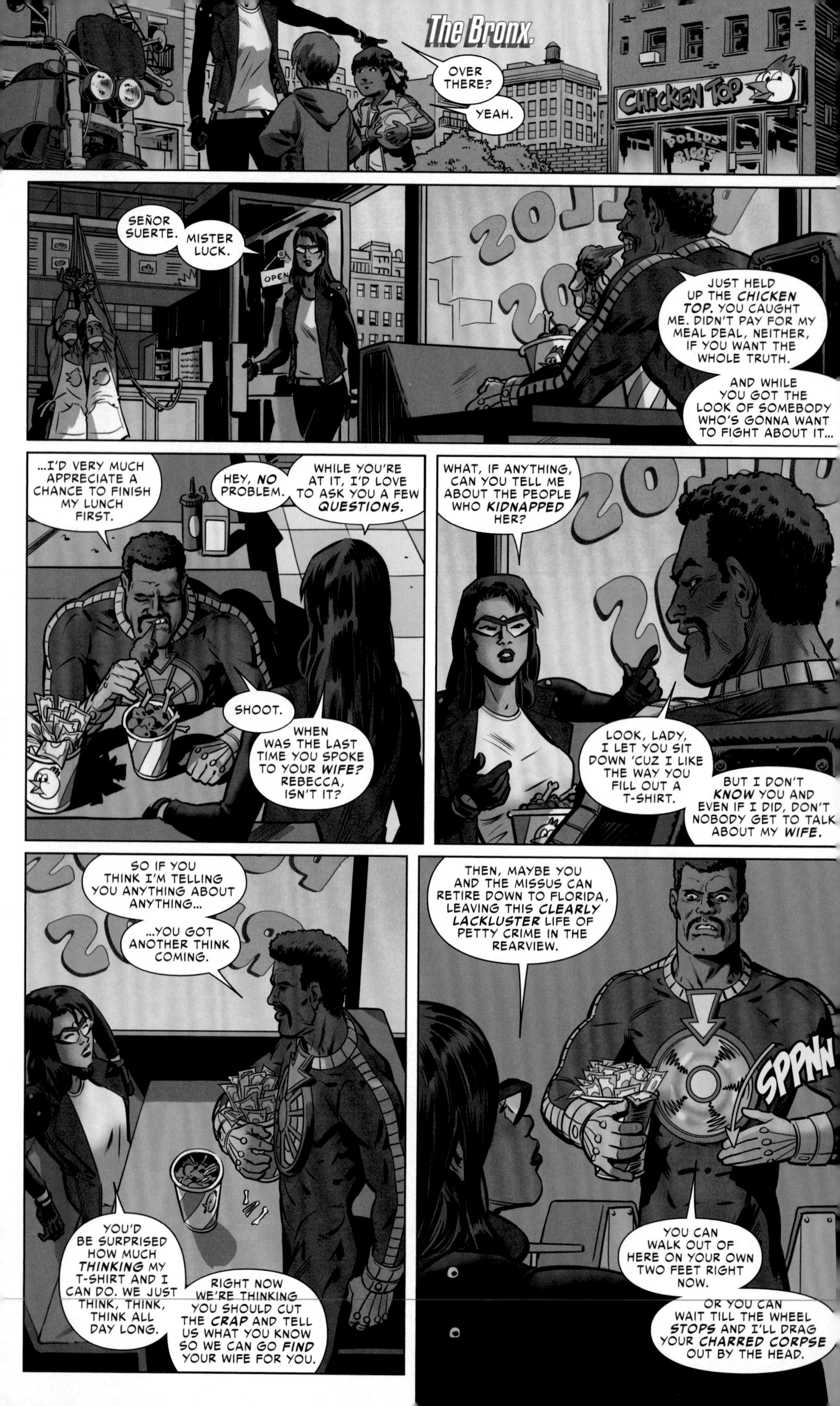
The Bronx.
OVER THERE?
YEAH.
CHICKEN TOP
POLLOS RICOS
SEÑOR SUERTE.
MISTER LUCK.
OPEN
JUST HELD UP THE CHICKEN TOP. YOU CAUGHT ME. DIDN'T PAY FOR MY MEAL DEAL, NEITHER, IF YOU WANT THE WHOLE TRUTH.
AND WHILE YOU GOT THE LOOK OF SOMEBODY WHO'S GONNA WANT TO FIGHT ABOUT IT...
...I'D VERY MUCH APPRECIATE A CHANCE TO FINISH MY LUNCH FIRST.
HEY, NO PROBLEM.
WHILE YOU'RE AT IT, I'D LOVE TO ASK YOU A FEW QUESTIONS.
SHOOT.
WHEN WAS THE LAST TIME YOU SPOKE TO YOUR WIFE? REBECCA, ISN'T IT?
WHAT, IF ANYTHING, CAN YOU TELL ME ABOUT THE PEOPLE WHO KIDNAPPED HER?
LOOK, LADY, I LET YOU SIT DOWN 'CUZ I LIKE THE WAY YOU FILL OUT A T-SHIRT.
BUT I DON'T KNOW YOU AND EVEN IF I DID, DON'T NOBODY GET TO TALK ABOUT MY WIFE.
SO IF YOU THINK I'M TELLING YOU ANYTHING ABOUT ANYTHING...
...YOU GOT ANOTHER THINK COMING.
YOU'D BE SURPRISED HOW MUCH THINKING MY T-SHIRT AND I CAN DO. WE JUST THINK, THINK, THINK ALL DAY LONG.
RIGHT NOW WE'RE THINKING YOU SHOULD CUT THE CRAP AND TELL US WHAT YOU KNOW SO WE CAN GO FIND YOUR WIFE FOR YOU.
THEN, MAYBE YOU AND THE MISSUS CAN RETIRE DOWN TO FLORIDA, LEAVING THIS CLEARLY LACKLUSTER LIFE OF PETTY CRIME IN THE REARVIEW.
SPPNN
YOU CAN WALK OUT OF HERE ON YOUR OWN TWO FEET RIGHT NOW.
OR YOU CAN WAIT TILL THE WHEEL STOPS AND I'LL DRAG YOUR CHARRED CORPSE OUT BY THE HEAD.

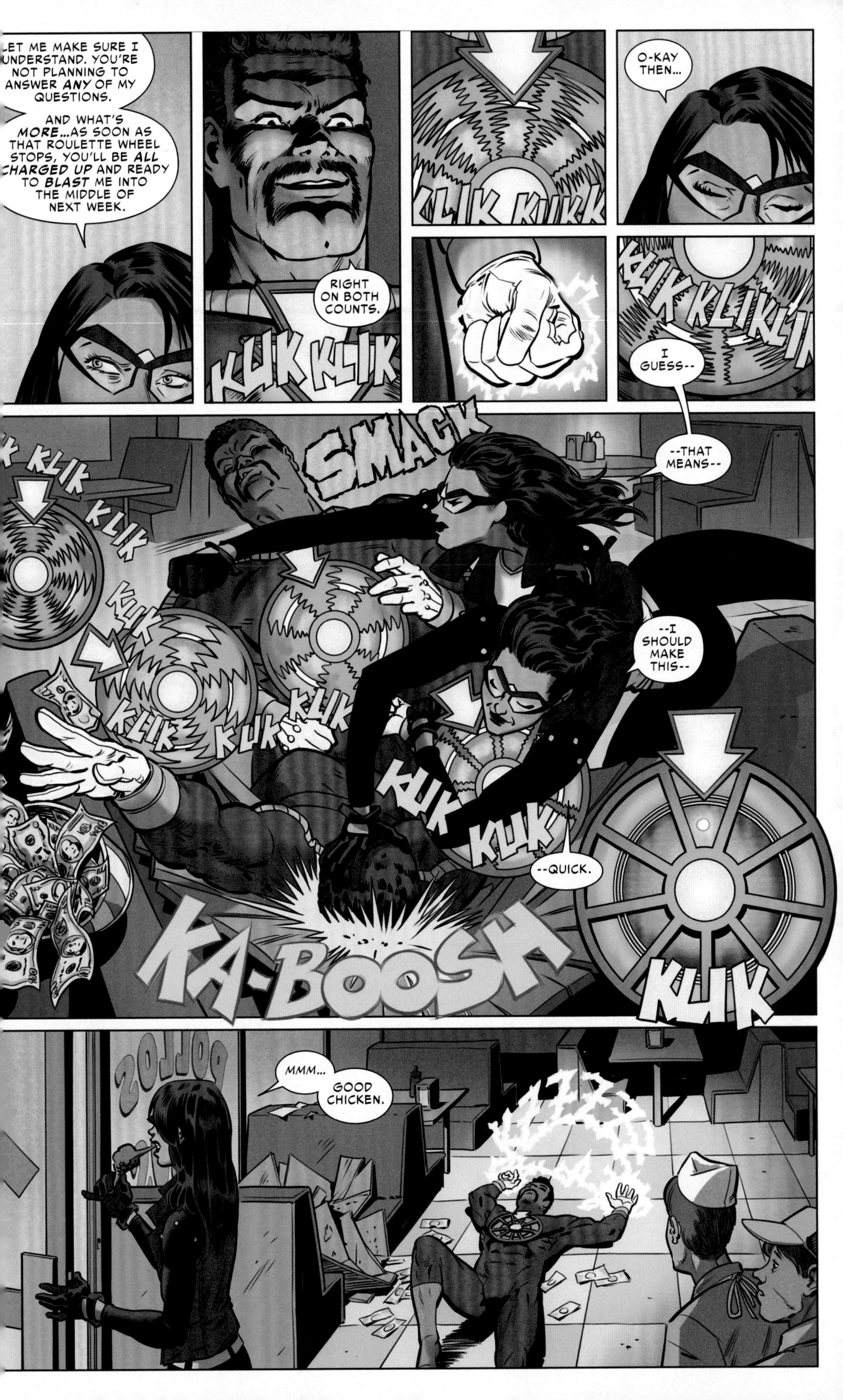
LET ME MAKE SURE I UNDERSTAND. YOU'RE NOT PLANNING TO ANSWER ANY OF MY QUESTIONS.
AND WHAT'S MORE...AS SOON AS THAT ROULETTE WHEEL STOPS, YOU'LL BE ALL CHARGED UP AND READY TO BLAST ME INTO THE MIDDLE OF NEXT WEEK.
RIGHT ON BOTH COUNTS.
KLIK KLIK
KLIK KLIKK
O-KAY THEN...
KLIK KLIKLIKLIK
I GUESS--
--THAT MEANS--
SMACK
KLIK KLIK
KLIK
KLIK
KLIK
KLIK
KLIK
--I SHOULD MAKE THIS--
KLIK
KLIK
--QUICK.
KA-BOOSH
KLIK
MMM... GOOD CHICKEN.

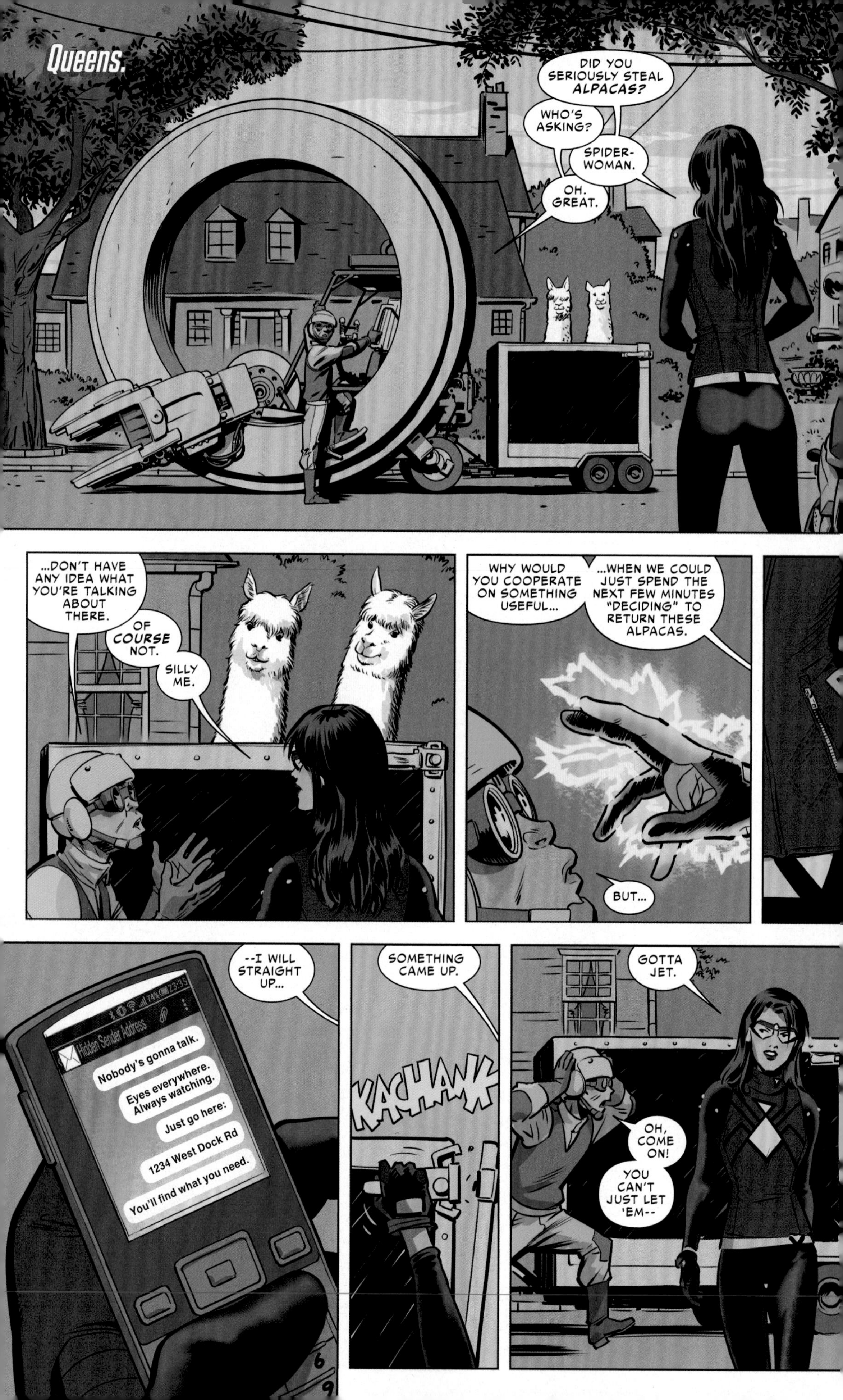
Queens.
DID YOU SERIOUSLY STEAL ALPACAS?
WHO'S ASKING?
SPIDER-WOMAN.
OH. GREAT.
...DON'T HAVE ANY IDEA WHAT YOU'RE TALKING ABOUT THERE.
OF COURSE NOT.
SILLY ME.
WHY WOULD YOU COOPERATE ON SOMETHING USEFUL...
...WHEN WE COULD JUST SPEND THE NEXT FEW MINUTES "DECIDING" TO RETURN THESE ALPACAS.
BUT...
--I WILL STRAIGHT UP...
Hidden Sender Address
Nobody's gonna talk.
Eyes everywhere. Always watching.
Just go here:
1234 West Dock Rd
You'll find what you need.
SOMETHING CAME UP.
KACHANK
GOTTA JET.
OH, COME ON!
YOU CAN'T JUST LET 'EM--

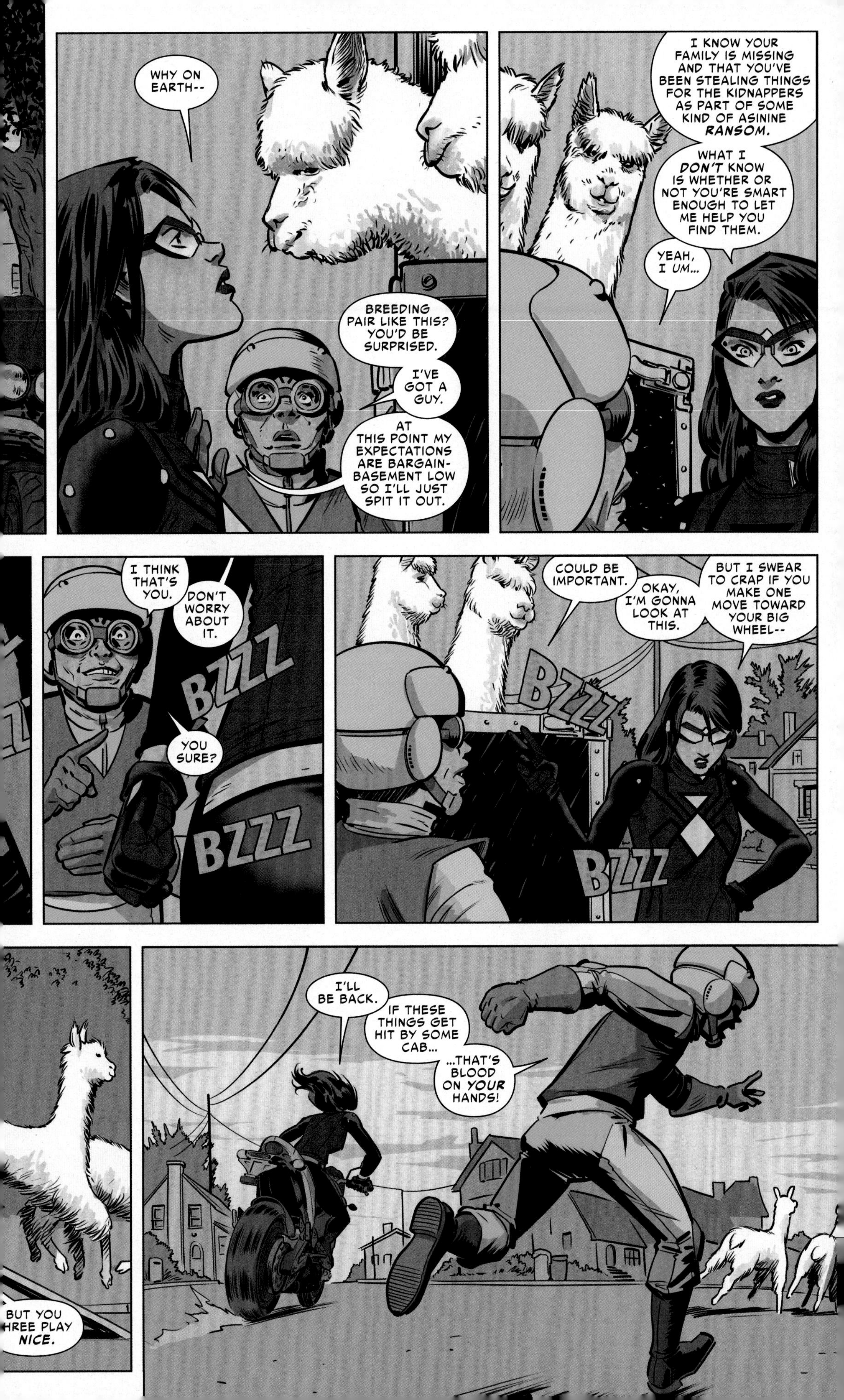
WHY ON EARTH--
BREEDING PAIR LIKE THIS? YOU'D BE SURPRISED.
I'VE GOT A GUY.
AT THIS POINT MY EXPECTATIONS ARE BARGAIN-BASEMENT LOW SO I'LL JUST SPIT IT OUT.
I KNOW YOUR FAMILY IS MISSING AND THAT YOU'VE BEEN STEALING THINGS FOR THE KIDNAPPERS AS PART OF SOME KIND OF ASININE RANSOM.
WHAT I DON'T KNOW IS WHETHER OR NOT YOU'RE SMART ENOUGH TO LET ME HELP YOU FIND THEM.
YEAH, I UM...
I THINK THAT'S YOU.
DON'T WORRY ABOUT IT.
BZZZ
YOU SURE?
BZZZ
COULD BE IMPORTANT.
OKAY, I'M GONNA LOOK AT THIS.
BUT I SWEAR TO CRAP IF YOU MAKE ONE MOVE TOWARD YOUR BIG WHEEL--
BZZZ
BZZZ
BUT YOU HREE PLAY NICE.
I'LL BE BACK.
IF THESE THINGS GET HIT BY SOME CAB...
...THAT'S BLOOD ON YOUR HANDS!

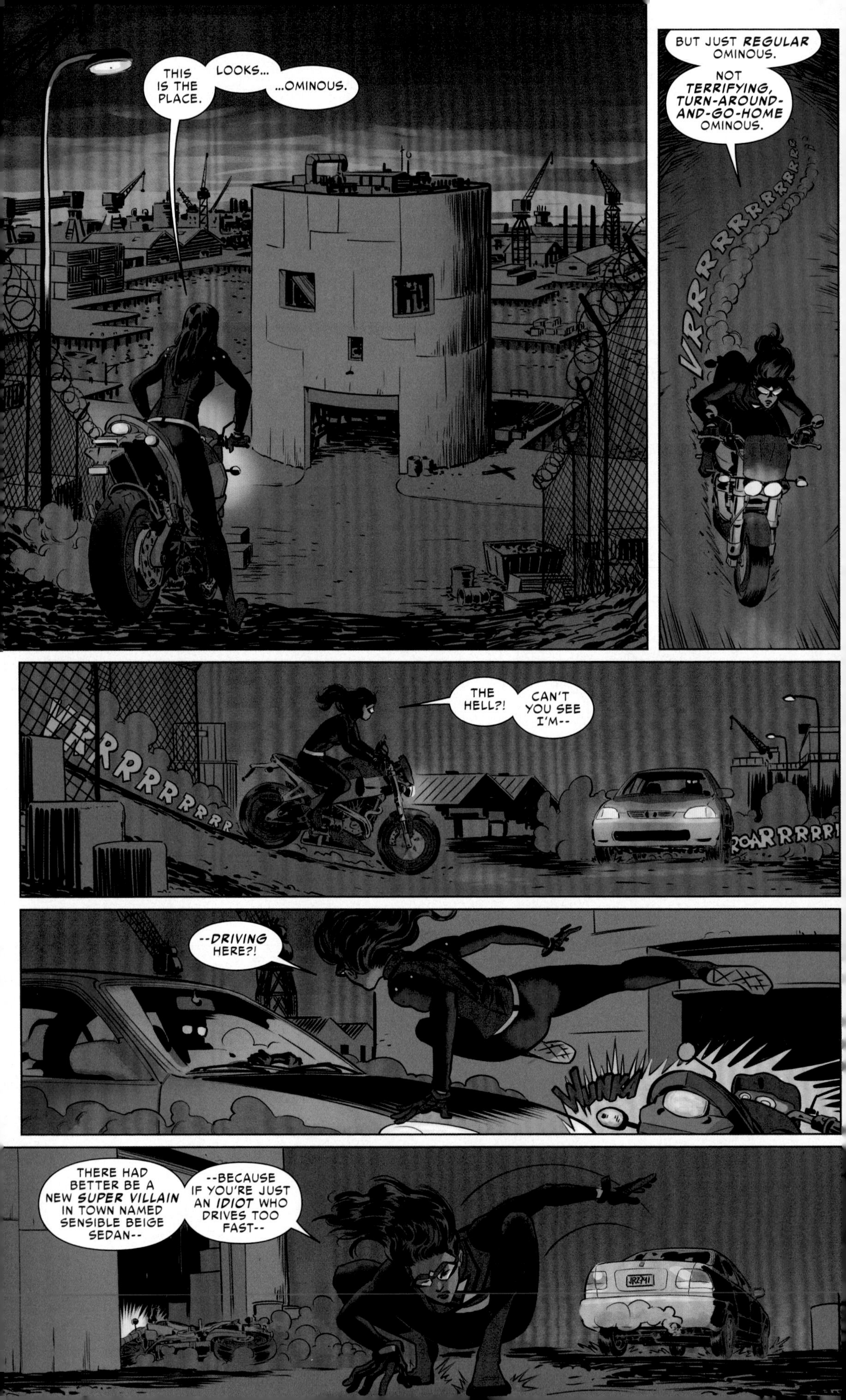
THIS IS THE PLACE.
LOOKS...
...OMINOUS.
BUT JUST REGULAR OMINOUS.
NOT TERRIFYING, TURN-AROUND-AND-GO-HOME OMINOUS.
THE HELL?!
CAN'T YOU SEE I'M--
--DRIVING HERE?!
THERE HAD BETTER BE A NEW SUPER VILLAIN IN TOWN NAMED SENSIBLE BEIGE SEDAN--
--BECAUSE IF YOU'RE JUST AN IDIOT WHO DRIVES TOO FAST--

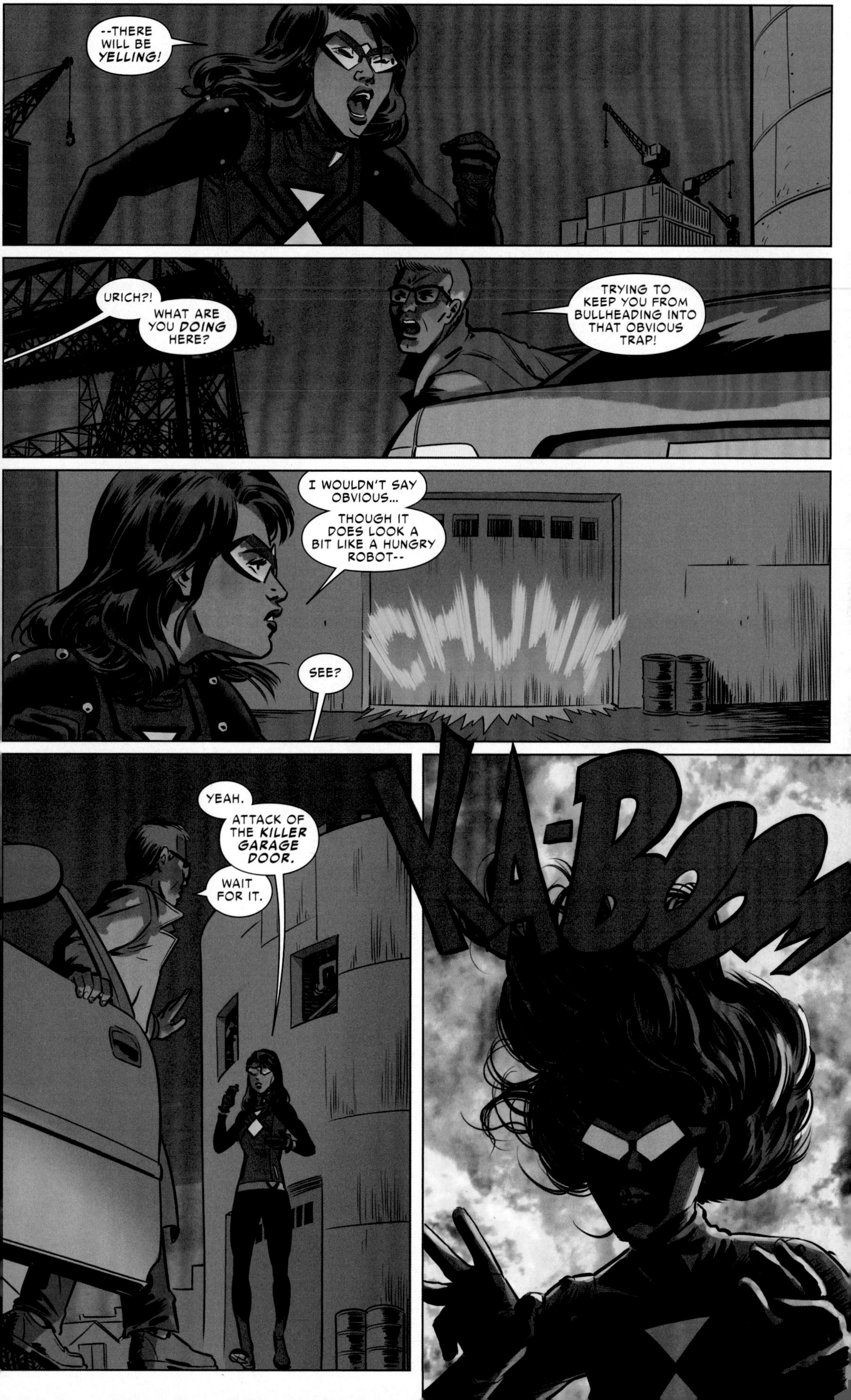

--THERE WILL BE YELLING!
URICH?! WHAT ARE YOU DOING HERE?
TRYING TO KEEP YOU FROM BULLHEADING INTO THAT OBVIOUS TRAP!
I WOULDN'T SAY OBVIOUS...
THOUGH IT DOES LOOK A BIT LIKE A HUNGRY ROBOT--
CHUNK
SEE?
YEAH.
ATTACK OF THE KILLER GARAGE DOOR.
WAIT FOR IT.
KA-BOOM

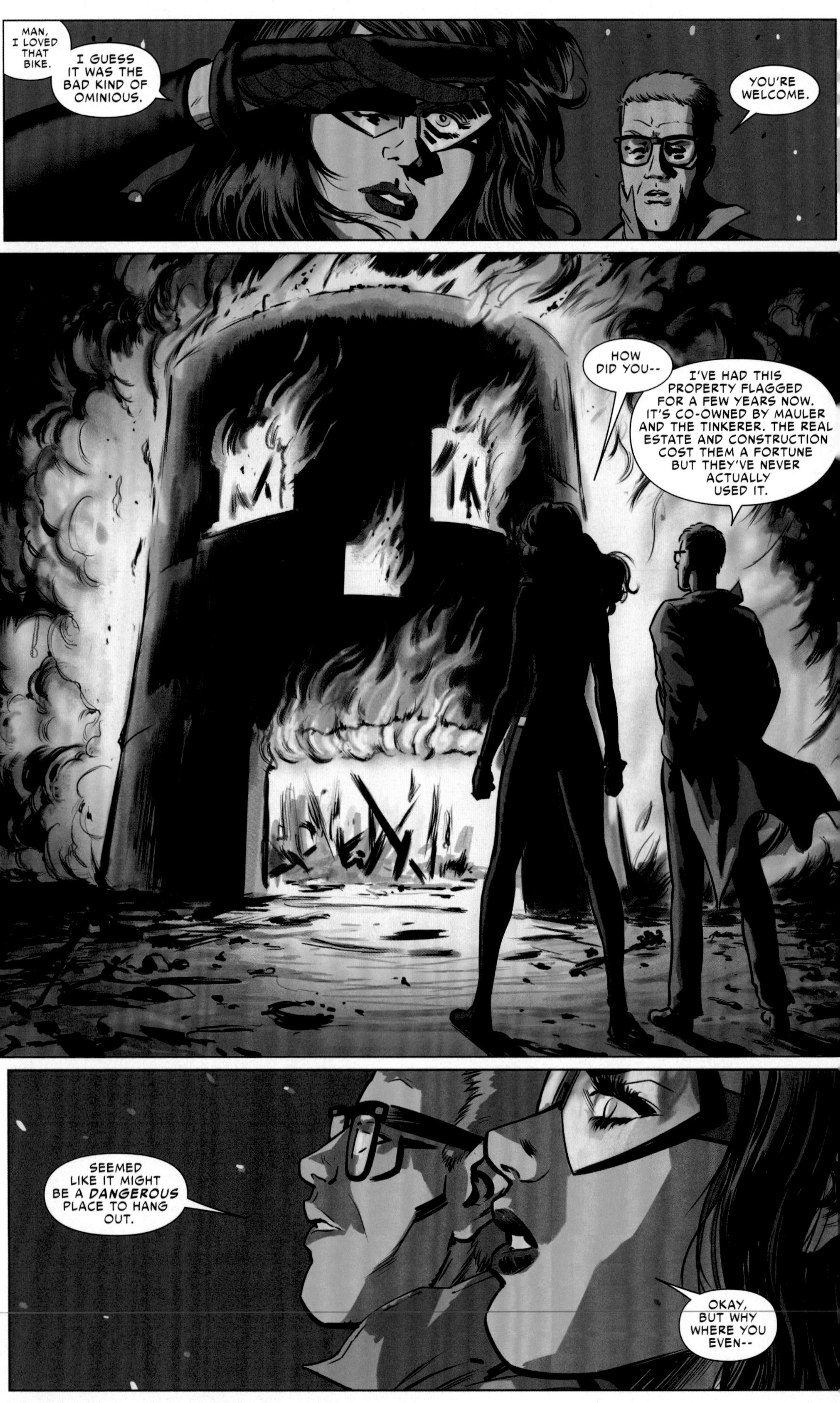

MAN, I LOVED THAT BIKE.
I GUESS IT WAS THE BAD KIND OF OMINIOUS.
YOU'RE WELCOME.
HOW DID YOU--
I'VE HAD THIS PROPERTY FLAGGED FOR A FEW YEARS NOW. IT'S CO-OWNED BY MAULER AND THE TINKERER. THE REAL ESTATE AND CONSTRUCTION COST THEM A FORTUNE BUT THEY'VE NEVER ACTUALLY USED IT.
SEEMED LIKE IT MIGHT BE A *DANGEROUS* PLACE TO HANG OUT.
OKAY, BUT WHY WHERE YOU EVEN--

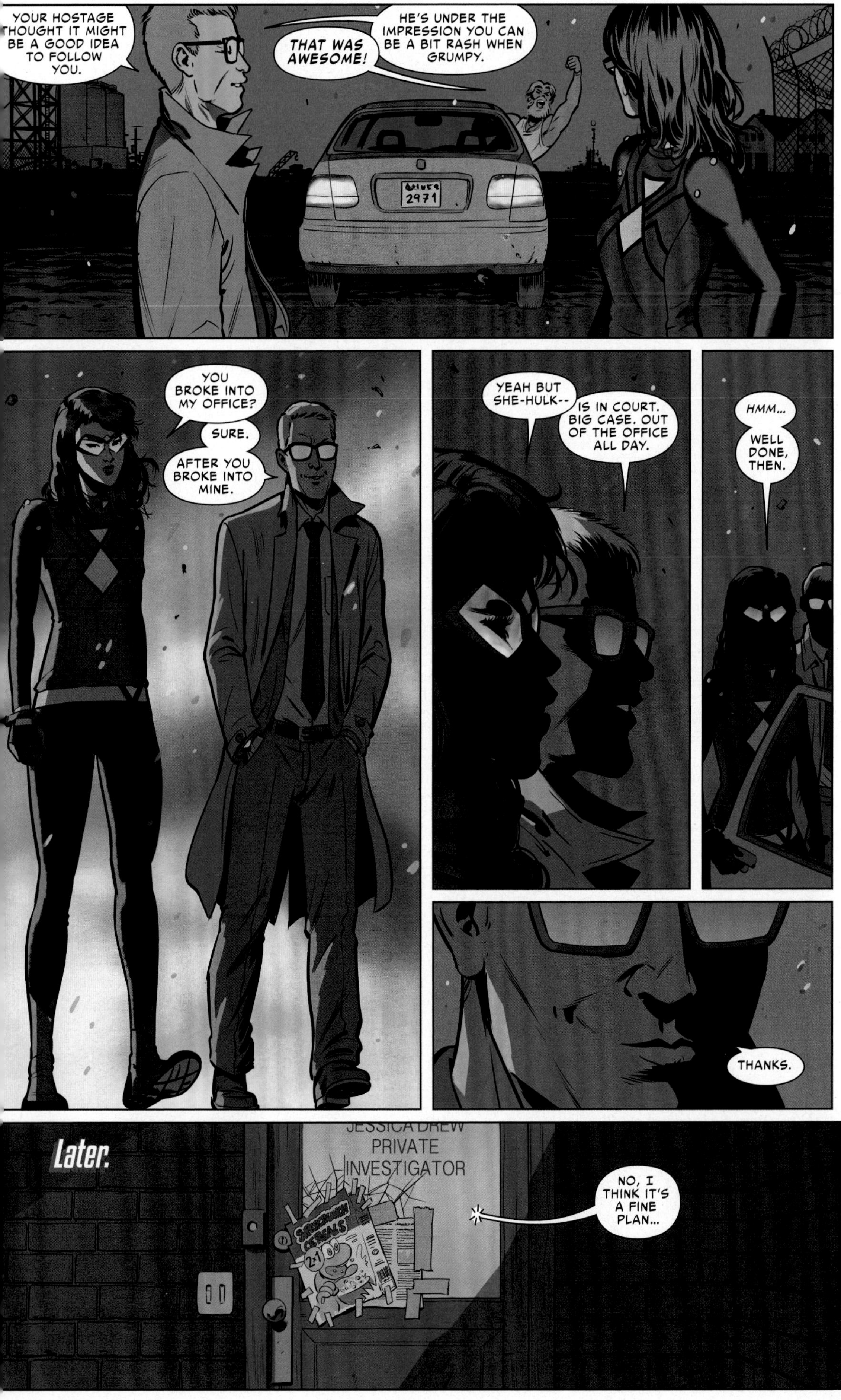
YOUR HOSTAGE THOUGHT IT MIGHT BE A GOOD IDEA TO FOLLOW YOU.
HE'S UNDER THE IMPRESSION YOU CAN BE A BIT RASH WHEN GRUMPY.
THAT WAS AWESOME!
2971
YOU BROKE INTO MY OFFICE?
SURE.
AFTER YOU BROKE INTO MINE.
YEAH BUT SHE-HULK--
IS IN COURT. BIG CASE. OUT OF THE OFFICE ALL DAY.
HMM...
WELL DONE, THEN.
THANKS.
Later.
JESSICA DREW
PRIVATE
INVESTIGATOR
NO, I THINK IT'S A FINE PLAN...

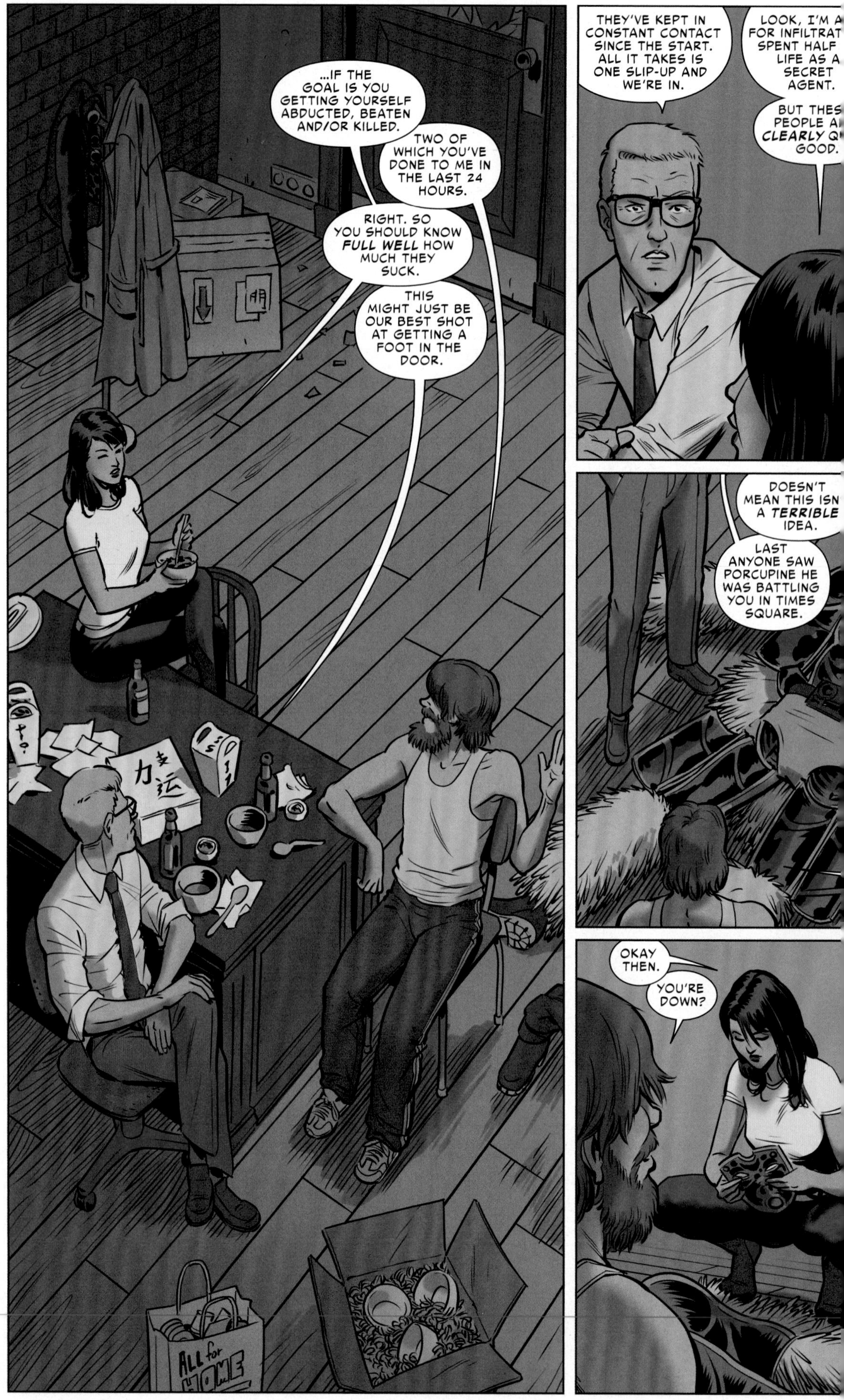

...IF THE GOAL IS YOU GETTING YOURSELF ABDUCTED, BEATEN AND/OR KILLED.
TWO OF WHICH YOU'VE DONE TO ME IN THE LAST 24 HOURS.
RIGHT. SO YOU SHOULD KNOW *FULL WELL* HOW MUCH THEY SUCK.
THIS MIGHT JUST BE OUR BEST SHOT AT GETTING A FOOT IN THE DOOR.
ALL for HOME
THEY'VE KEPT IN CONSTANT CONTACT SINCE THE START. ALL IT TAKES IS ONE SLIP-UP AND WE'RE IN.
LOOK, I'M A
FOR INFILTRAT
SPENT HALF
LIFE AS A
SECRET
AGENT.
BUT THES
PEOPLE A
CLEARLY Q
GOOD.
DOESN'T
MEAN THIS ISN
A *TERRIBLE*
IDEA.
LAST ANYONE SAW PORCUPINE HE WAS BATTLING YOU IN TIMES SQUARE.
OKAY THEN.
YOU'RE DOWN?

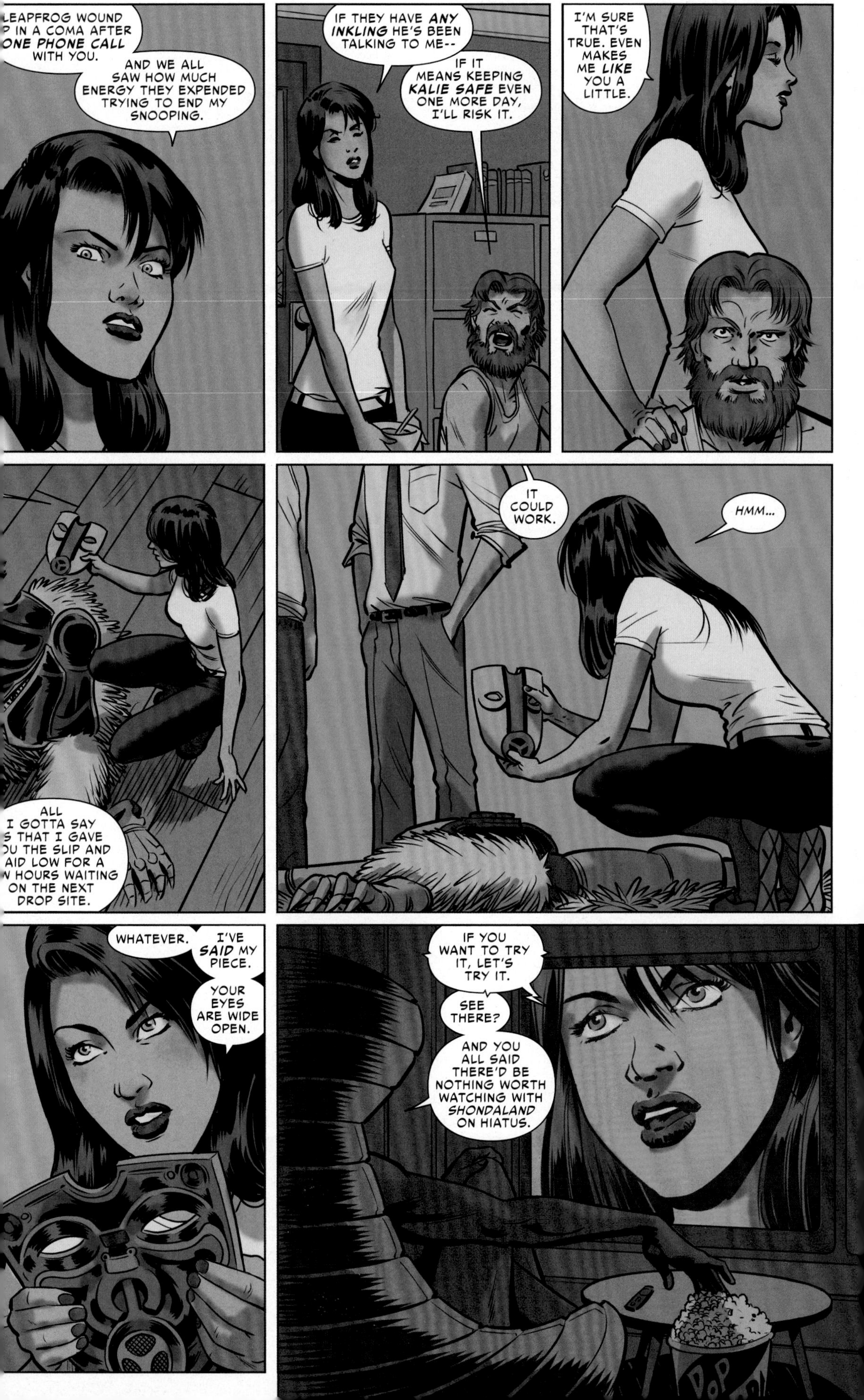
LEAPFROG WOUND P IN A COMA AFTER ONE PHONE CALL WITH YOU.
AND WE ALL SAW HOW MUCH ENERGY THEY EXPENDED TRYING TO END MY SNOOPING.
IF THEY HAVE ANY INKLING HE'S BEEN TALKING TO ME--
IF IT MEANS KEEPING KALIE SAFE EVEN ONE MORE DAY, I'LL RISK IT.
I'M SURE THAT'S TRUE. EVEN MAKES ME LIKE YOU A LITTLE.
ALL I GOTTA SAY S THAT I GAVE OU THE SLIP AND AID LOW FOR A W HOURS WAITING ON THE NEXT DROP SITE.
IT COULD WORK.
HMM...
WHATEVER.
I'VE SAID MY PIECE.
YOUR EYES ARE WIDE OPEN.
IF YOU WANT TO TRY IT, LET'S TRY IT.
SEE THERE?
AND YOU ALL SAID THERE'D BE NOTHING WORTH WATCHING WITH SHONDALAND ON HIATUS.

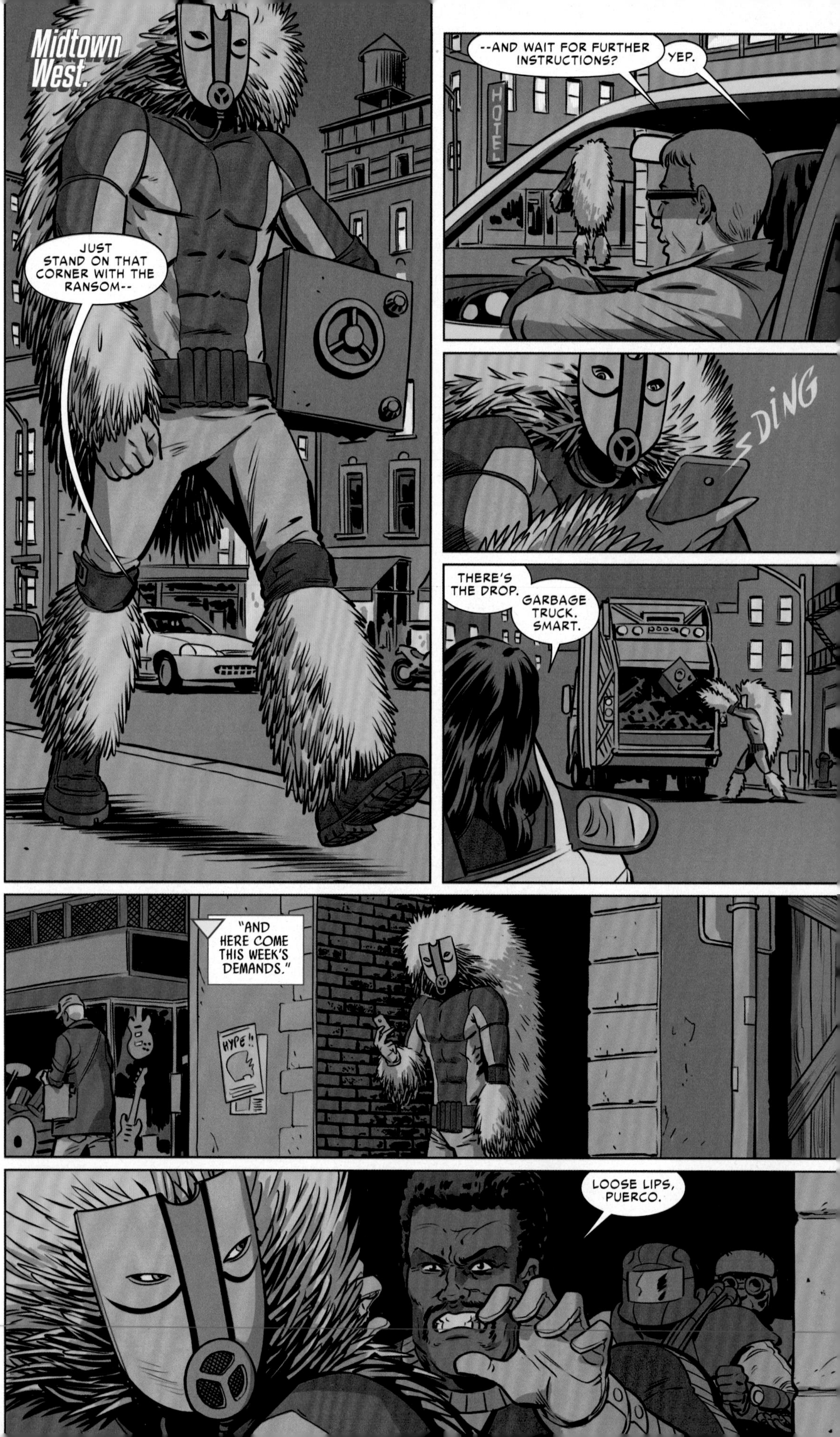

Midtown West.
JUST STAND ON THAT CORNER WITH THE RANSOM--
--AND WAIT FOR FURTHER INSTRUCTIONS?
YEP.
HOTEL
SDING
THERE'S THE DROP.
GARBAGE TRUCK. SMART.
"AND HERE COME THIS WEEK'S DEMANDS."
HYPE!!
LOOSE LIPS, PUERCO.

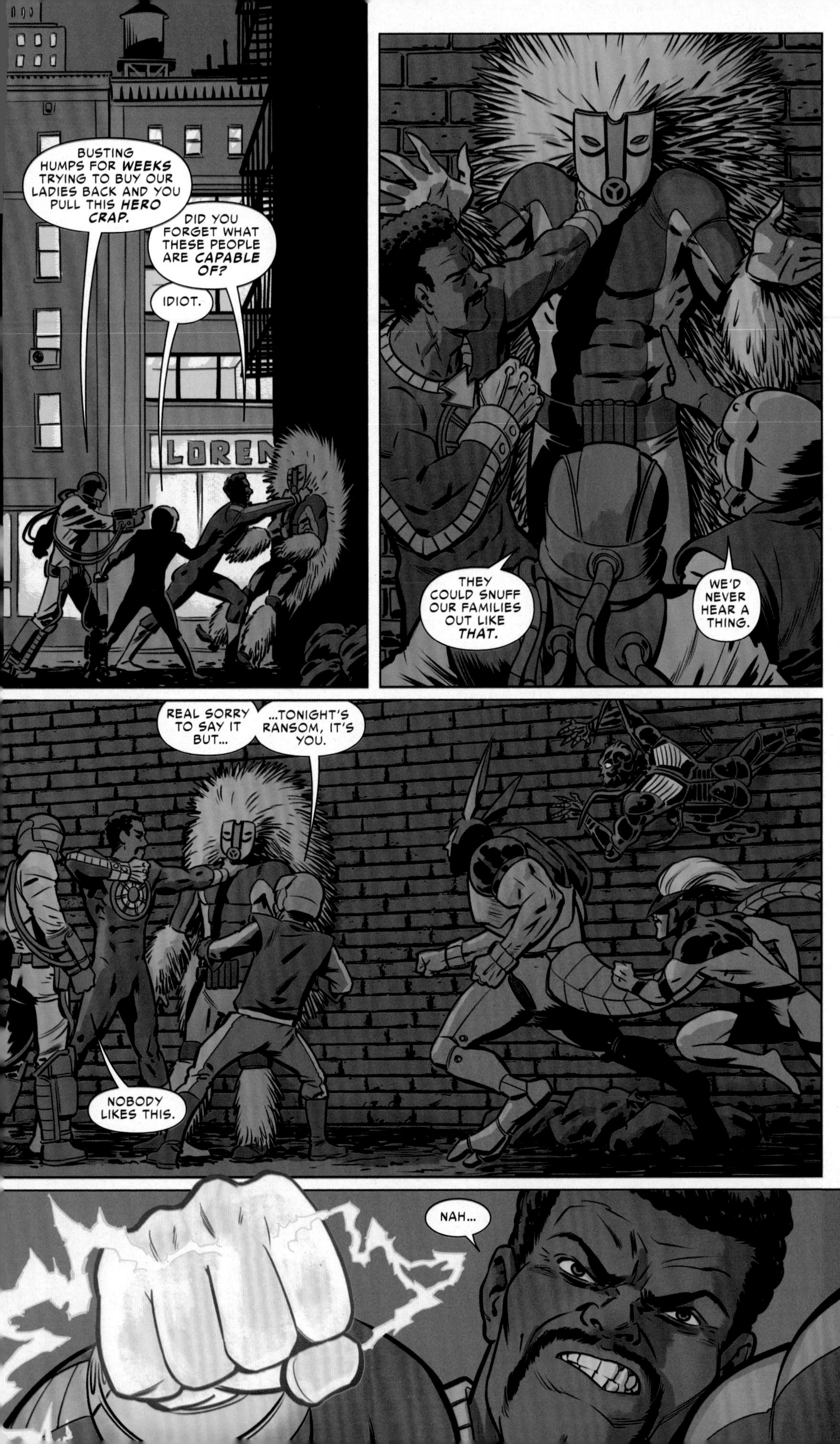
BUSTING HUMPS FOR WEEKS TRYING TO BUY OUR LADIES BACK AND YOU PULL THIS HERO CRAP.
DID YOU FORGET WHAT THESE PEOPLE ARE CAPABLE OF?
IDIOT.
LOREN
THEY COULD SNUFF OUR FAMILIES OUT LIKE THAT.
WE'D NEVER HEAR A THING.
REAL SORRY TO SAY IT BUT...
...TONIGHT'S RANSOM, IT'S YOU.
NOBODY LIKES THIS.
NAH...

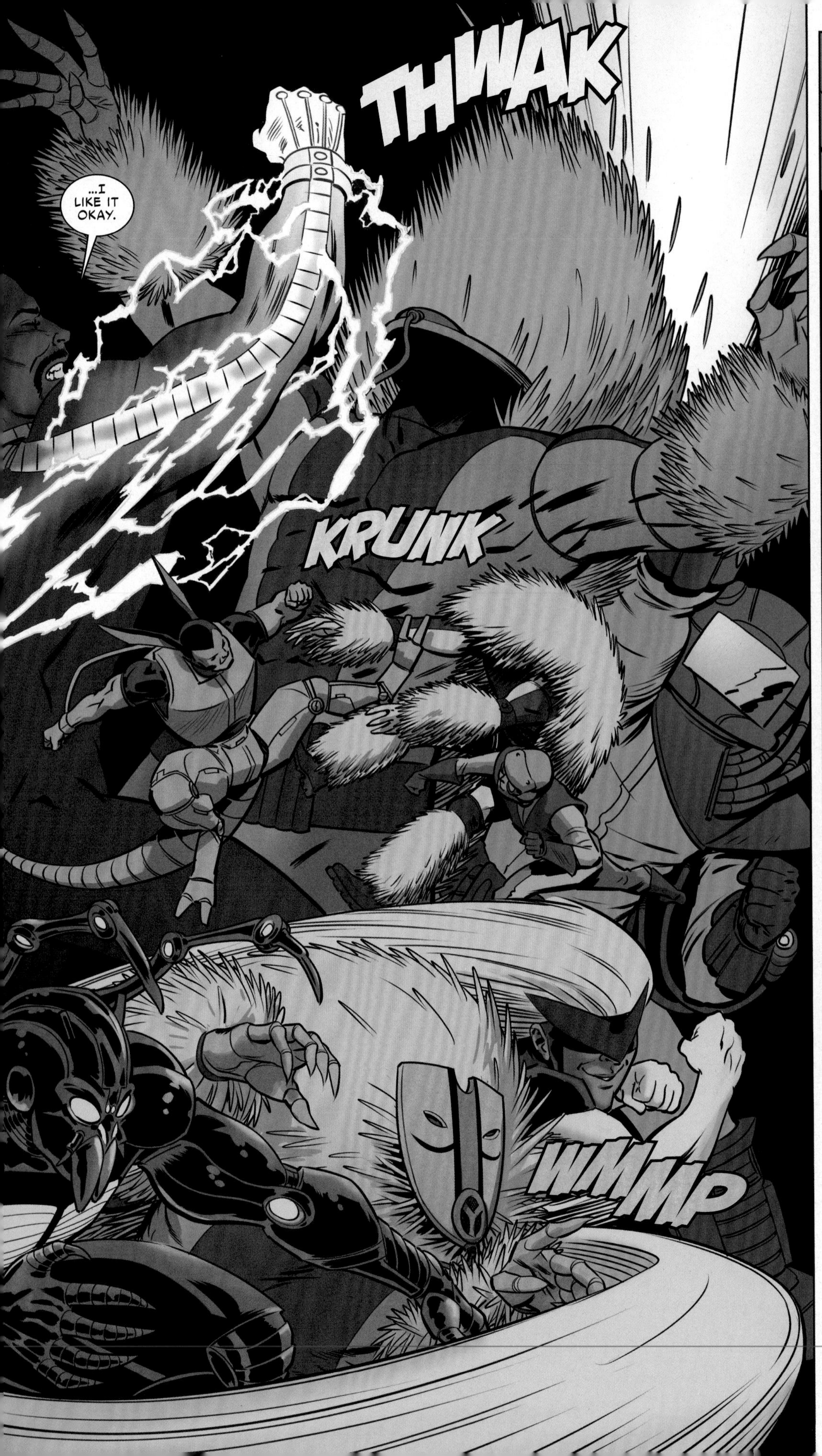
THWAK
...I LIKE IT OKAY.
KRUNK
WMMP

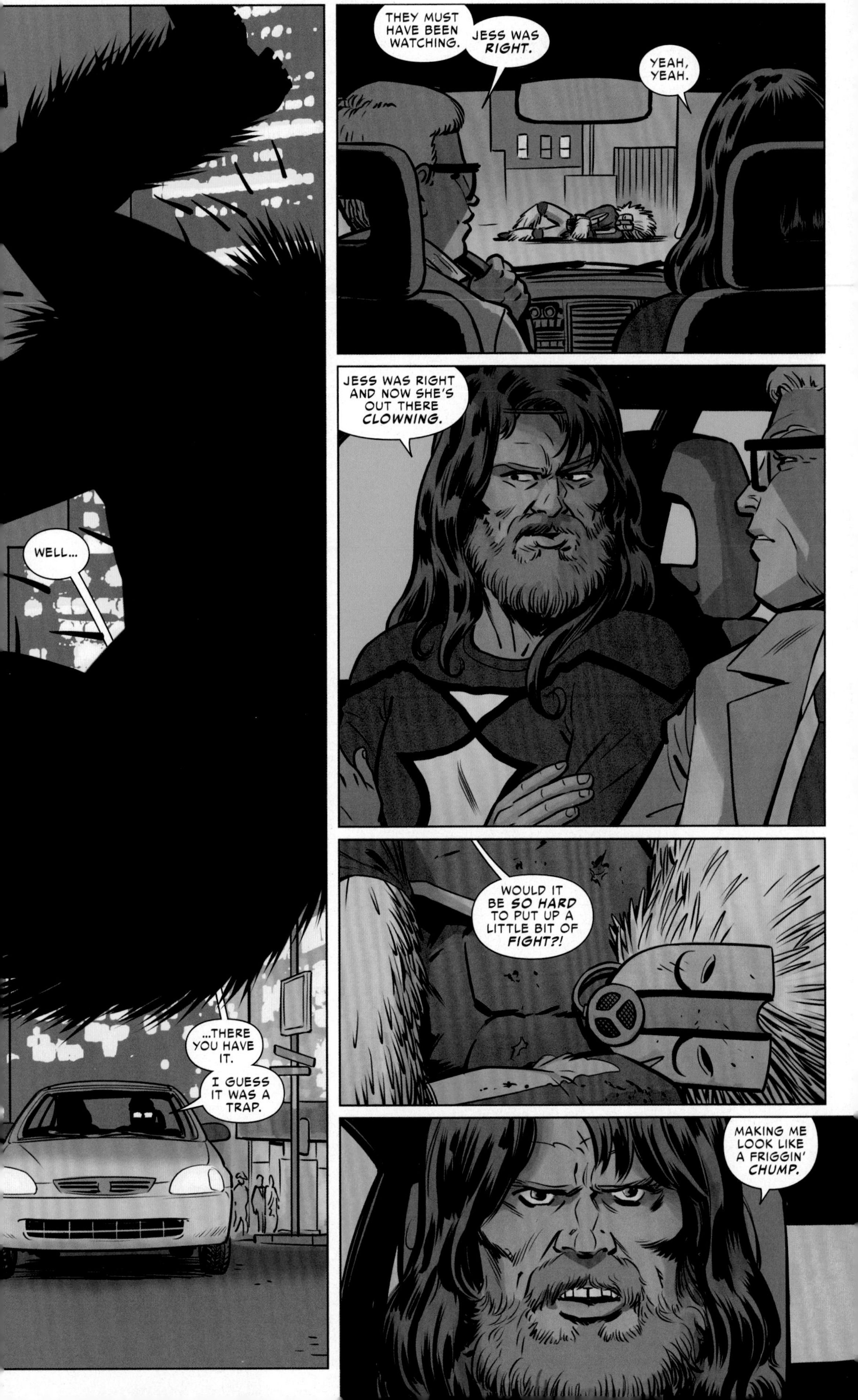
WELL...
...THERE YOU HAVE IT.
I GUESS IT WAS A TRAP.
THEY MUST HAVE BEEN WATCHING.
JESS WAS RIGHT.
YEAH, YEAH.
JESS WAS RIGHT AND NOW SHE'S OUT THERE CLOWNING.
WOULD IT BE SO HARD TO PUT UP A LITTLE BIT OF FIGHT?!
MAKING ME LOOK LIKE A FRIGGIN' CHUMP.

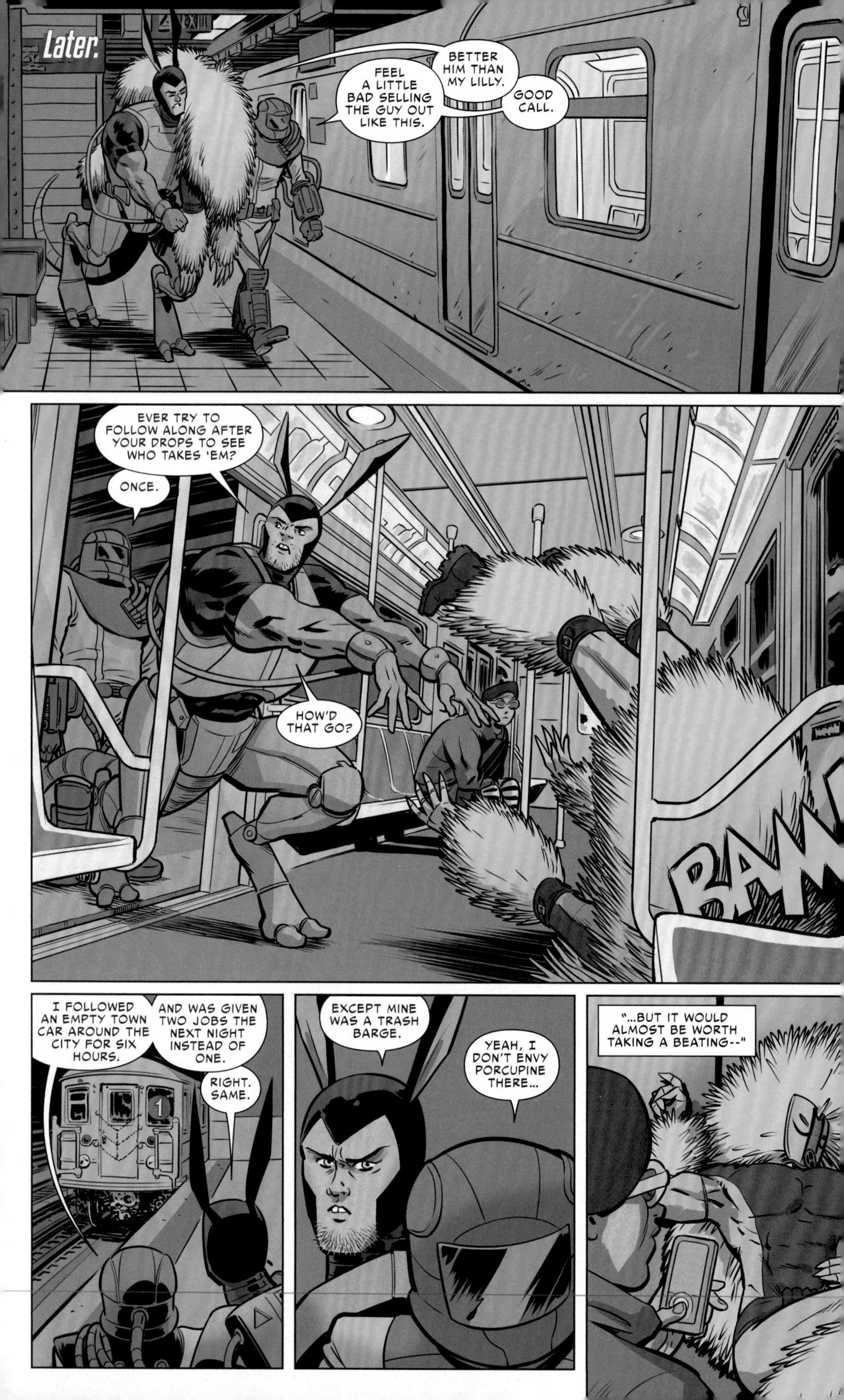
Later.
FEEL A LITTLE BAD SELLING THE GUY OUT LIKE THIS.
BETTER HIM THAN MY LILLY.
GOOD CALL.
EVER TRY TO FOLLOW ALONG AFTER YOUR DROPS TO SEE WHO TAKES 'EM?
ONCE.
HOW'D THAT GO?
BAM
I FOLLOWED AN EMPTY TOWN CAR AROUND THE CITY FOR SIX HOURS.
AND WAS GIVEN TWO JOBS THE NEXT NIGHT INSTEAD OF ONE.
RIGHT. SAME.
EXCEPT MINE WAS A TRASH BARGE.
YEAH, I DON'T ENVY PORCUPINE THERE...
"...BUT IT WOULD ALMOST BE WORTH TAKING A BEATING--"

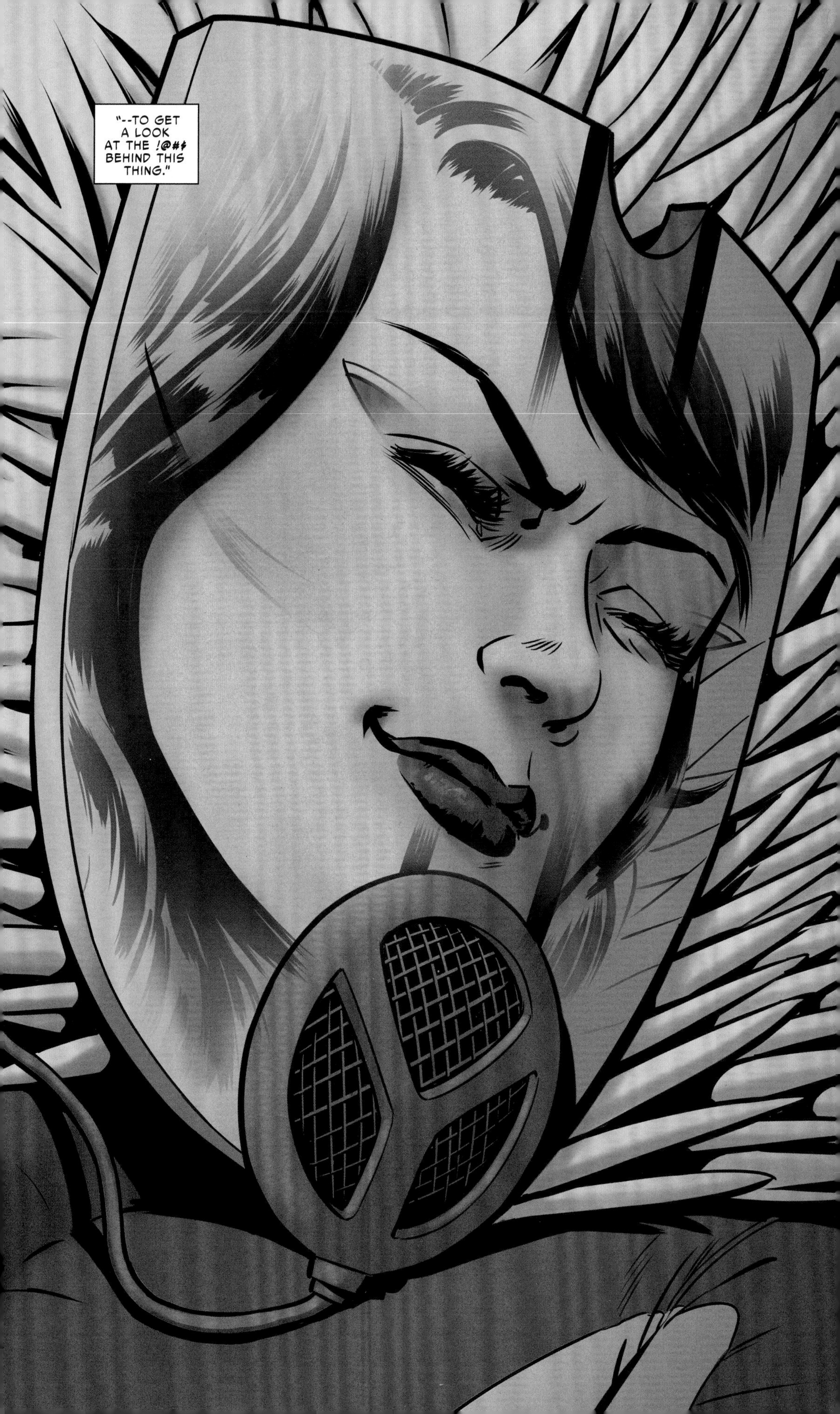
"--TO GET A LOOK AT THE !@#$ BEHIND THIS THING."

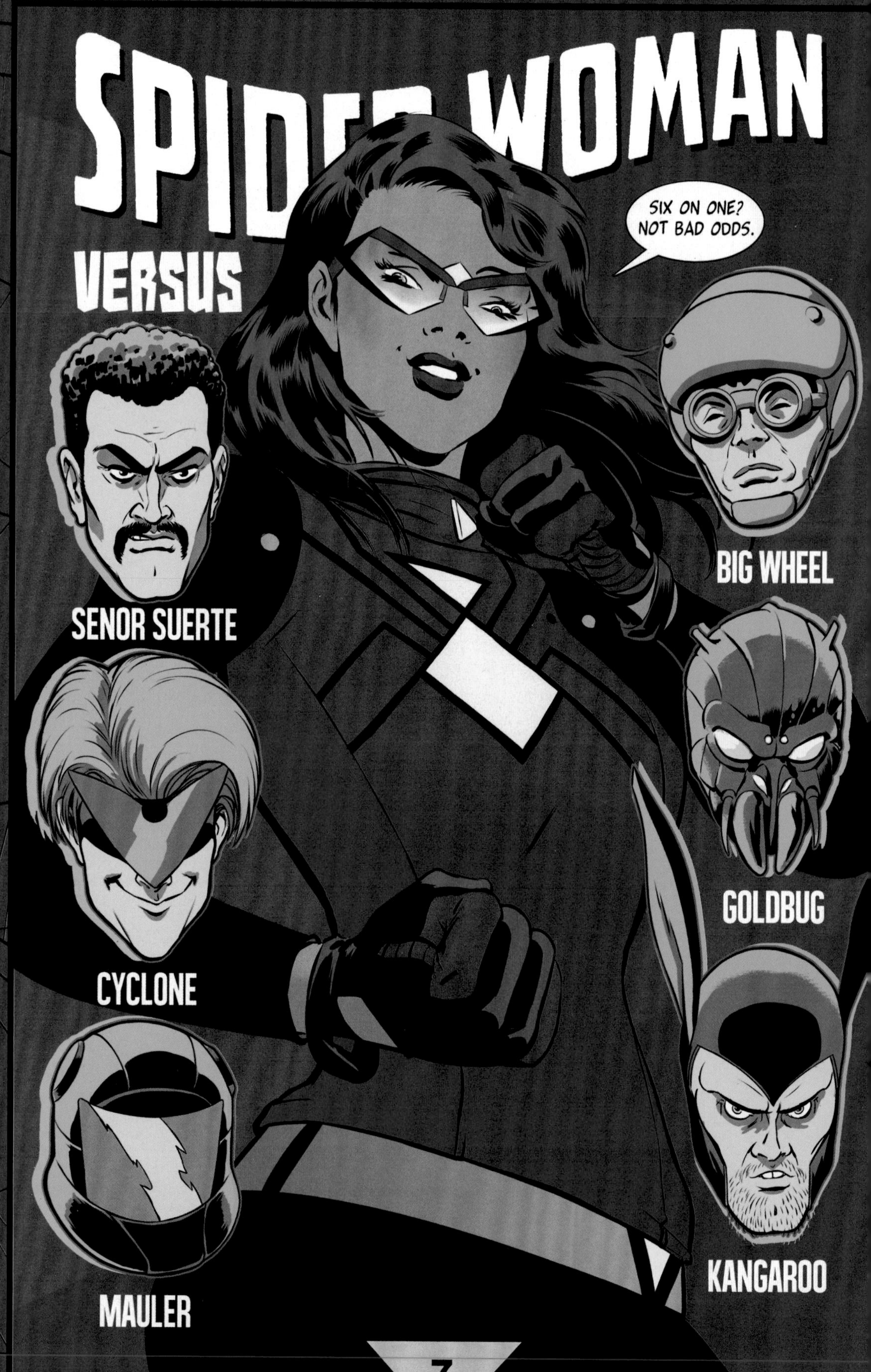
SPIDER-WOMAN
VERSUS
SIX ON ONE? NOT BAD ODDS.
SENOR SUERTE
CYCLONE
MAULER
BIG WHEEL
GOLDBUG
KANGAROO

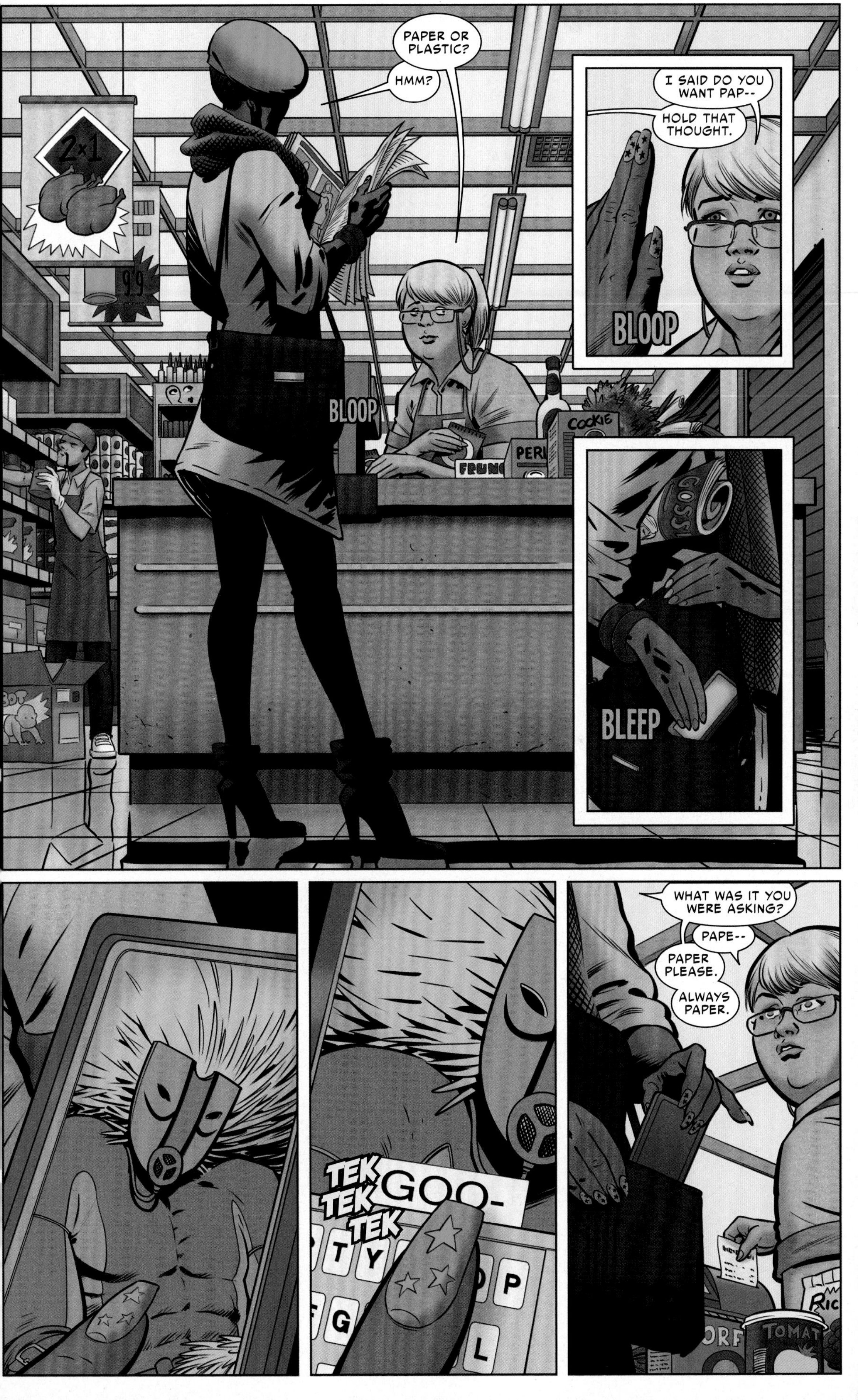

PAPER OR PLASTIC?
HMM?
I SAID DO YOU WANT PAP--
HOLD THAT THOUGHT.
BLOOP
BLOOP
BLEEP
TEK TEK TEK
GOO-
WHAT WAS IT YOU WERE ASKING?
PAPE--
PAPER PLEASE.
ALWAYS PAPER.

GOOD.

DO IT.

ALL RIGHT, I GET IT.

LIE ON THE FLOOR OF THE SUBWAY WEARING ROGER'S ASININE PINECONE SUIT...PHOTOS WILL BE TAKEN.

BUT I'VE HAD A FIERCE NOSE TICKLE GOING ON FOR ABOUT 12 MINUTES THAT I CAN'T RISK SCRATCHING.

SO RASPBERRY BERET NEEDS TO WALK AWAY BEFORE SHE SNAPS MY LAST NERVE.

GOOD GIRL. OFF YOU GO.

LET ME FEIGN UNCONSCIOUSNESS IN...

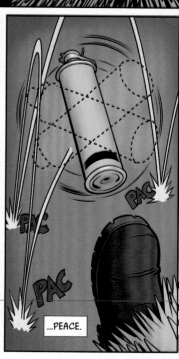

...PEACE.

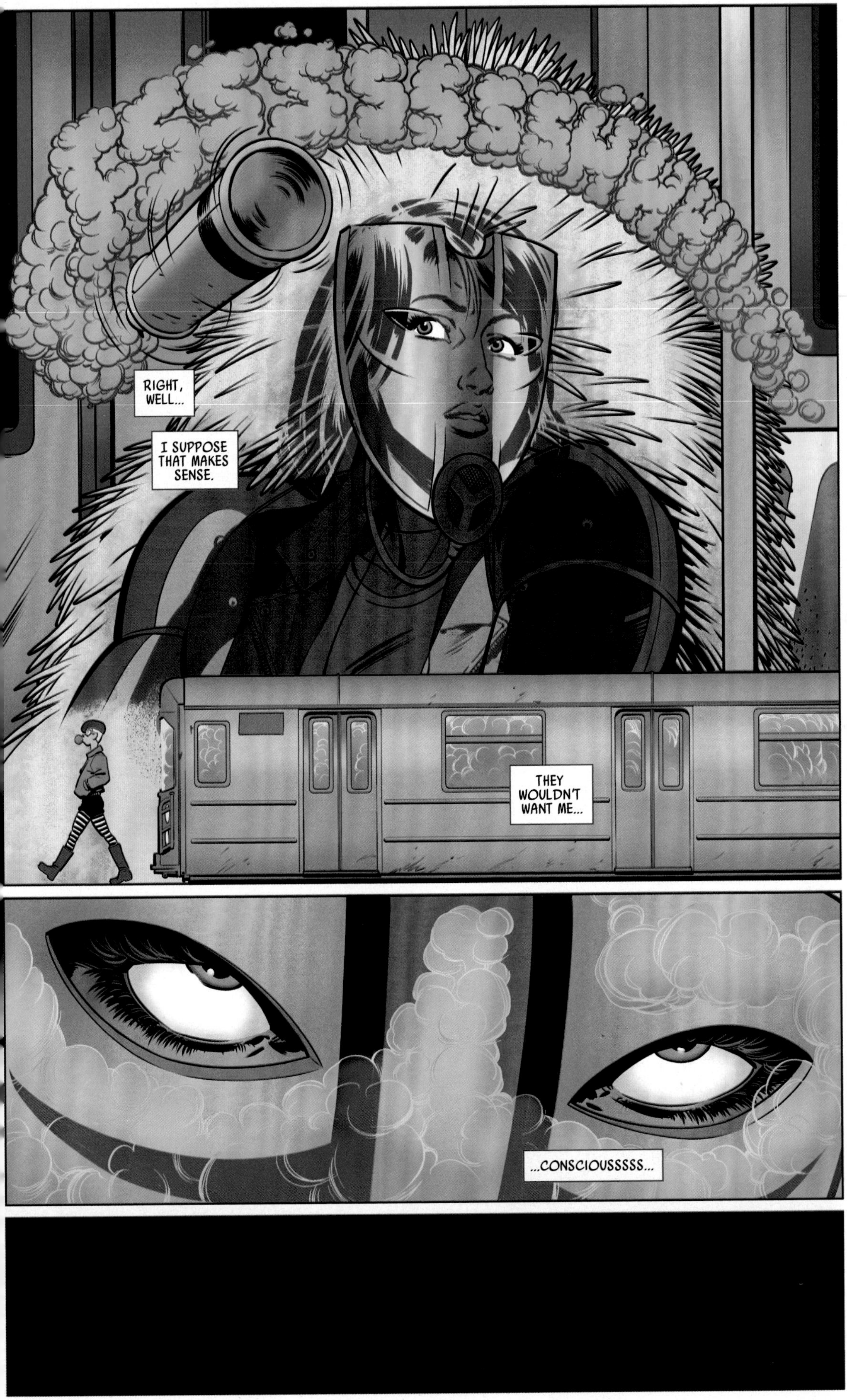
RIGHT, WELL...
I SUPPOSE THAT MAKES SENSE.
THEY WOULDN'T WANT ME...
...CONSCIOUSSSSS...

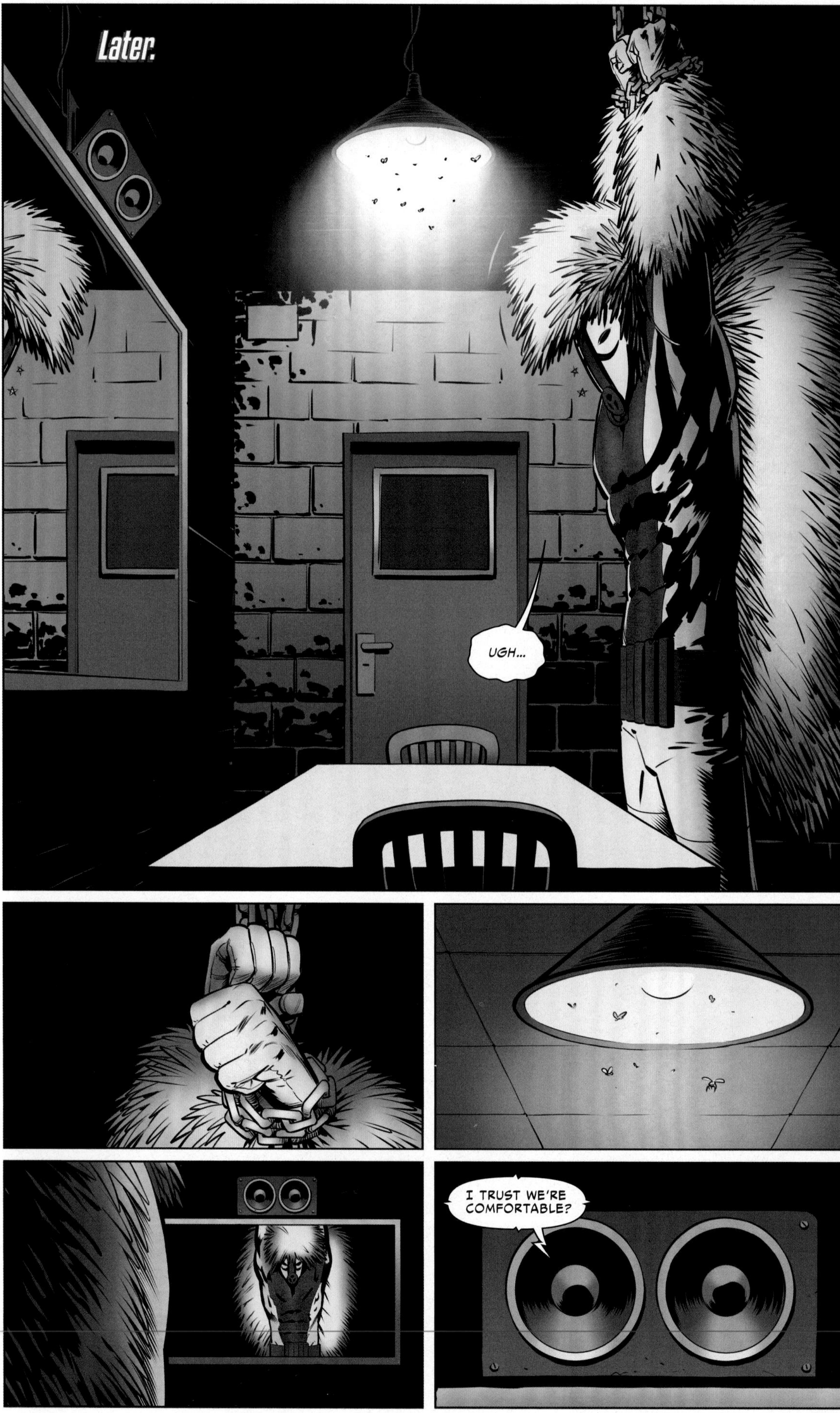
Later.
UGH...
I TRUST WE'RE COMFORTABLE?

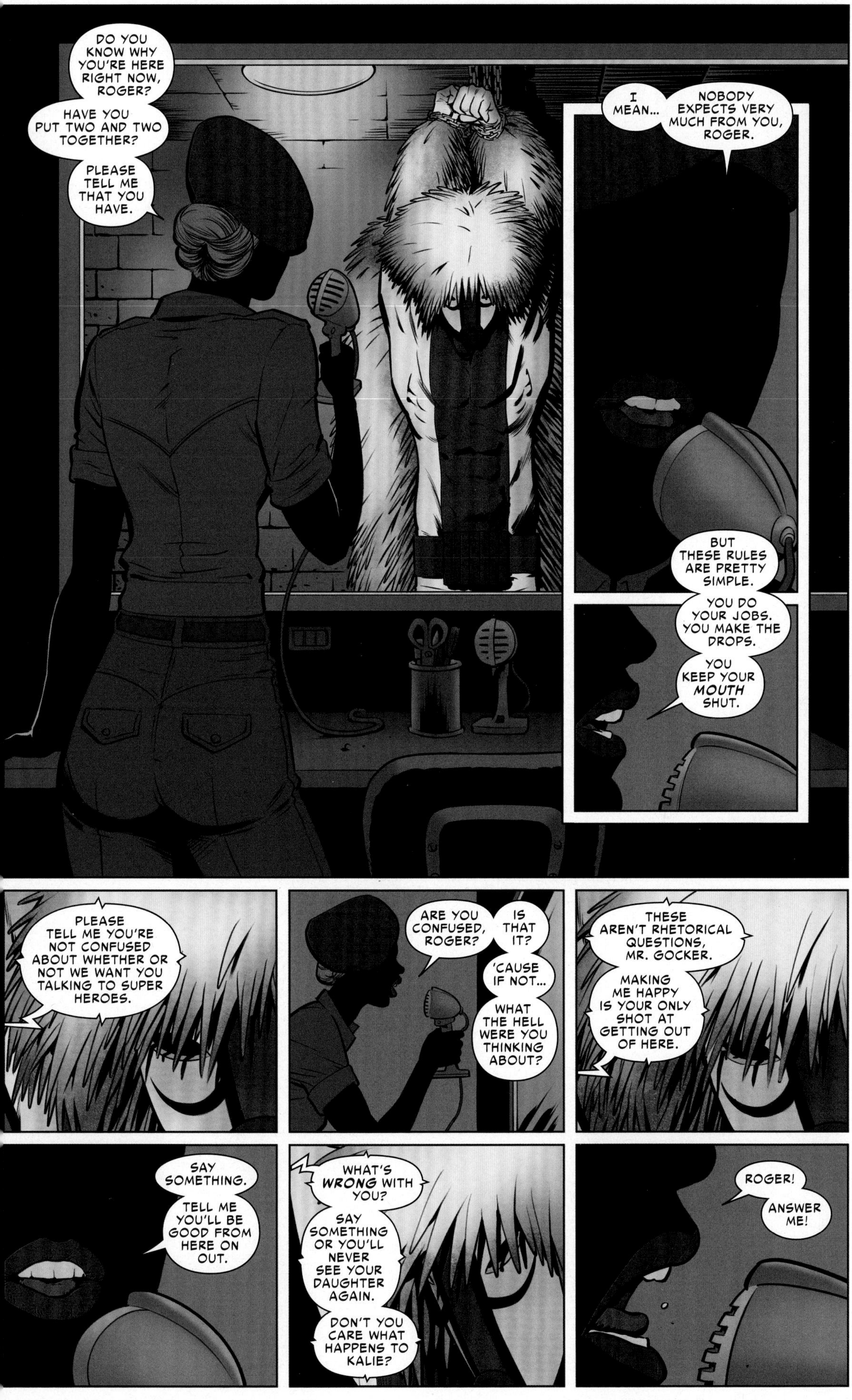
DO YOU KNOW WHY YOU'RE HERE RIGHT NOW, ROGER?
HAVE YOU PUT TWO AND TWO TOGETHER?
PLEASE TELL ME THAT YOU HAVE.
I MEAN...
NOBODY EXPECTS VERY MUCH FROM YOU, ROGER.
BUT THESE RULES ARE PRETTY SIMPLE.
YOU DO YOUR JOBS. YOU MAKE THE DROPS.
YOU KEEP YOUR *MOUTH* SHUT.
PLEASE TELL ME YOU'RE NOT CONFUSED ABOUT WHETHER OR NOT WE WANT YOU TALKING TO SUPER HEROES.
ARE YOU CONFUSED, ROGER?
IS THAT IT?
'CAUSE IF NOT...
WHAT THE HELL WERE YOU THINKING ABOUT?
THESE AREN'T RHETORICAL QUESTIONS, MR. GOCKER.
MAKING ME HAPPY IS YOUR ONLY SHOT AT GETTING OUT OF HERE.
SAY SOMETHING.
TELL ME YOU'LL BE GOOD FROM HERE ON OUT.
WHAT'S *WRONG* WITH YOU?
SAY SOMETHING OR YOU'LL NEVER SEE YOUR DAUGHTER AGAIN.
DON'T YOU CARE WHAT HAPPENS TO KALIE?
ROGER!
ANSWER ME!

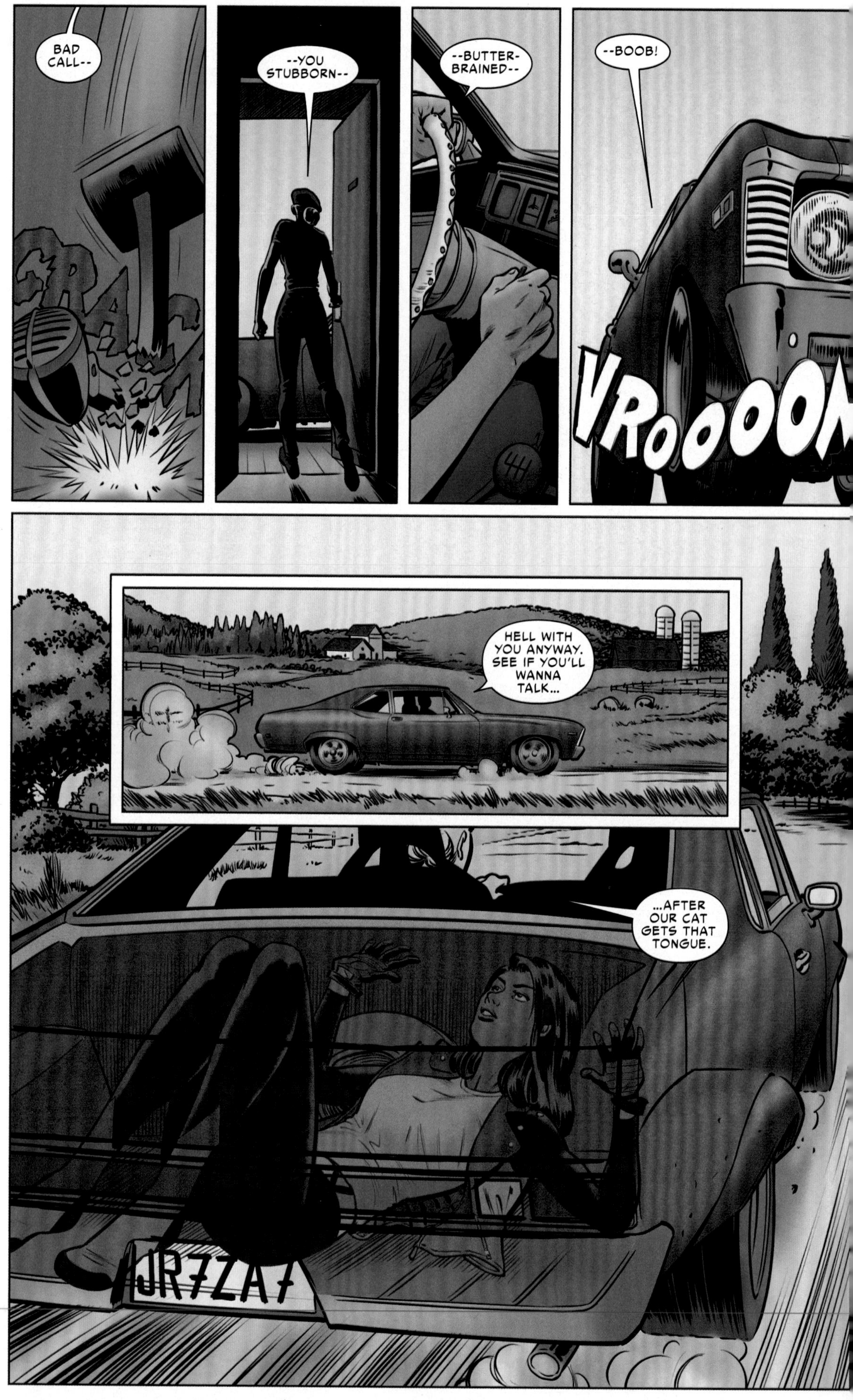
BAD CALL--
CRAK
--YOU STUBBORN--
--BUTTER-BRAINED--
--BOOB!
VROOOOM
HELL WITH YOU ANYWAY. SEE IF YOU'LL WANNA TALK...
...AFTER OUR CAT GETS THAT TONGUE.
JR7ZA7

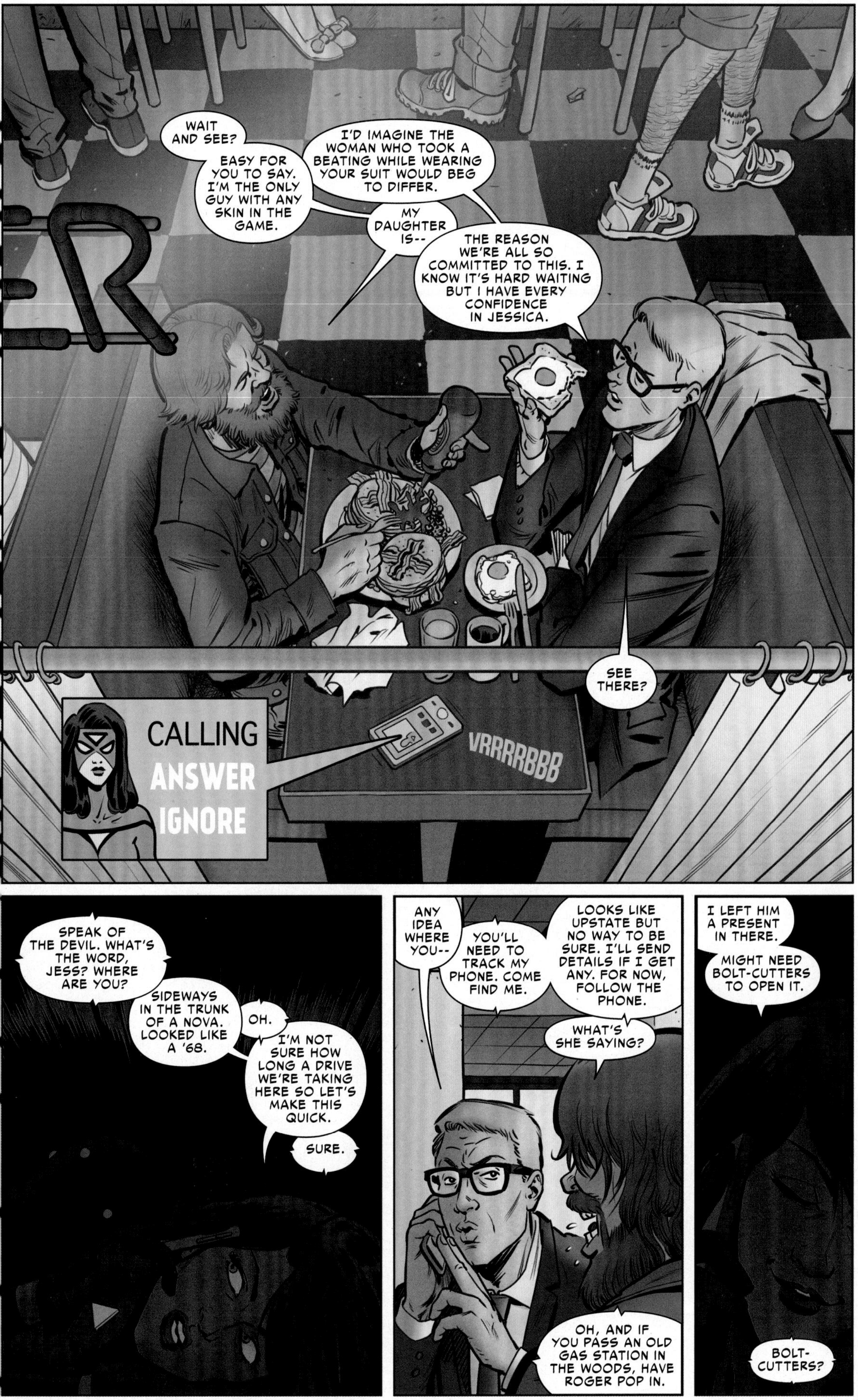

WAIT AND SEE?
EASY FOR YOU TO SAY. I'M THE ONLY GUY WITH ANY SKIN IN THE GAME.
I'D IMAGINE THE WOMAN WHO TOOK A BEATING WHILE WEARING YOUR SUIT WOULD BEG TO DIFFER.
MY DAUGHTER IS--
THE REASON WE'RE ALL SO COMMITTED TO THIS. I KNOW IT'S HARD WAITING BUT I HAVE EVERY CONFIDENCE IN JESSICA.
SEE THERE?
CALLING
ANSWER
IGNORE
VRRRRBBB
SPEAK OF THE DEVIL. WHAT'S THE WORD, JESS? WHERE ARE YOU?
SIDEWAYS IN THE TRUNK OF A NOVA. LOOKED LIKE A '68.
OH.
I'M NOT SURE HOW LONG A DRIVE WE'RE TAKING HERE SO LET'S MAKE THIS QUICK.
SURE.
ANY IDEA WHERE YOU--
YOU'LL NEED TO TRACK MY PHONE. COME FIND ME.
LOOKS LIKE UPSTATE BUT NO WAY TO BE SURE. I'LL SEND DETAILS IF I GET ANY. FOR NOW, FOLLOW THE PHONE.
WHAT'S SHE SAYING?
OH, AND IF YOU PASS AN OLD GAS STATION IN THE WOODS, HAVE ROGER POP IN.
I LEFT HIM A PRESENT IN THERE.
MIGHT NEED BOLT-CUTTERS TO OPEN IT.
BOLT-CUTTERS?

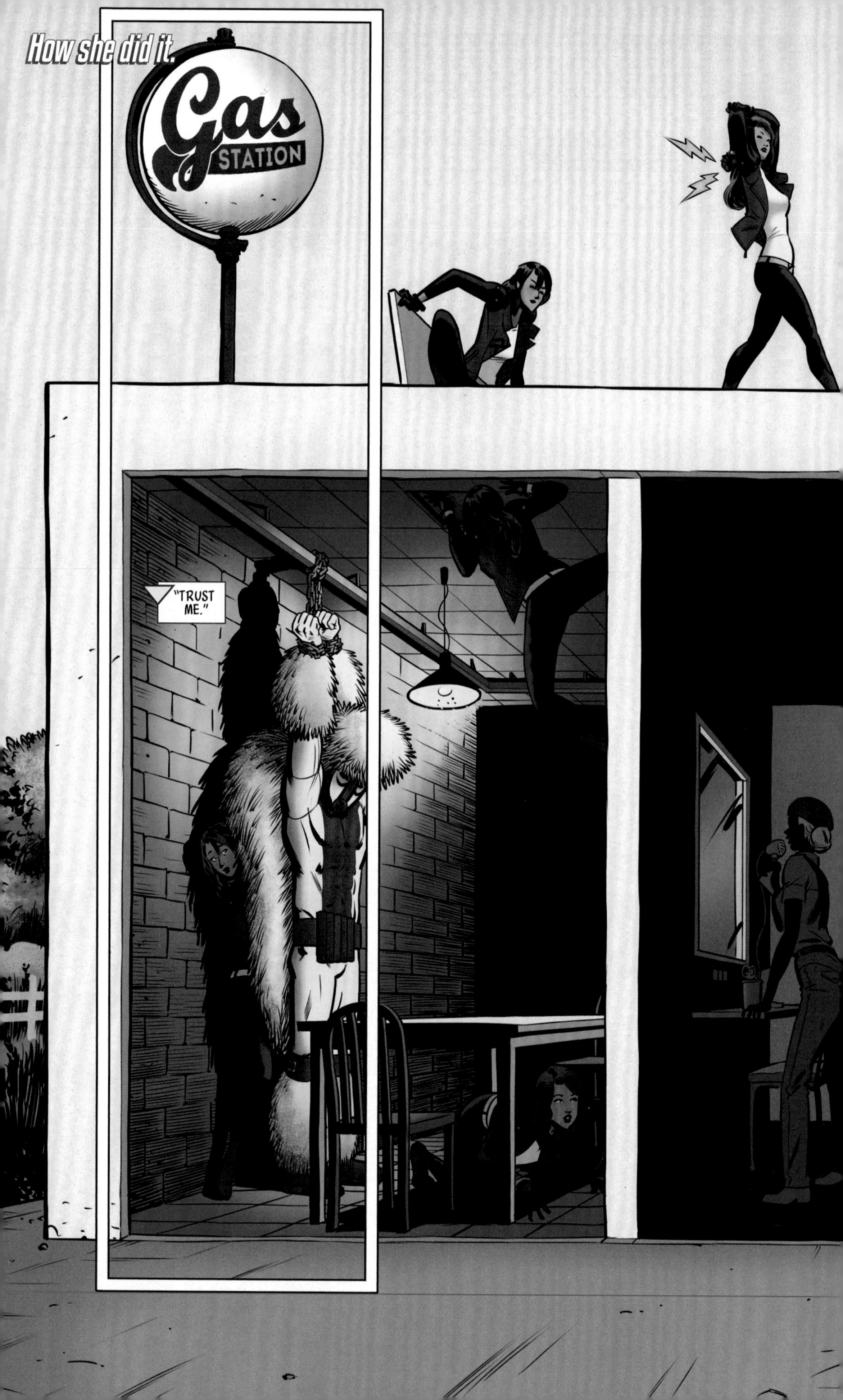
How she did it.
Gas
STATION
"TRUST ME."

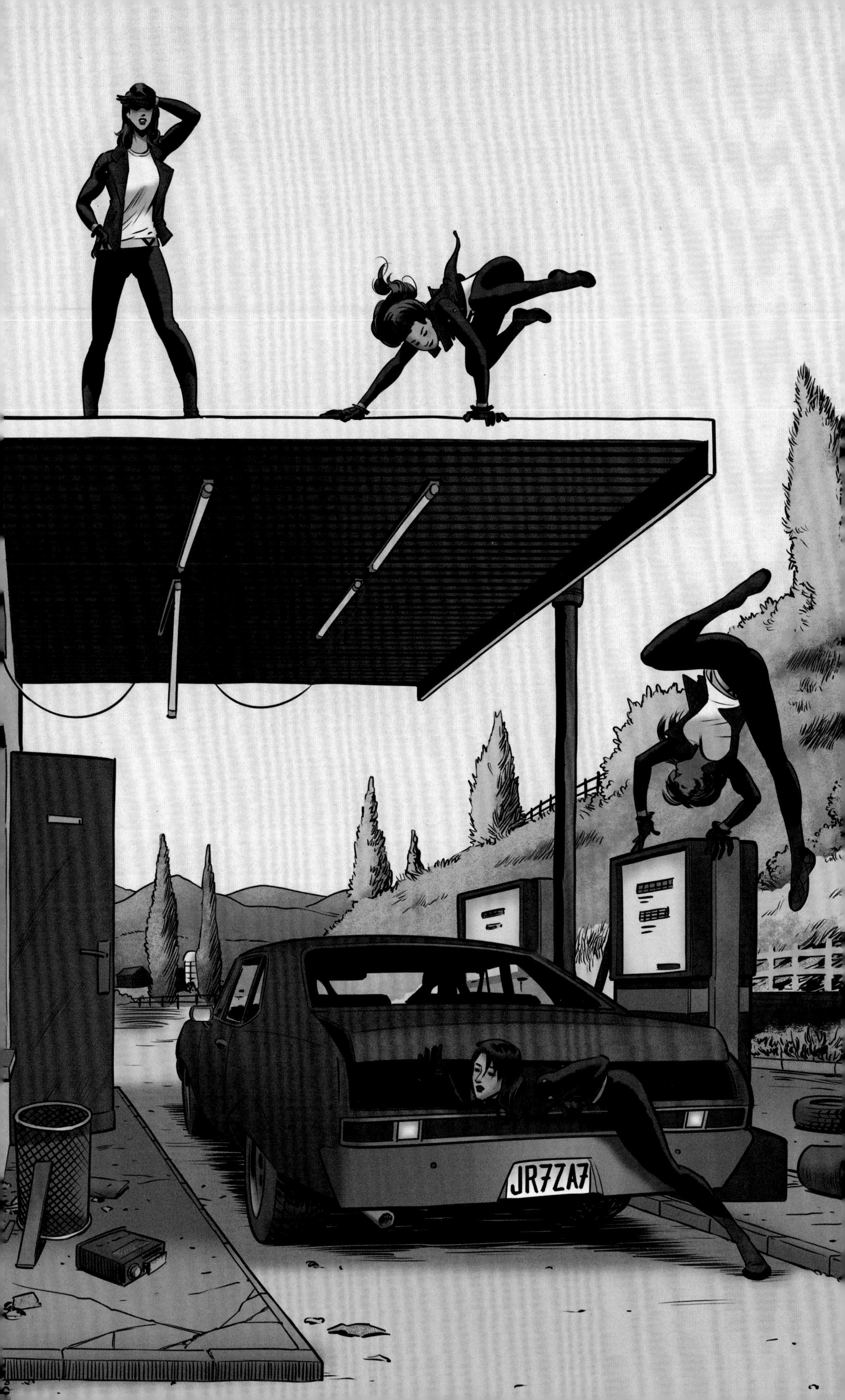
JR7ZA7

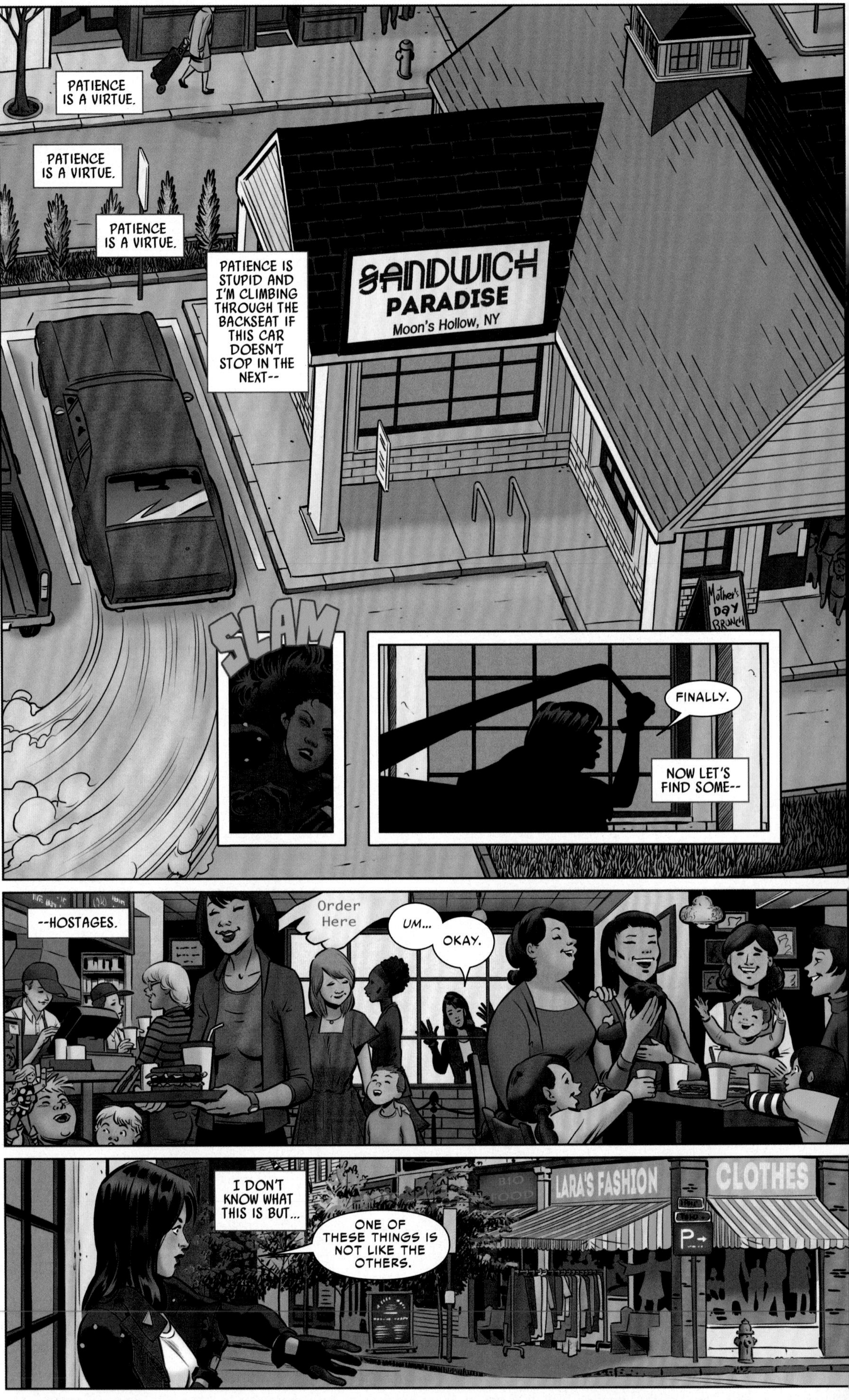
PATIENCE IS A VIRTUE.
PATIENCE IS A VIRTUE.
PATIENCE IS A VIRTUE.
PATIENCE IS STUPID AND I'M CLIMBING THROUGH THE BACKSEAT IF THIS CAR DOESN'T STOP IN THE NEXT--
SANDWICH PARADISE
Moon's Hollow, NY
Mother's Day Brunch
SLAM
FINALLY.
NOW LET'S FIND SOME--
--HOSTAGES.
Order Here
UM...
OKAY.
I DON'T KNOW WHAT THIS IS BUT...
ONE OF THESE THINGS IS NOT LIKE THE OTHERS.
LARA'S FASHION
CLOTHES

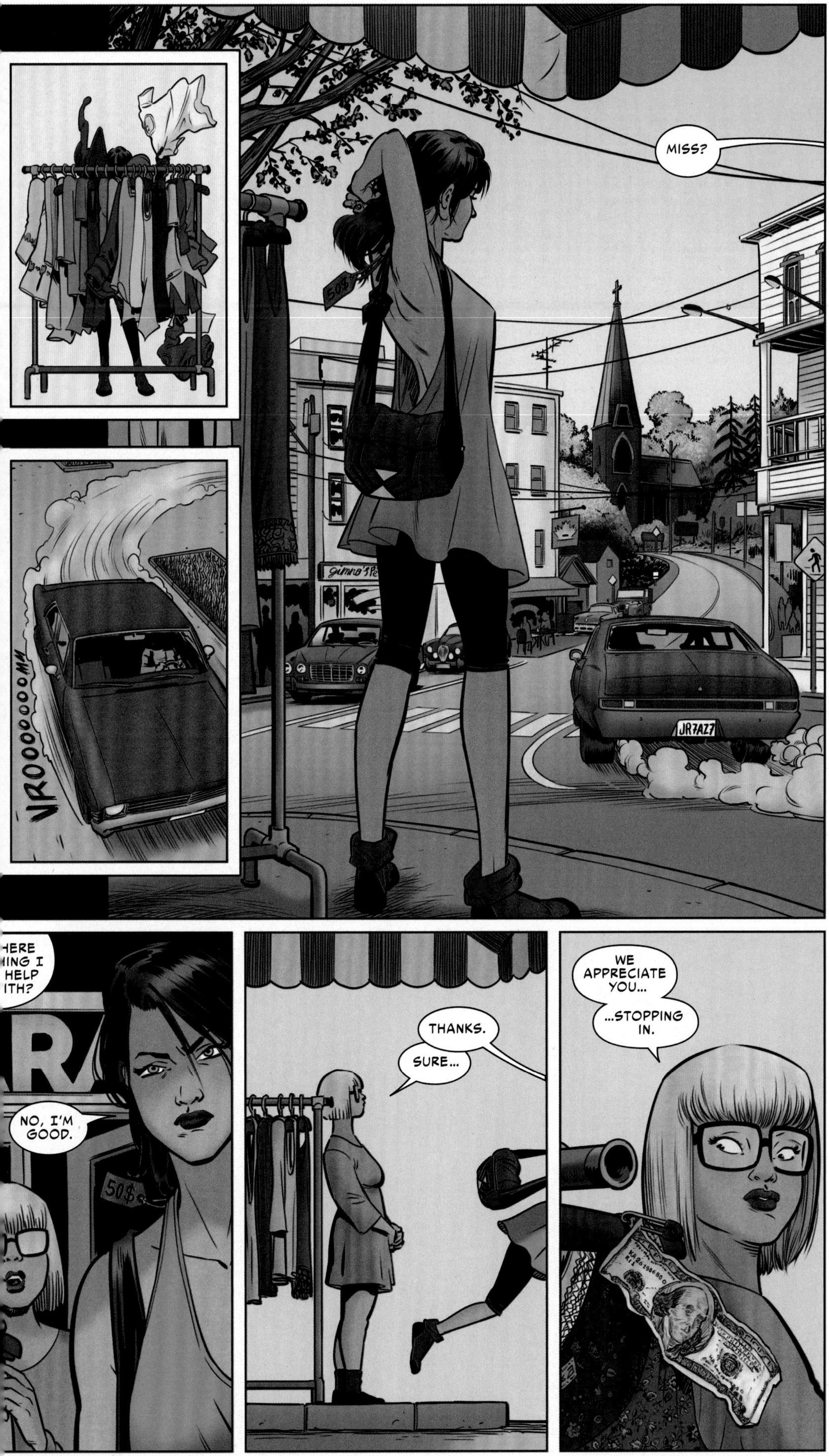
VROOOOOOOOMM
JR7AZ7
MISS?
HERE HING I HELP ITH?
NO, I'M GOOD.
THANKS.
SURE...
WE APPRECIATE YOU...
...STOPPING IN.

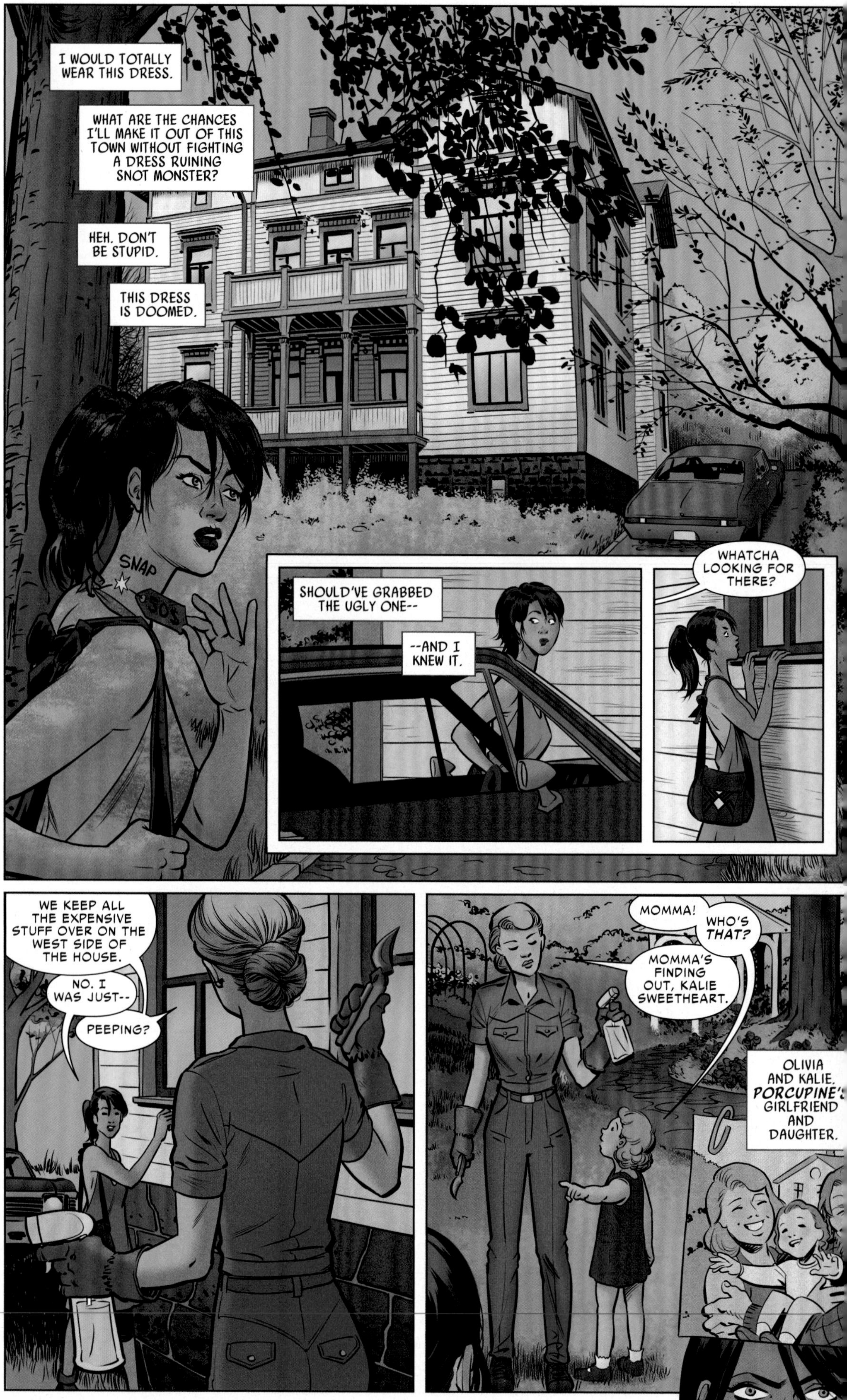
I WOULD TOTALLY WEAR THIS DRESS.
WHAT ARE THE CHANCES I'LL MAKE IT OUT OF THIS TOWN WITHOUT FIGHTING A DRESS RUINING SNOT MONSTER?
HEH. DON'T BE STUPID.
THIS DRESS IS DOOMED.
SNAP
SOS
SHOULD'VE GRABBED THE UGLY ONE--
--AND I KNEW IT.
WHATCHA LOOKING FOR THERE?
WE KEEP ALL THE EXPENSIVE STUFF OVER ON THE WEST SIDE OF THE HOUSE.
NO. I WAS JUST--
PEEPING?
MOMMA!
WHO'S THAT?
MOMMA'S FINDING OUT, KALIE SWEETHEART.
OLIVIA AND KALIE. PORCUPINE'S GIRLFRIEND AND DAUGHTER.

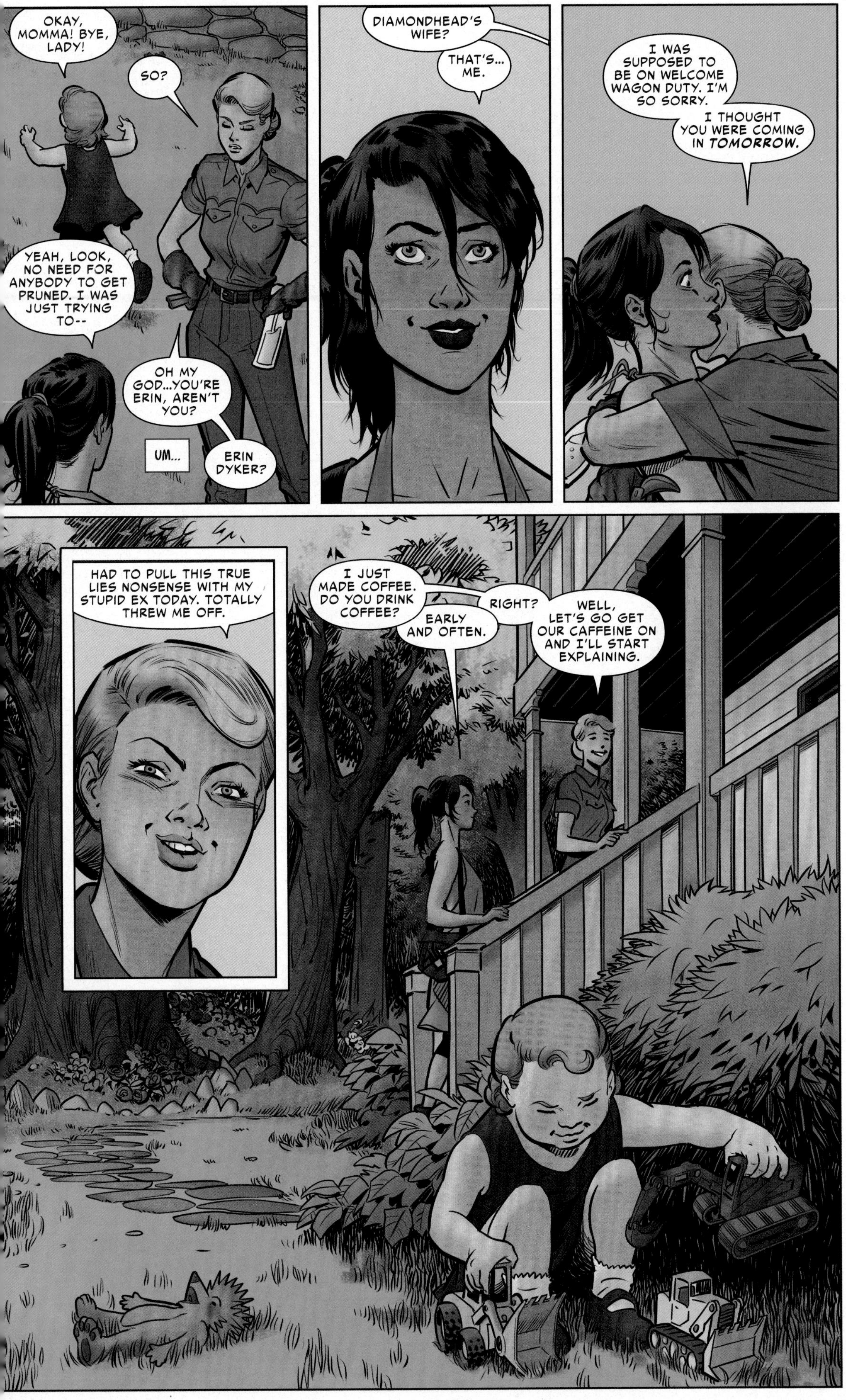

OKAY, MOMMA! BYE, LADY!
SO?
YEAH, LOOK, NO NEED FOR ANYBODY TO GET PRUNED. I WAS JUST TRYING TO--
OH MY GOD...YOU'RE ERIN, AREN'T YOU?
UM...
ERIN DYKER?
DIAMONDHEAD'S WIFE?
THAT'S... ME.
I WAS SUPPOSED TO BE ON WELCOME WAGON DUTY. I'M SO SORRY.
I THOUGHT YOU WERE COMING IN TOMORROW.
HAD TO PULL THIS TRUE LIES NONSENSE WITH MY STUPID EX TODAY. TOTALLY THREW ME OFF.
I JUST MADE COFFEE. DO YOU DRINK COFFEE?
RIGHT?
EARLY AND OFTEN.
WELL, LET'S GO GET OUR CAFFEINE ON AND I'LL START EXPLAINING.

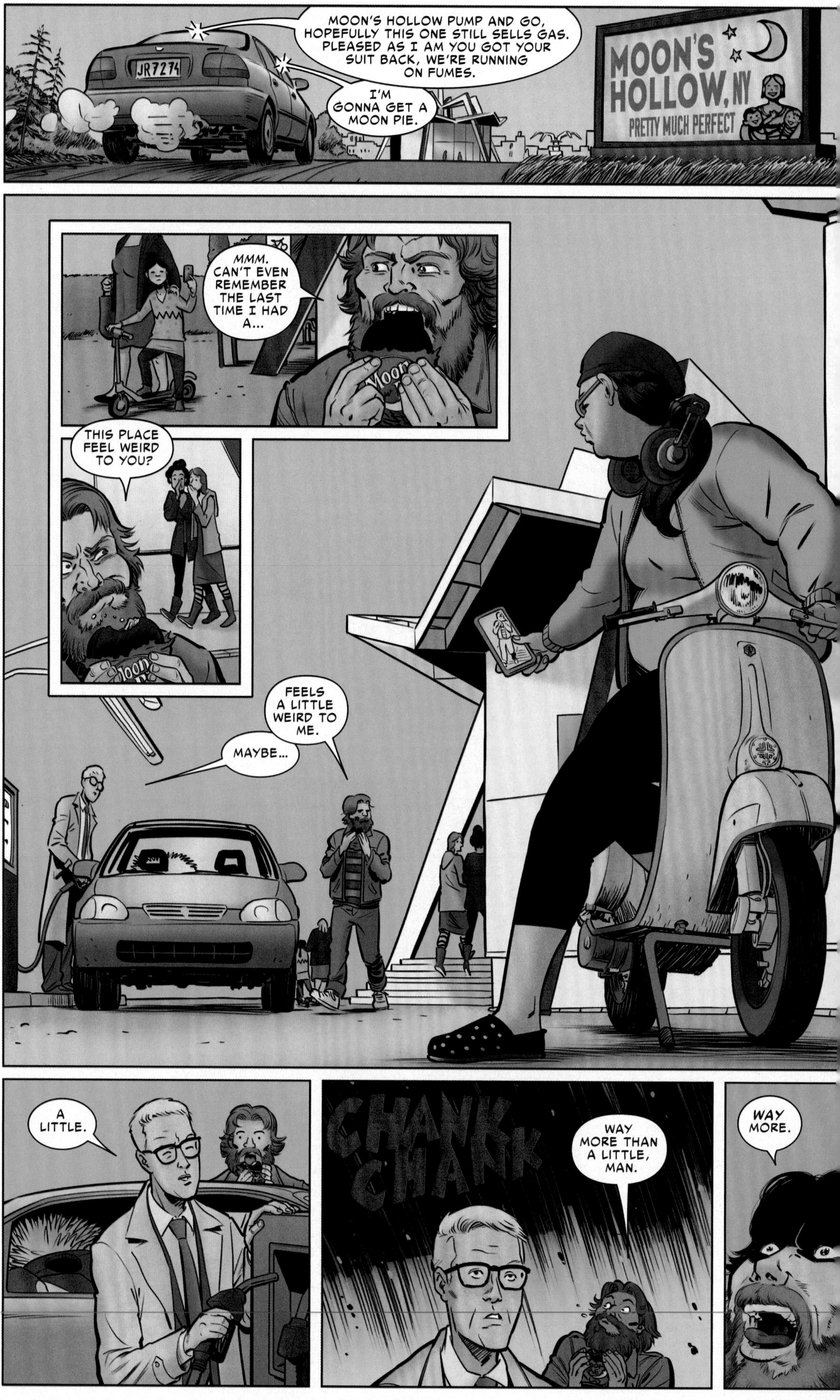

MOON'S HOLLOW PUMP AND GO, HOPEFULLY THIS ONE STILL SELLS GAS. PLEASED AS I AM YOU GOT YOUR SUIT BACK, WE'RE RUNNING ON FUMES.
I'M GONNA GET A MOON PIE.
MOON'S HOLLOW, NY
PRETTY MUCH PERFECT
JR7274
MMM. CAN'T EVEN REMEMBER THE LAST TIME I HAD A...
THIS PLACE FEEL WEIRD TO YOU?
FEELS A LITTLE WEIRD TO ME.
MAYBE...
A LITTLE.
CHANK CHANK
WAY MORE THAN A LITTLE, MAN.
WAY MORE.

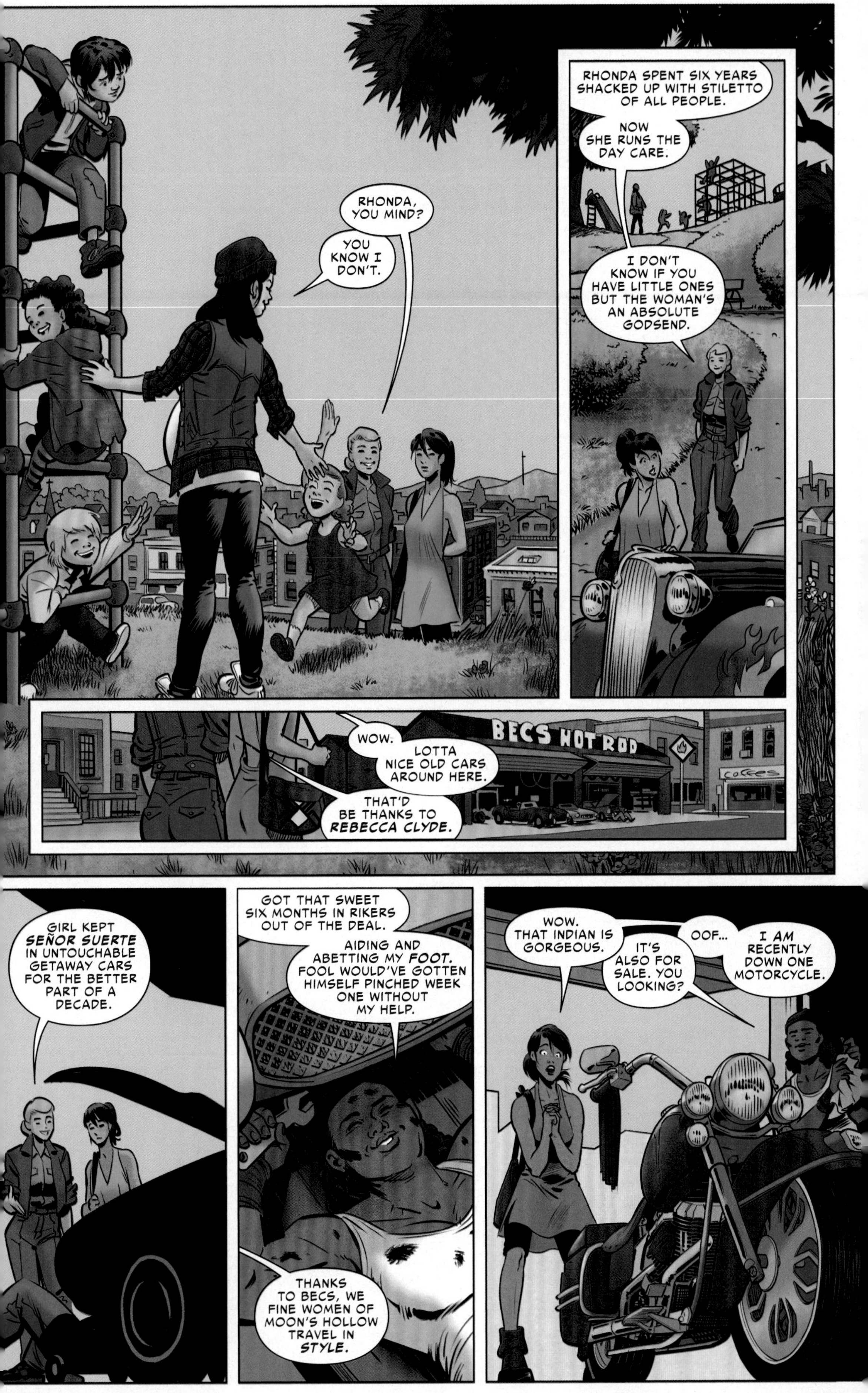
RHONDA, YOU MIND?
YOU KNOW I DON'T.
RHONDA SPENT SIX YEARS SHACKED UP WITH STILETTO OF ALL PEOPLE.
NOW SHE RUNS THE DAY CARE.
I DON'T KNOW IF YOU HAVE LITTLE ONES BUT THE WOMAN'S AN ABSOLUTE GODSEND.
BECS HOT ROD
COFFEE
WOW.
LOTTA NICE OLD CARS AROUND HERE.
THAT'D BE THANKS TO *REBECCA CLYDE*.
GIRL KEPT *SEÑOR SUERTE* IN UNTOUCHABLE GETAWAY CARS FOR THE BETTER PART OF A DECADE.
GOT THAT SWEET SIX MONTHS IN RIKERS OUT OF THE DEAL.
AIDING AND ABETTING MY *FOOT*. FOOL WOULD'VE GOTTEN HIMSELF PINCHED WEEK ONE WITHOUT MY HELP.
THANKS TO BECS, WE FINE WOMEN OF MOON'S HOLLOW TRAVEL IN *STYLE*.
WOW. THAT INDIAN IS GORGEOUS.
IT'S ALSO FOR SALE. YOU LOOKING?
OOF...
I *AM* RECENTLY DOWN ONE MOTORCYCLE.

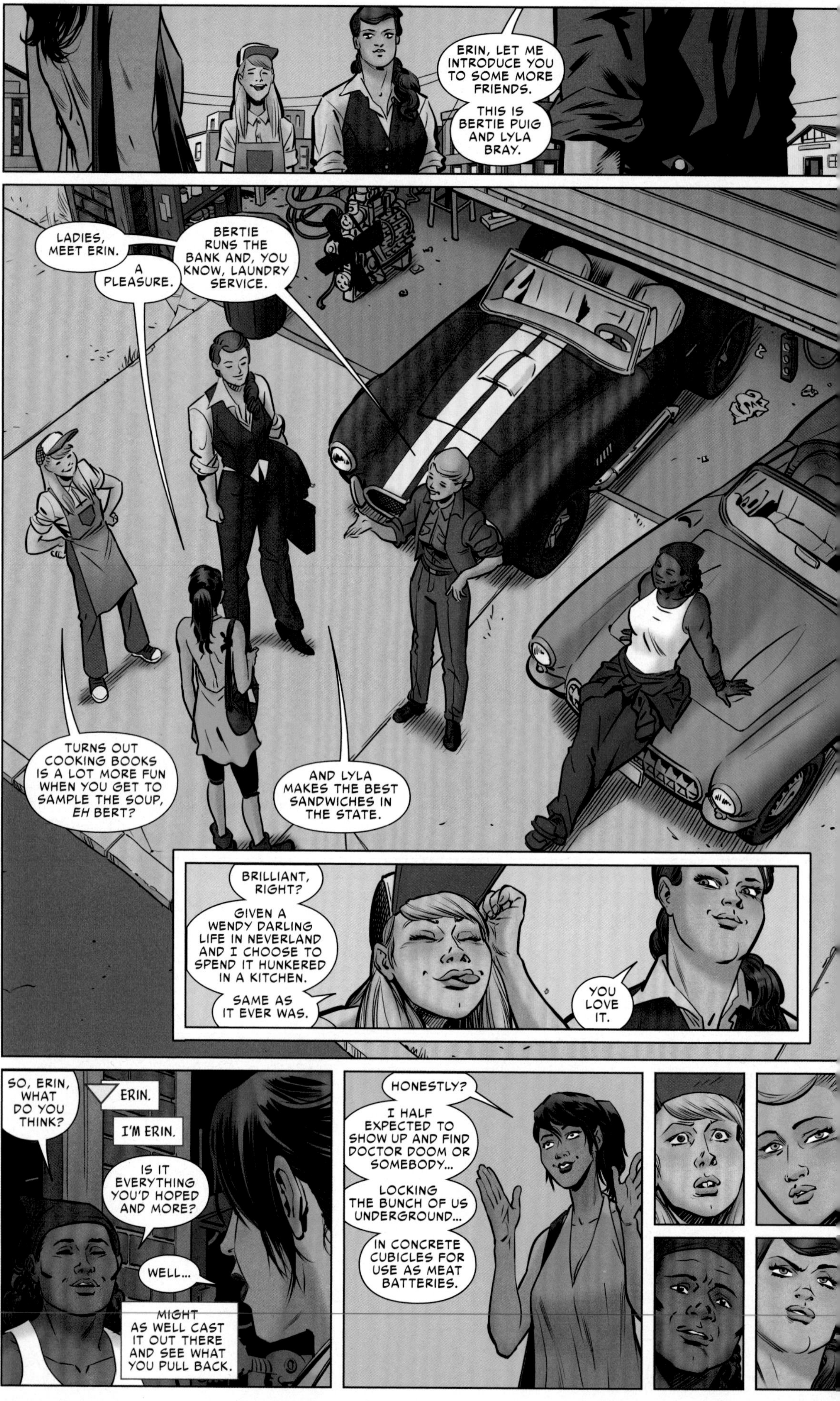

ERIN, LET ME INTRODUCE YOU TO SOME MORE FRIENDS.
THIS IS BERTIE PUIG AND LYLA BRAY.
LADIES, MEET ERIN.
A PLEASURE.
BERTIE RUNS THE BANK AND, YOU KNOW, LAUNDRY SERVICE.
TURNS OUT COOKING BOOKS IS A LOT MORE FUN WHEN YOU GET TO SAMPLE THE SOUP, EH BERT?
AND LYLA MAKES THE BEST SANDWICHES IN THE STATE.
BRILLIANT, RIGHT?
GIVEN A WENDY DARLING LIFE IN NEVERLAND AND I CHOOSE TO SPEND IT HUNKERED IN A KITCHEN.
SAME AS IT EVER WAS.
YOU LOVE IT.
SO, ERIN, WHAT DO YOU THINK?
ERIN.
I'M ERIN.
IS IT EVERYTHING YOU'D HOPED AND MORE?
WELL...
MIGHT AS WELL CAST IT OUT THERE AND SEE WHAT YOU PULL BACK.
HONESTLY?
I HALF EXPECTED TO SHOW UP AND FIND DOCTOR DOOM OR SOMEBODY...
LOCKING THE BUNCH OF US UNDERGROUND...
IN CONCRETE CUBICLES FOR USE AS MEAT BATTERIES.

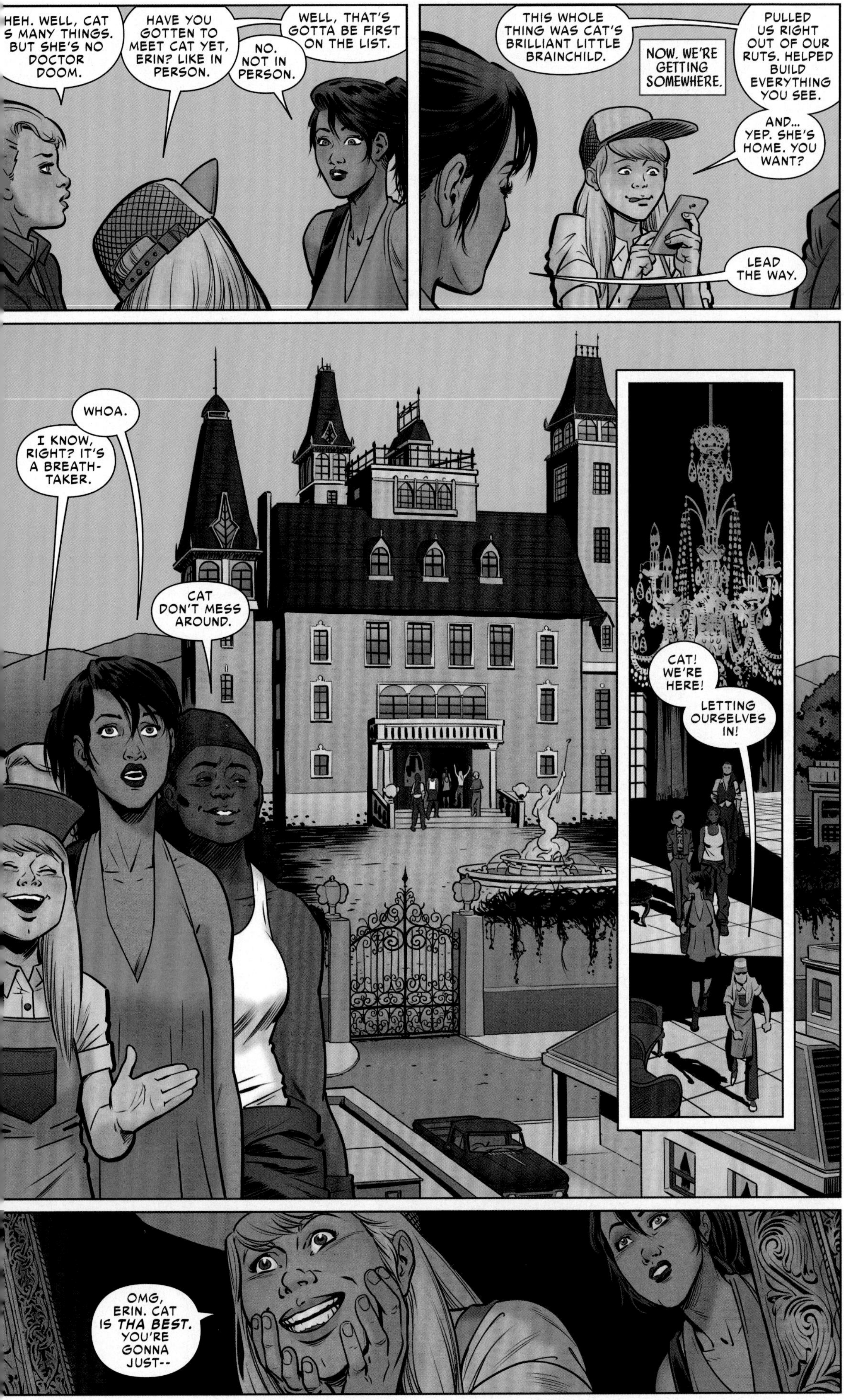

HEH. WELL, CAT IS MANY THINGS. BUT SHE'S NO DOCTOR DOOM.
HAVE YOU GOTTEN TO MEET CAT YET, ERIN? LIKE IN PERSON.
NO. NOT IN PERSON.
WELL, THAT'S GOTTA BE FIRST ON THE LIST.
THIS WHOLE THING WAS CAT'S BRILLIANT LITTLE BRAINCHILD.
PULLED US RIGHT OUT OF OUR RUTS. HELPED BUILD EVERYTHING YOU SEE.
NOW. WE'RE GETTING SOMEWHERE.
AND... YEP. SHE'S HOME. YOU WANT?
LEAD THE WAY.
WHOA.
I KNOW, RIGHT? IT'S A BREATH-TAKER.
CAT DON'T MESS AROUND.
CAT! WE'RE HERE!
LETTING OURSELVES IN!
OMG, ERIN. CAT IS *THA BEST.* YOU'RE GONNA JUST--

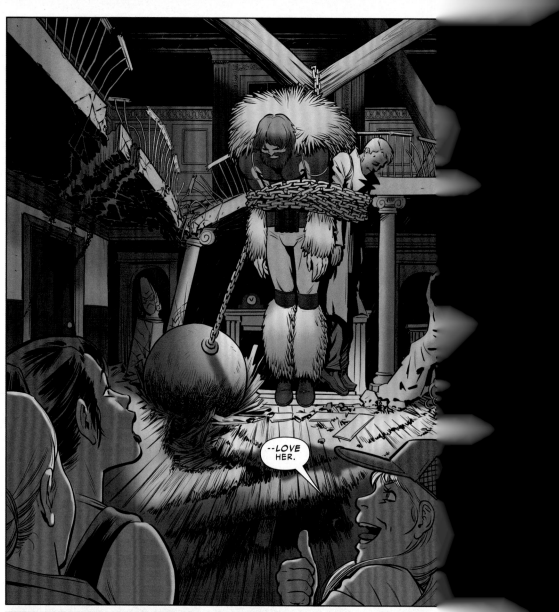

--LOVE HER.

ROGER!

BEN, WHAT?

BE...HIND...

YOU.

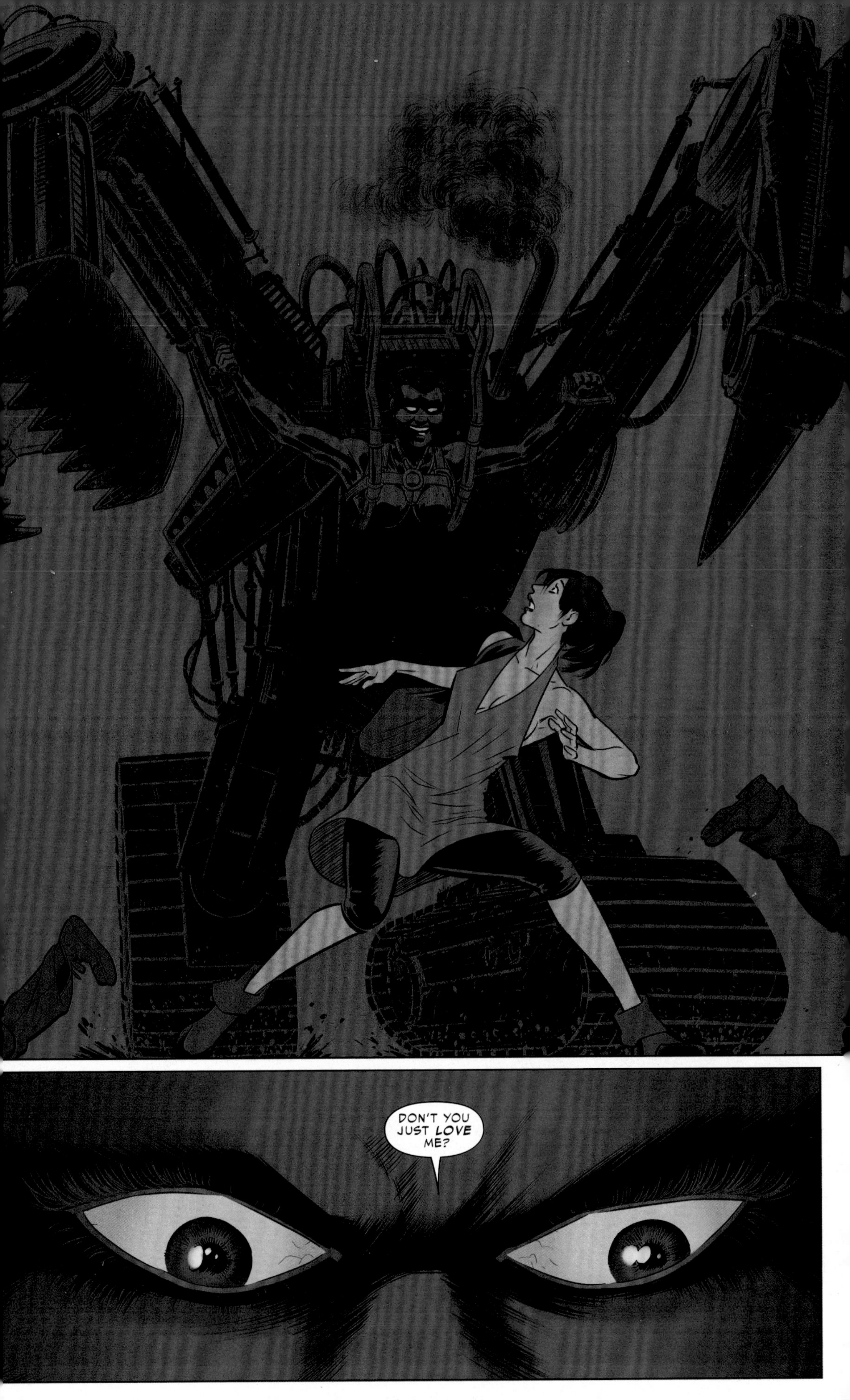
DON'T YOU JUST LOVE ME?

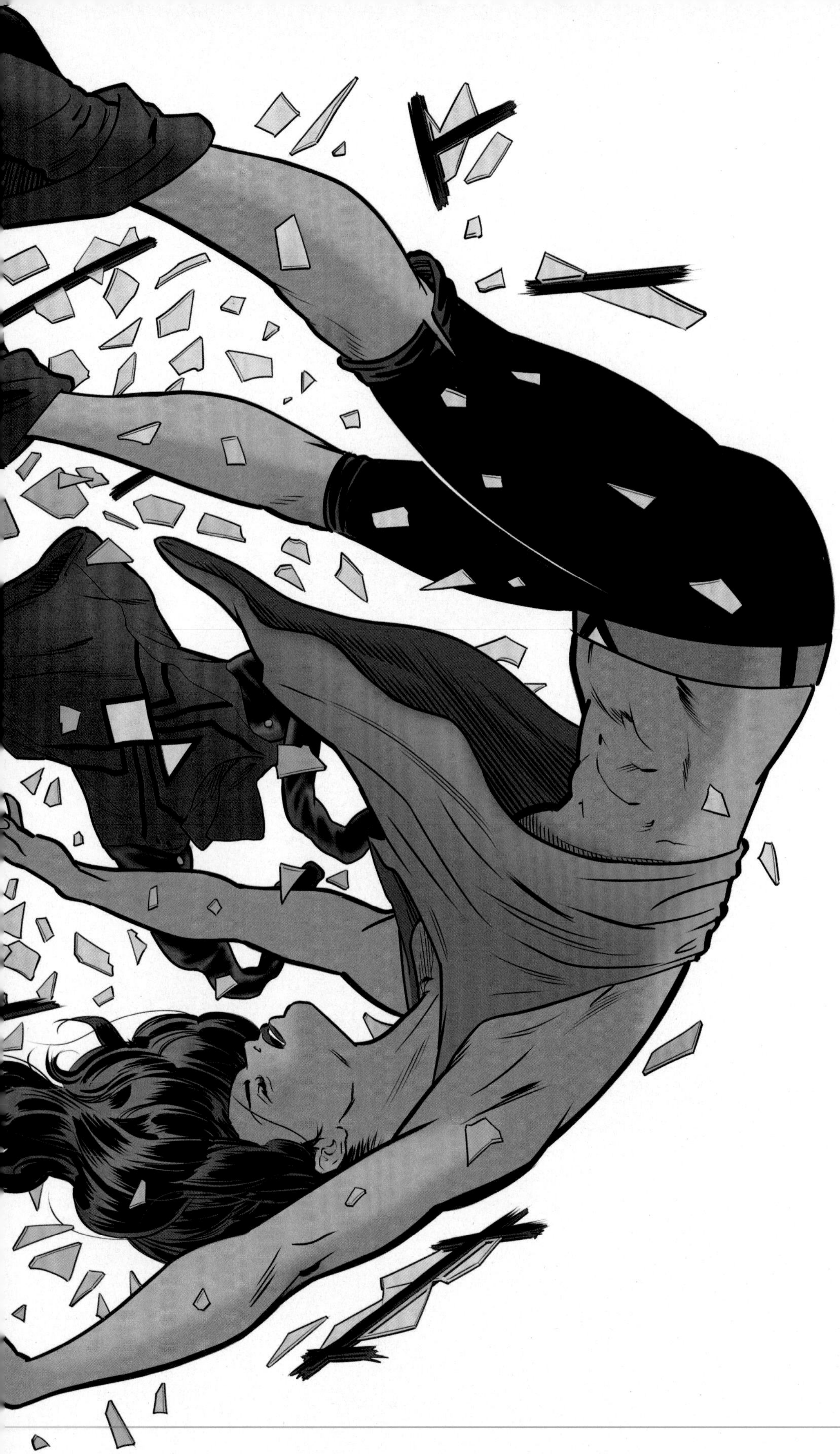

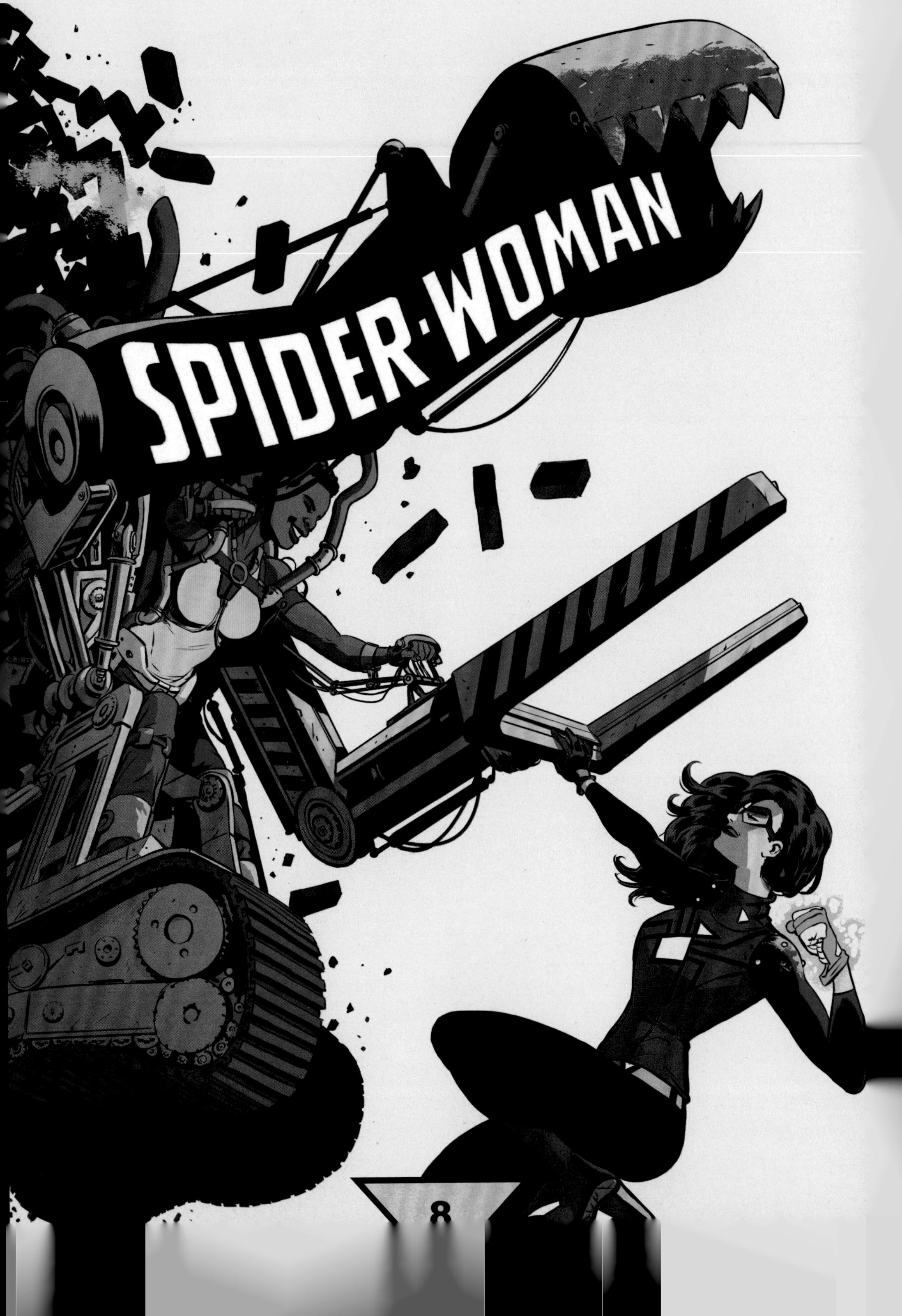
SPIDER-WOMAN
8

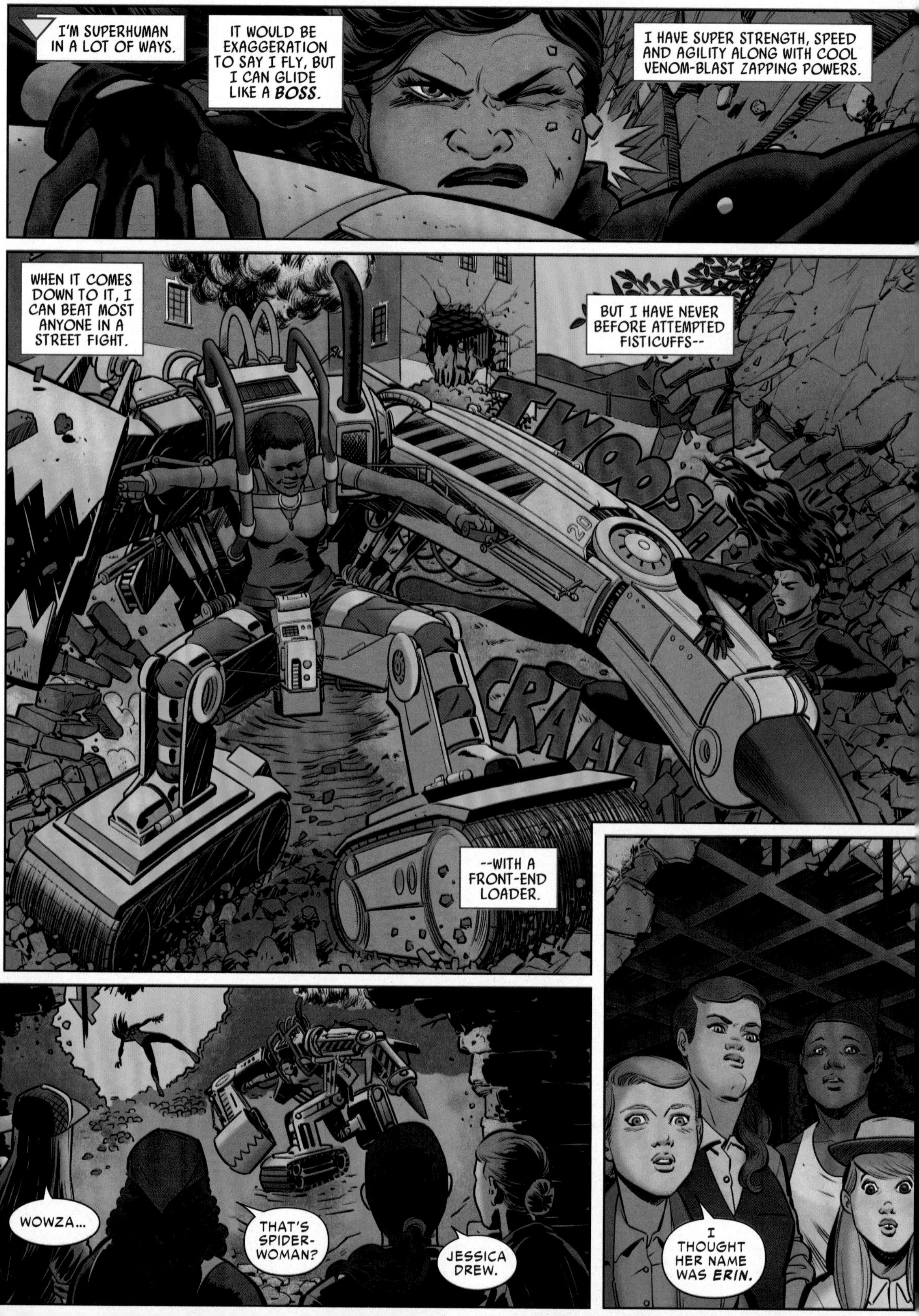

I'M SUPERHUMAN IN A LOT OF WAYS.
IT WOULD BE EXAGGERATION TO SAY I FLY, BUT I CAN GLIDE LIKE A BOSS.
I HAVE SUPER STRENGTH, SPEED AND AGILITY ALONG WITH COOL VENOM-BLAST ZAPPING POWERS.
WHEN IT COMES DOWN TO IT, I CAN BEAT MOST ANYONE IN A STREET FIGHT.
BUT I HAVE NEVER BEFORE ATTEMPTED FISTICUFFS--
TWOOSH
20
CRAAAA
--WITH A FRONT-END LOADER.
WOWZA...
THAT'S SPIDER-WOMAN?
JESSICA DREW.
I THOUGHT HER NAME WAS ERIN.

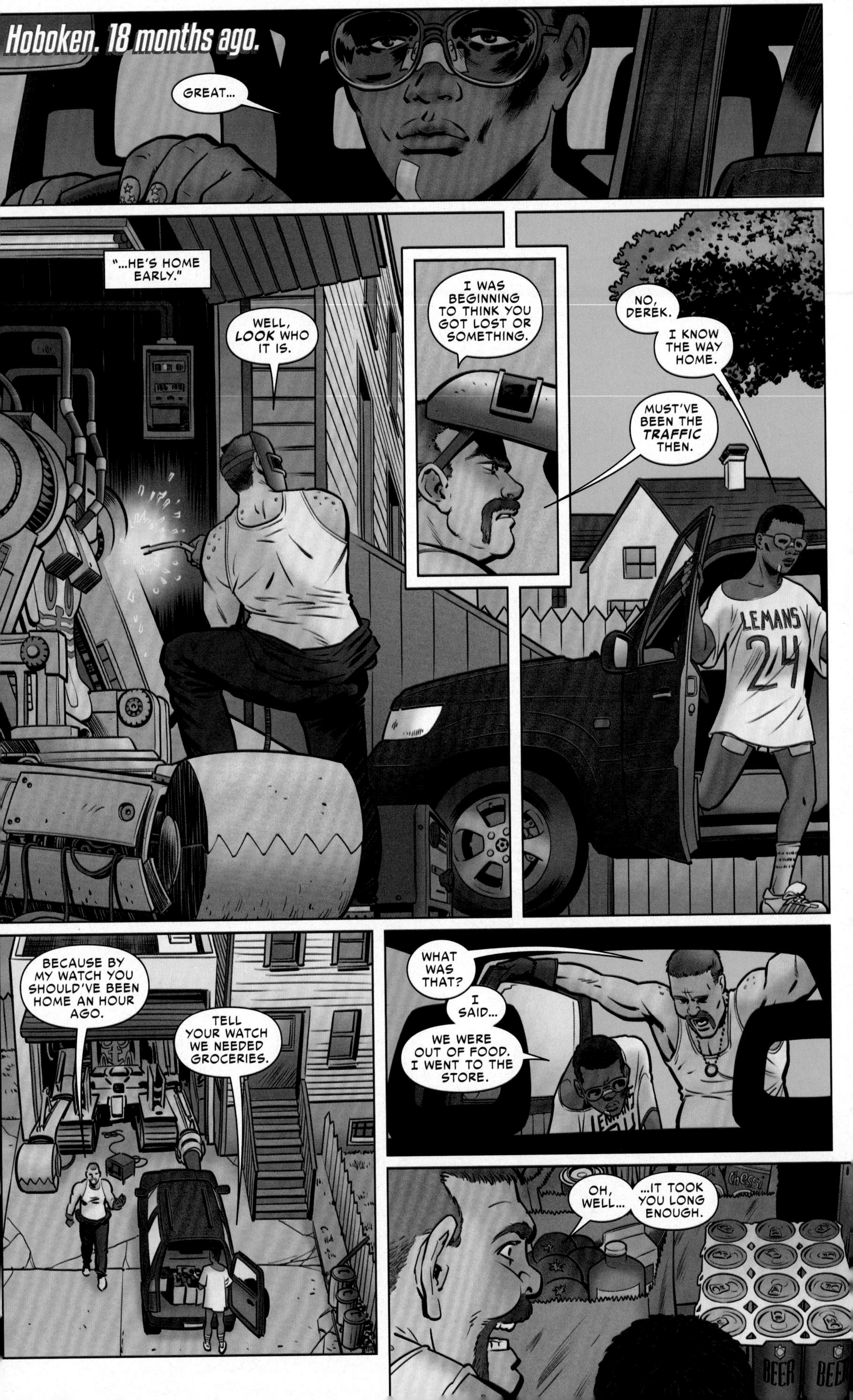
Hoboken. 18 months ago.
GREAT...
"...HE'S HOME EARLY."
WELL, LOOK WHO IT IS.
I WAS BEGINNING TO THINK YOU GOT LOST OR SOMETHING.
NO, DEREK.
I KNOW THE WAY HOME.
MUST'VE BEEN THE TRAFFIC THEN.
LEMANS 24
BECAUSE BY MY WATCH YOU SHOULD'VE BEEN HOME AN HOUR AGO.
TELL YOUR WATCH WE NEEDED GROCERIES.
WHAT WAS THAT?
I SAID...
WE WERE OUT OF FOOD. I WENT TO THE STORE.
OH, WELL...
...IT TOOK YOU LONG ENOUGH.
BEER
BEER

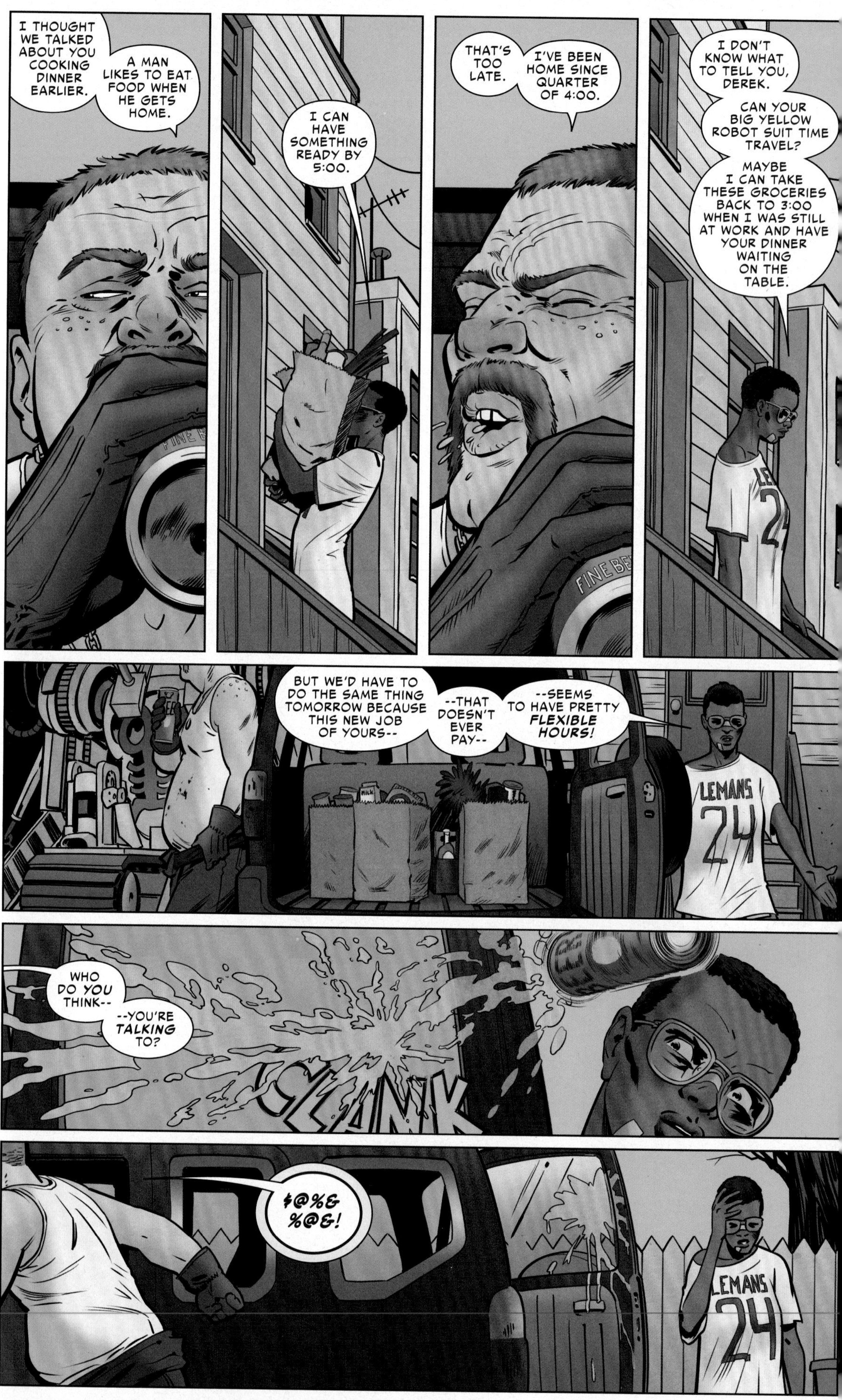
I THOUGHT WE TALKED ABOUT YOU COOKING DINNER EARLIER.
A MAN LIKES TO EAT FOOD WHEN HE GETS HOME.
FINE BE
I CAN HAVE SOMETHING READY BY 5:00.
THAT'S TOO LATE.
I'VE BEEN HOME SINCE QUARTER OF 4:00.
FINE BE
I DON'T KNOW WHAT TO TELL YOU, DEREK.
CAN YOUR BIG YELLOW ROBOT SUIT TIME TRAVEL?
MAYBE I CAN TAKE THESE GROCERIES BACK TO 3:00 WHEN I WAS STILL AT WORK AND HAVE YOUR DINNER WAITING ON THE TABLE.
BUT WE'D HAVE TO DO THE SAME THING TOMORROW BECAUSE THIS NEW JOB OF YOURS--
--THAT DOESN'T EVER PAY--
--SEEMS TO HAVE PRETTY *FLEXIBLE HOURS!*
MILK
LEMANS 24
WHO DO *YOU* THINK--
--YOU'RE *TALKING* TO?
CLANK
$@%& %@&!
LEMANS 24

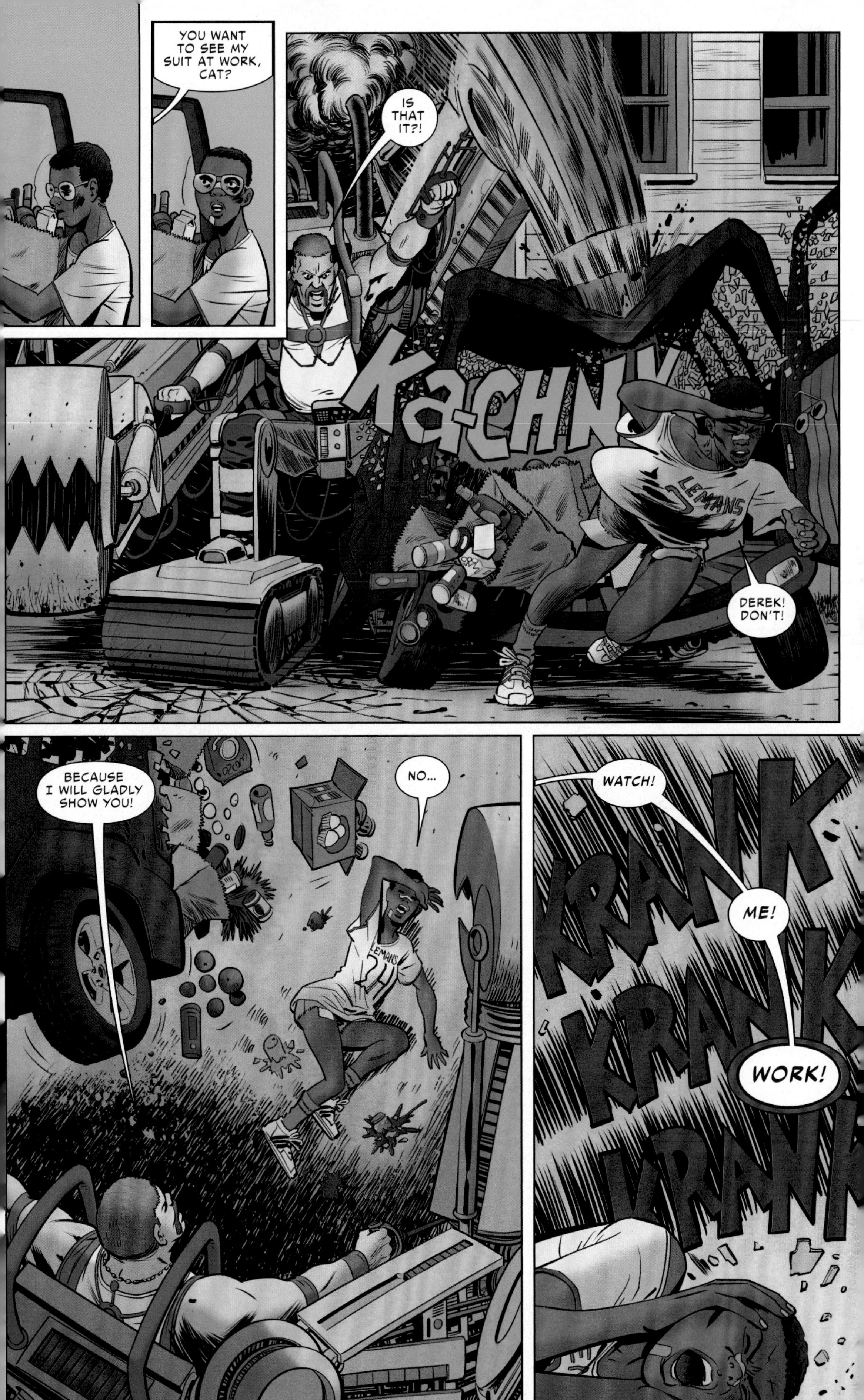
YOU WANT TO SEE MY SUIT AT WORK, CAT?
IS THAT IT?!
KA-CHNK
DEREK! DON'T!
BECAUSE I WILL GLADLY SHOW YOU!
NO...
WATCH!
ME!
WORK!
KRANK
KRANK
KRANK

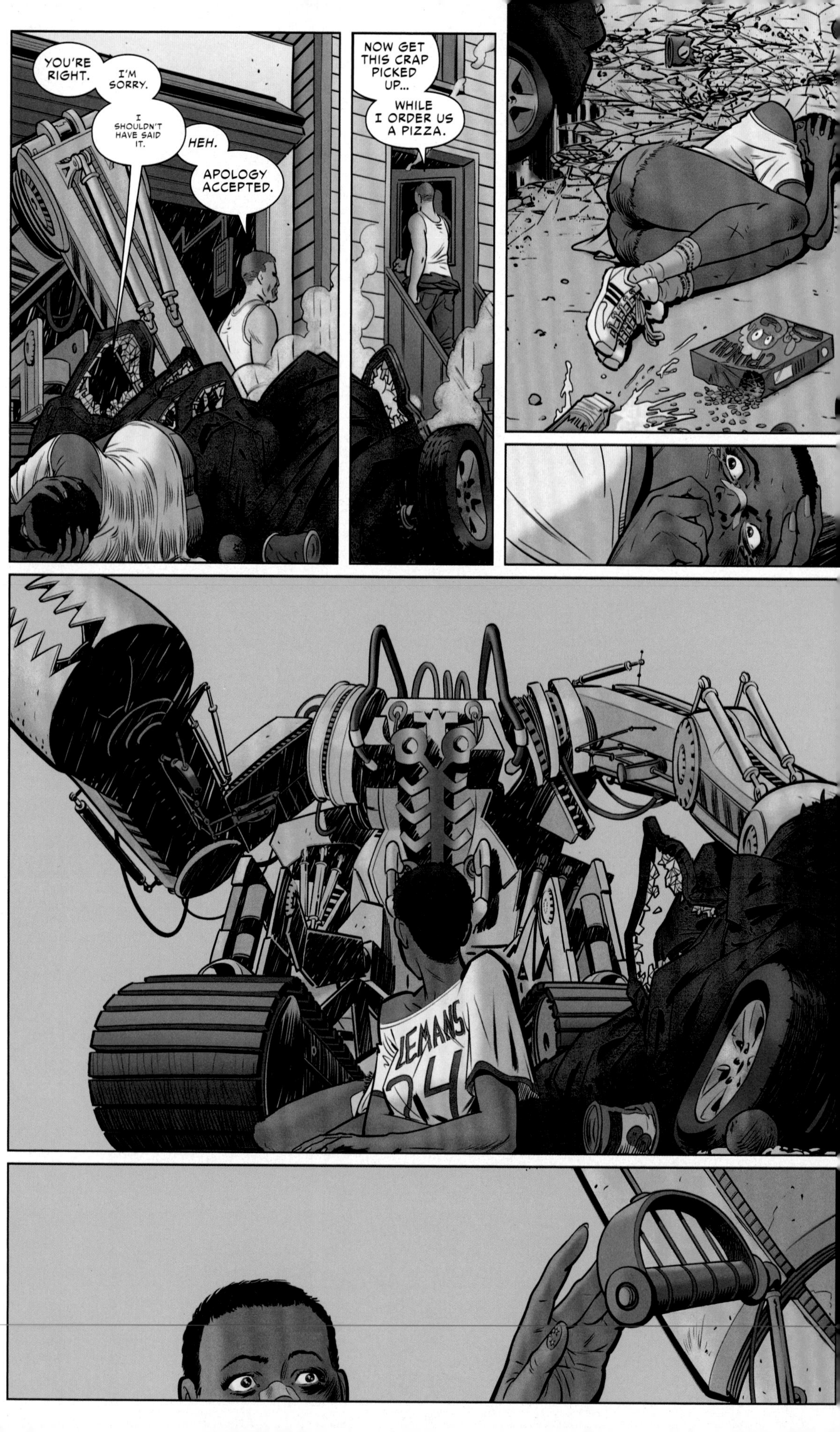

YOU'RE RIGHT.
I'M SORRY.
I SHOULDN'T HAVE SAID IT.
HEH.
APOLOGY ACCEPTED.
NOW GET THIS CRAP PICKED UP...
WHILE I ORDER US A PIZZA.
CRUNCH
MILK
LEMANS
24

WHAT GIVES YOU THE RIGHT, JESSICA DREW?

CKCLACK

TO COME UP HERE--

YA-CHNK

--AND TAKE AWAY--

--EVERYTHING WE'VE *BUILT*?!

Lottu's Ho

THA-HRRTS

WHAT GIVES YOU THE RIGHT?

UGH...

OH GOD...

AARRGGH!!

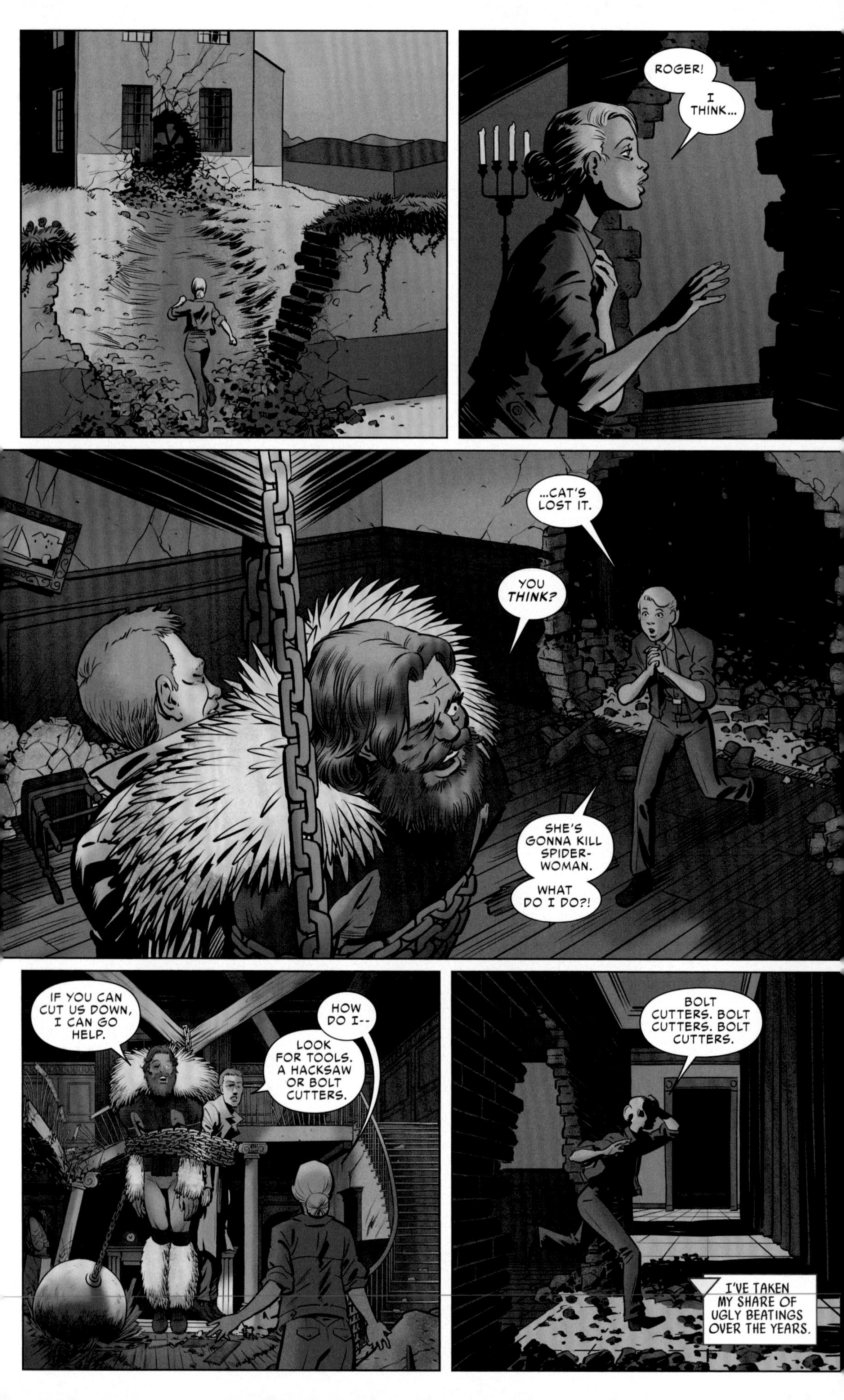
ROGER!
I THINK...
...CAT'S LOST IT.
YOU *THINK?*
SHE'S GONNA KILL SPIDER-WOMAN.
WHAT DO I DO?!
IF YOU CAN CUT US DOWN, I CAN GO HELP.
HOW DO I--
LOOK FOR TOOLS. A HACKSAW OR BOLT CUTTERS.
BOLT CUTTERS. BOLT CUTTERS. BOLT CUTTERS.
I'VE TAKEN MY SHARE OF UGLY BEATINGS OVER THE YEARS.

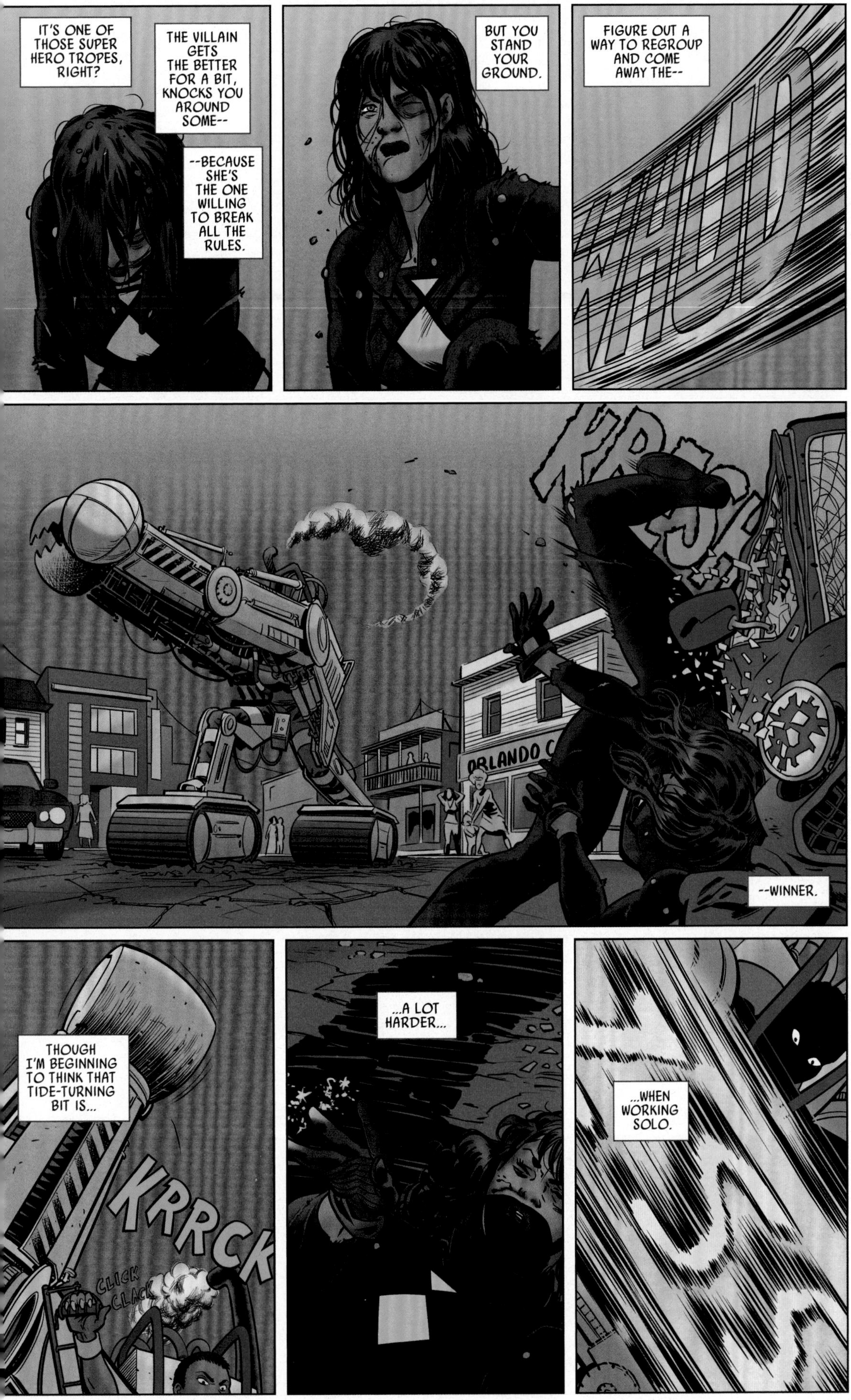
IT'S ONE OF THOSE SUPER HERO TROPES, RIGHT?
THE VILLAIN GETS THE BETTER FOR A BIT, KNOCKS YOU AROUND SOME--
--BECAUSE SHE'S THE ONE WILLING TO BREAK ALL THE RULES.
BUT YOU STAND YOUR GROUND.
FIGURE OUT A WAY TO REGROUP AND COME AWAY THE--
WHUD
KRESH
ORLANDO C
--WINNER.
THOUGH I'M BEGINNING TO THINK THAT TIDE-TURNING BIT IS...
KRRCK
CLICK
CLACK
...A LOT HARDER...
...WHEN WORKING SOLO.

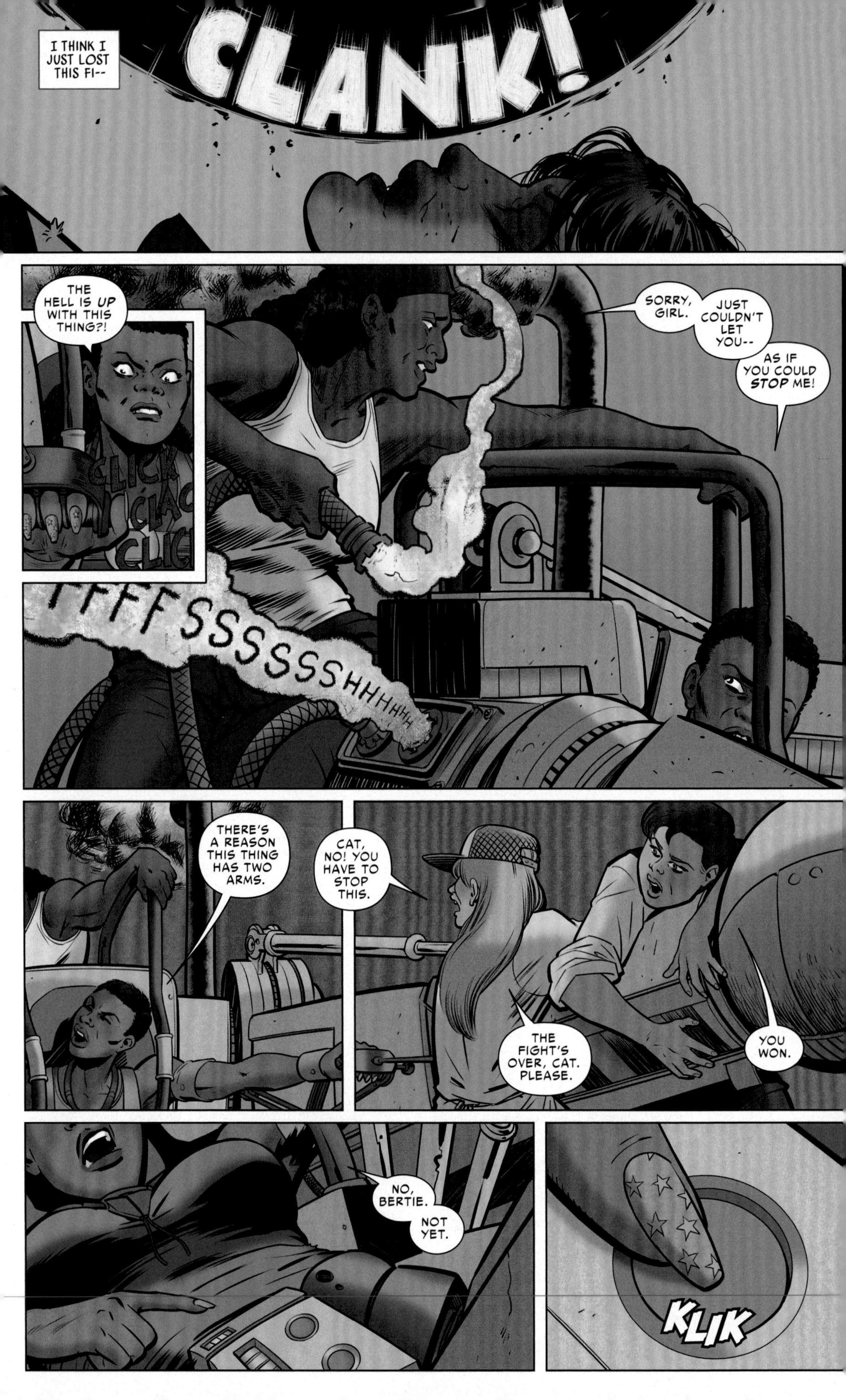

I THINK I JUST LOST THIS FI--
CLANK!
THE HELL IS *UP* WITH THIS THING?!
CLICK
CLAC
CLIC
SORRY, GIRL.
JUST COULDN'T LET YOU--
AS IF YOU COULD *STOP* ME!
FFFFSSSSSSSHHHHH
THERE'S A REASON THIS THING HAS TWO ARMS.
CAT, NO! YOU HAVE TO STOP THIS.
THE FIGHT'S OVER, CAT. PLEASE.
YOU WON.
NO, BERTIE.
NOT YET.
KLIK

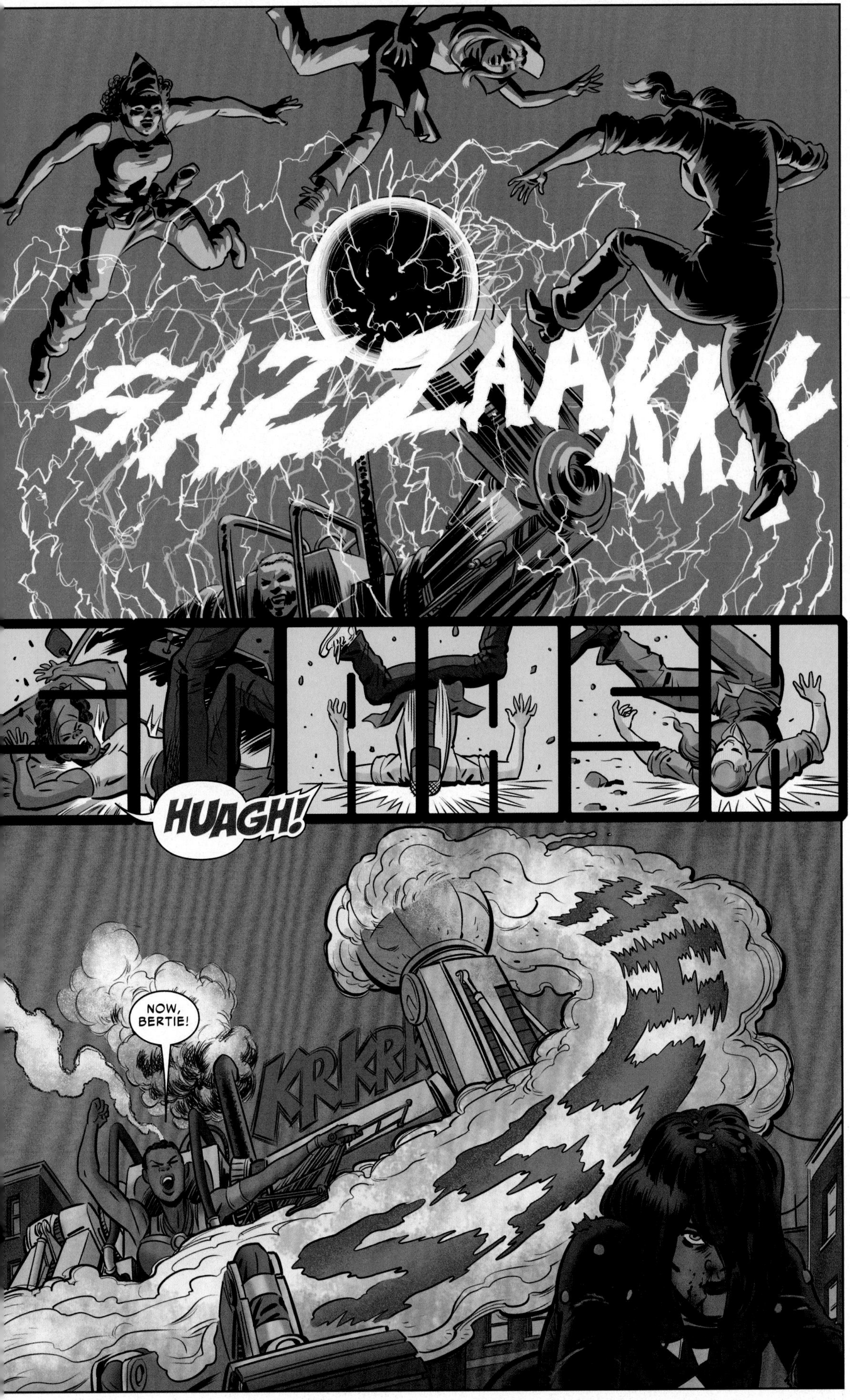
SAZZAAKK!
HUAGH!
NOW, BERTIE!
KRKRK

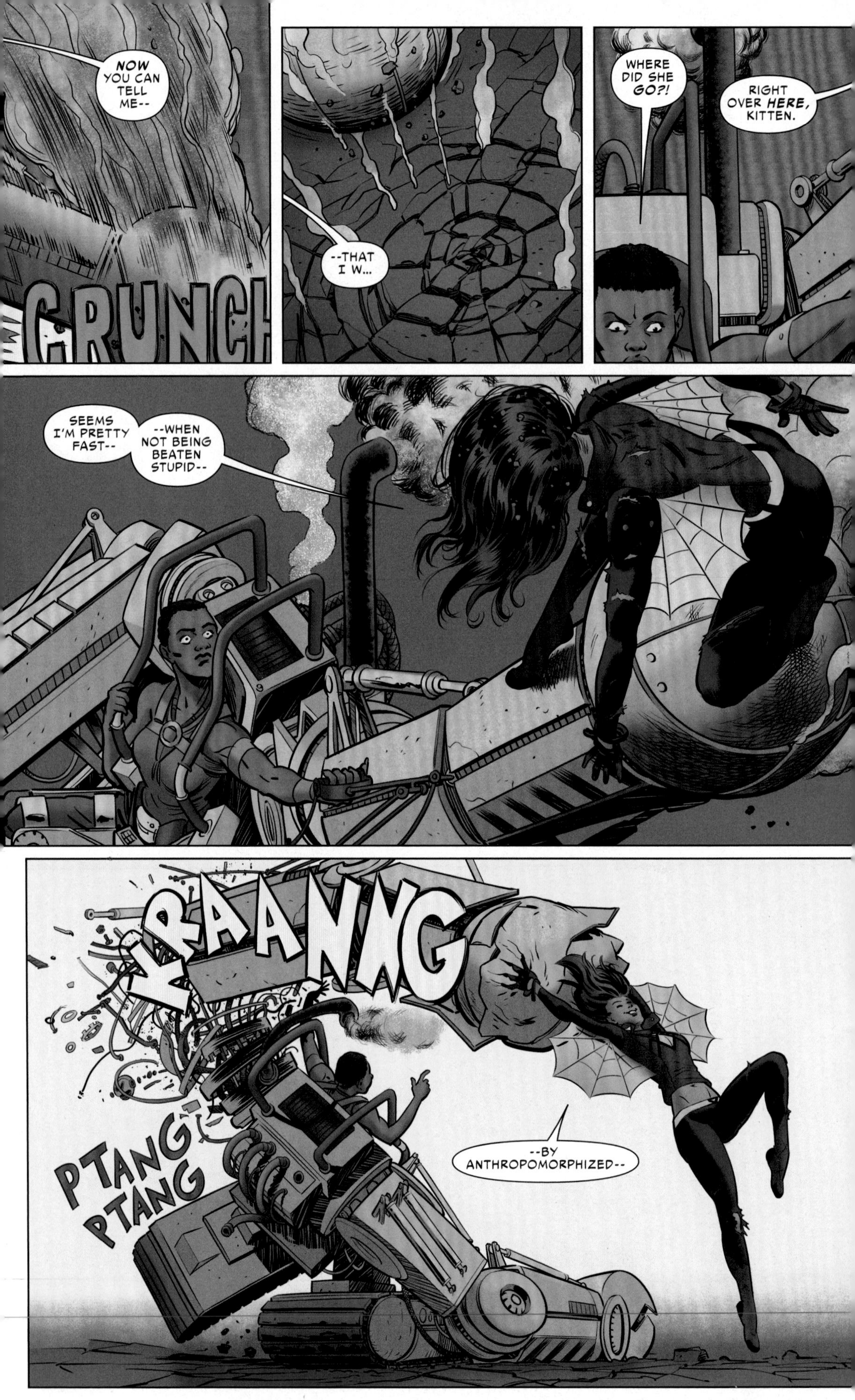

NOW YOU CAN TELL ME--
CRUNCH
--THAT I W...
WHERE DID SHE GO?!
RIGHT OVER HERE, KITTEN.
SEEMS I'M PRETTY FAST--
--WHEN NOT BEING BEATEN STUPID--
KRAANNG
PTANG PTANG
--BY ANTHROPOMORPHIZED--

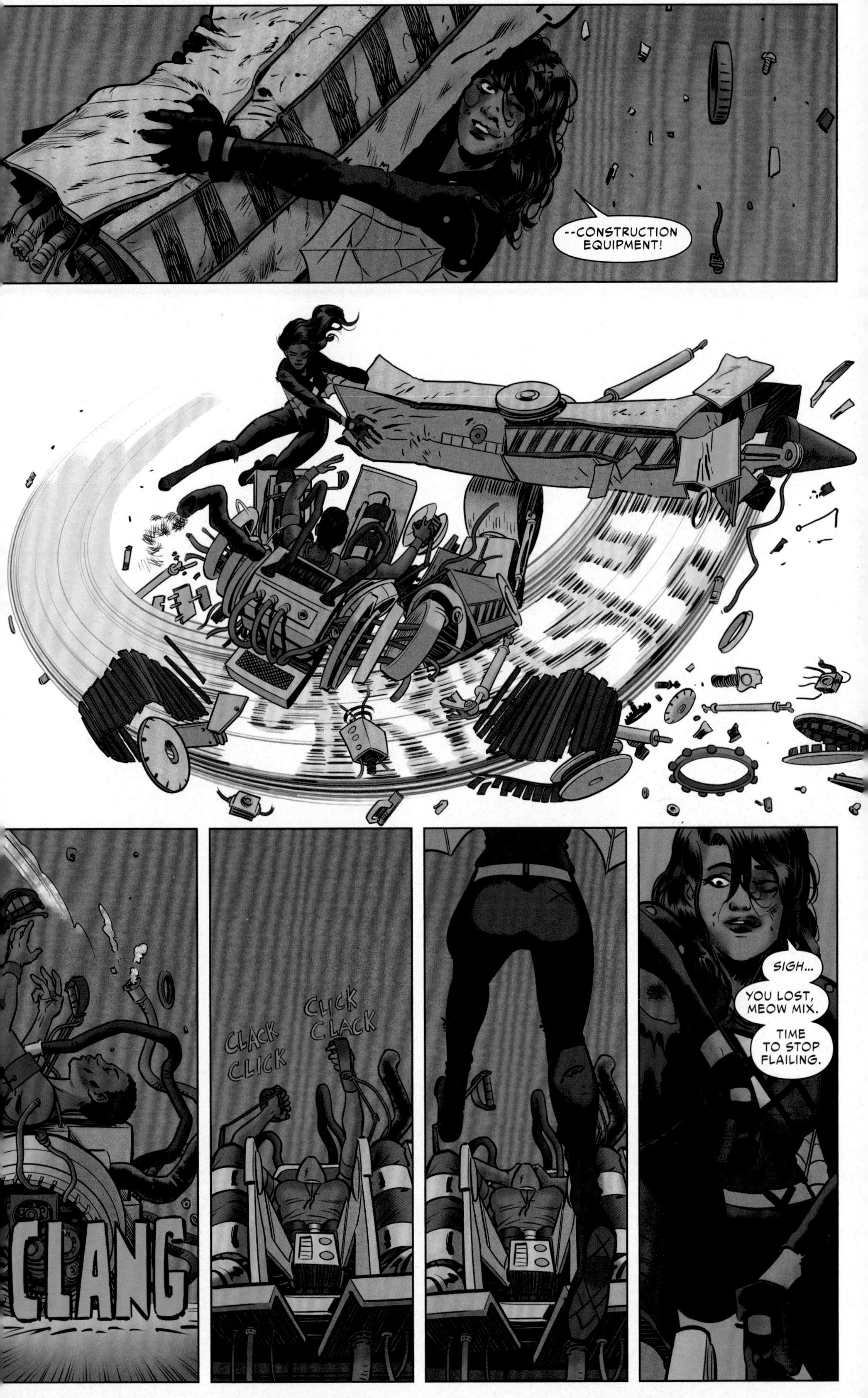
--CONSTRUCTION EQUIPMENT!
CLANG
CLACK CLICK
CLICK CLACK
SIGH...
YOU LOST, MEOW MIX.
TIME TO STOP FLAILING.

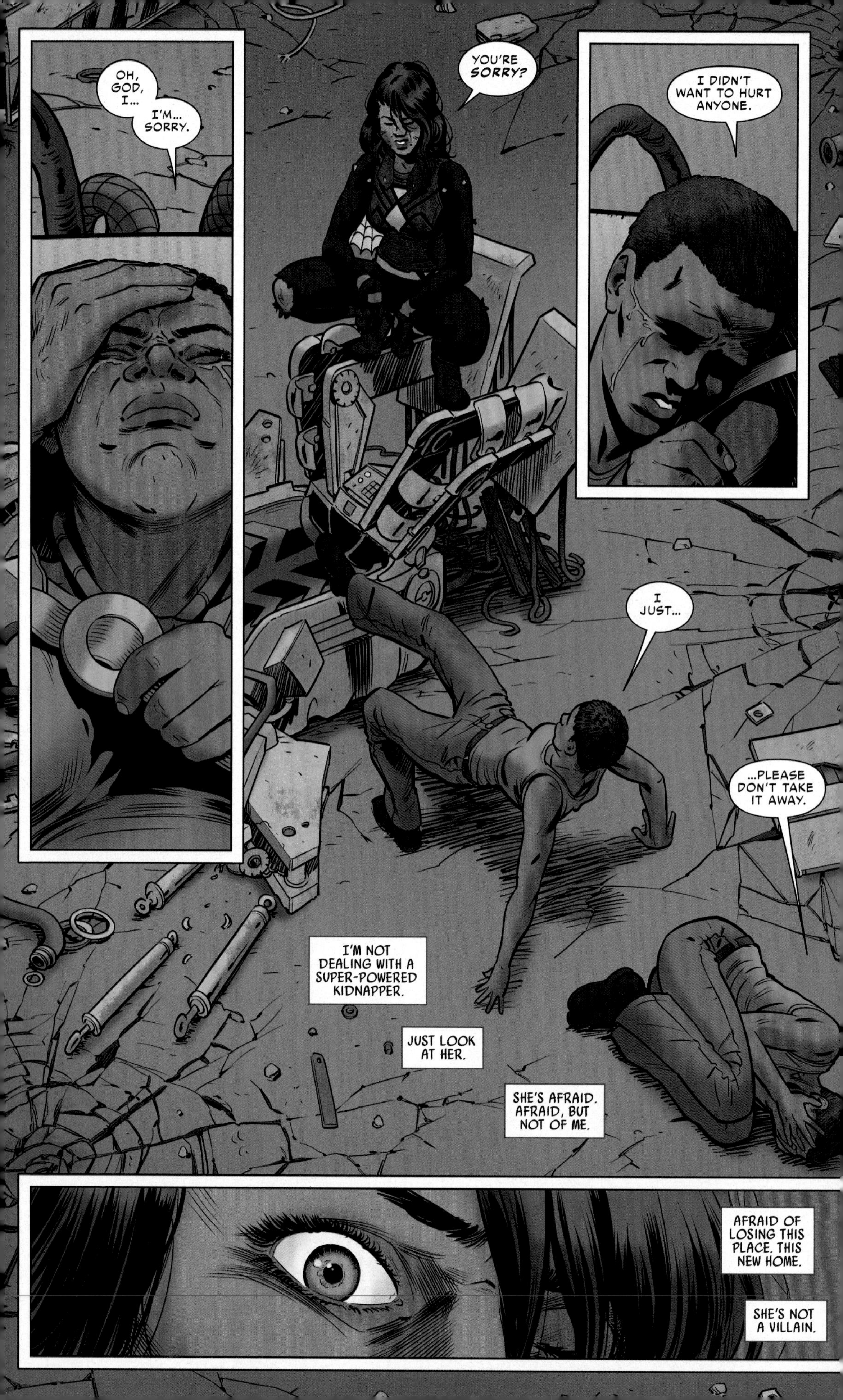

OH, GOD, I...
I'M... SORRY.
YOU'RE SORRY?
I DIDN'T WANT TO HURT ANYONE.
I JUST...
...PLEASE DON'T TAKE IT AWAY.
I'M NOT DEALING WITH A SUPER-POWERED KIDNAPPER.
JUST LOOK AT HER.
SHE'S AFRAID. AFRAID, BUT NOT OF ME.
AFRAID OF LOSING THIS PLACE. THIS NEW HOME.
SHE'S NOT A VILLAIN.

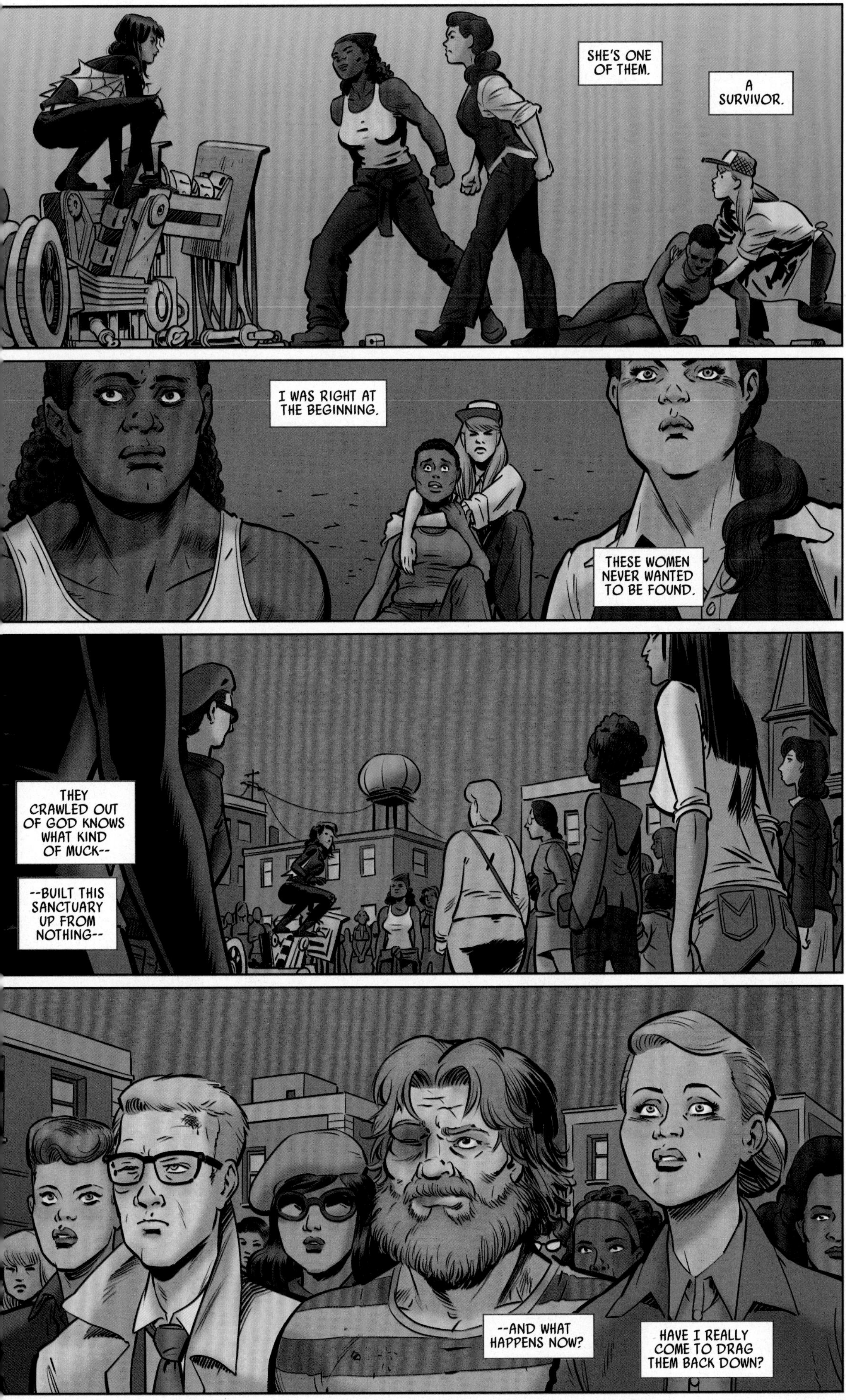
SHE'S ONE OF THEM.
A SURVIVOR.
I WAS RIGHT AT THE BEGINNING.
THESE WOMEN NEVER WANTED TO BE FOUND.
THEY CRAWLED OUT OF GOD KNOWS WHAT KIND OF MUCK--
--BUILT THIS SANCTUARY UP FROM NOTHING--
--AND WHAT HAPPENS NOW?
HAVE I REALLY COME TO DRAG THEM BACK DOWN?

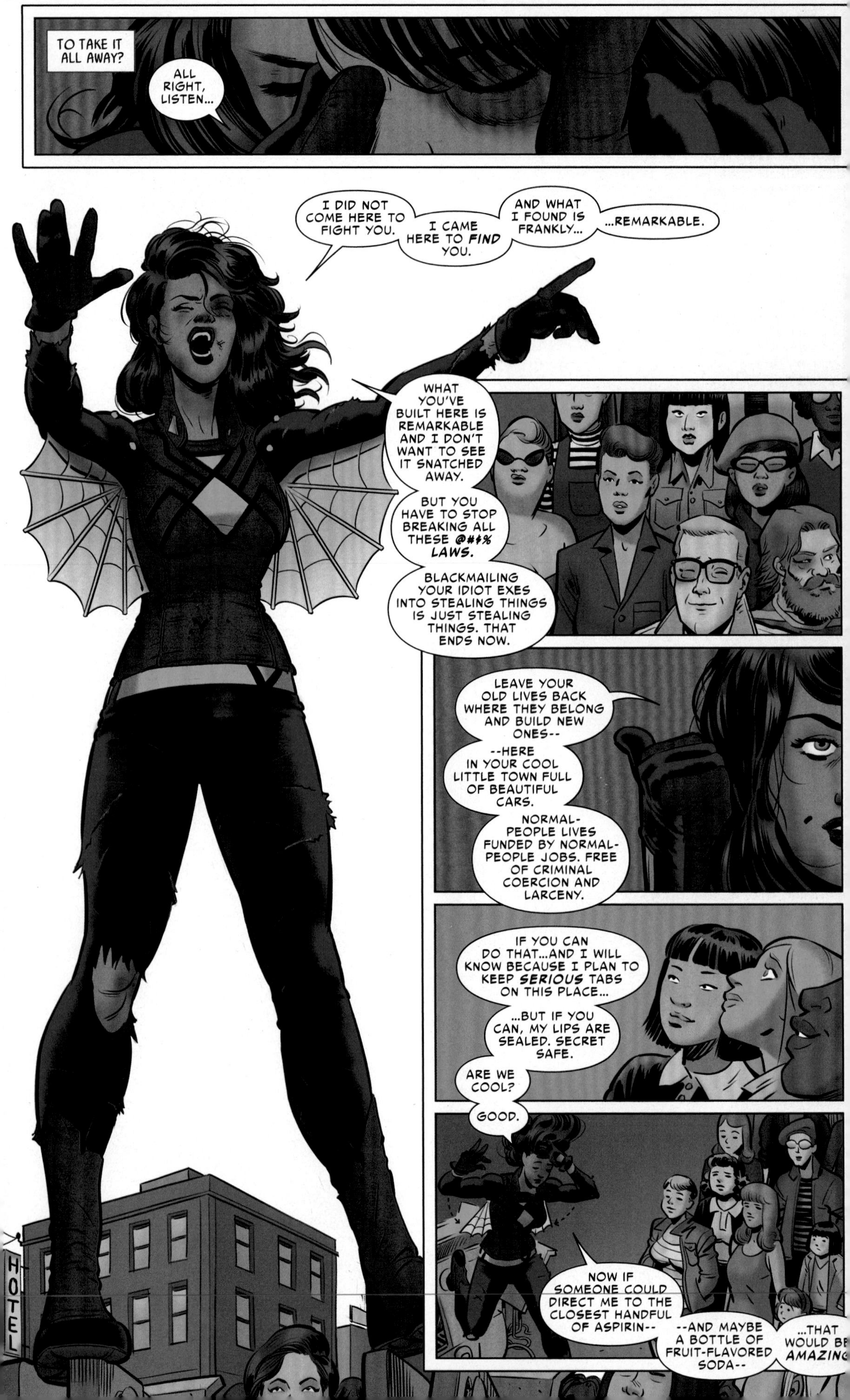
TO TAKE IT ALL AWAY?
ALL RIGHT, LISTEN...
I DID NOT COME HERE TO FIGHT YOU.
I CAME HERE TO FIND YOU.
AND WHAT I FOUND IS FRANKLY...
...REMARKABLE.
WHAT YOU'VE BUILT HERE IS REMARKABLE AND I DON'T WANT TO SEE IT SNATCHED AWAY.
BUT YOU HAVE TO STOP BREAKING ALL THESE @#$% LAWS.
BLACKMAILING YOUR IDIOT EXES INTO STEALING THINGS IS JUST STEALING THINGS. THAT ENDS NOW.
LEAVE YOUR OLD LIVES BACK WHERE THEY BELONG AND BUILD NEW ONES--
--HERE IN YOUR COOL LITTLE TOWN FULL OF BEAUTIFUL CARS.
NORMAL-PEOPLE LIVES FUNDED BY NORMAL-PEOPLE JOBS. FREE OF CRIMINAL COERCION AND LARCENY.
IF YOU CAN DO THAT...AND I WILL KNOW BECAUSE I PLAN TO KEEP SERIOUS TABS ON THIS PLACE...
...BUT IF YOU CAN, MY LIPS ARE SEALED. SECRET SAFE.
ARE WE COOL?
GOOD.
HOTEL
NOW IF SOMEONE COULD DIRECT ME TO THE CLOSEST HANDFUL OF ASPIRIN--
--AND MAYBE A BOTTLE OF FRUIT-FLAVORED SODA--
...THAT WOULD BE AMAZING

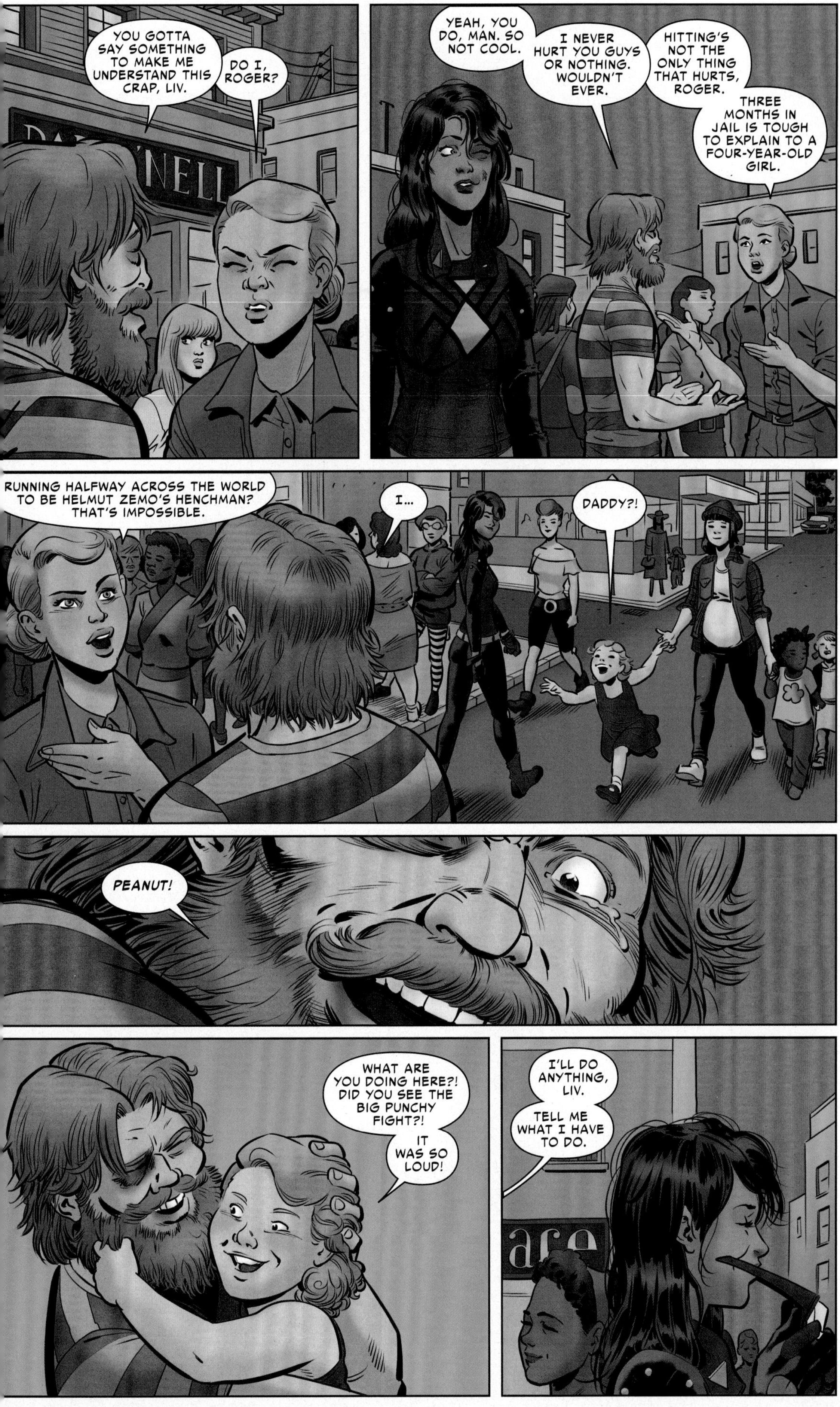
YOU GOTTA SAY SOMETHING TO MAKE ME UNDERSTAND THIS CRAP, LIV.
DO I, ROGER?
YEAH, YOU DO, MAN. SO NOT COOL.
I NEVER HURT YOU GUYS OR NOTHING. WOULDN'T EVER.
HITTING'S NOT THE ONLY THING THAT HURTS, ROGER.
THREE MONTHS IN JAIL IS TOUGH TO EXPLAIN TO A FOUR-YEAR-OLD GIRL.
RUNNING HALFWAY ACROSS THE WORLD TO BE HELMUT ZEMO'S HENCHMAN? THAT'S IMPOSSIBLE.
I...
DADDY?!
PEANUT!
WHAT ARE YOU DOING HERE?! DID YOU SEE THE BIG PUNCHY FIGHT?!
IT WAS SO LOUD!
I'LL DO ANYTHING, LIV.
TELL ME WHAT I HAVE TO DO.

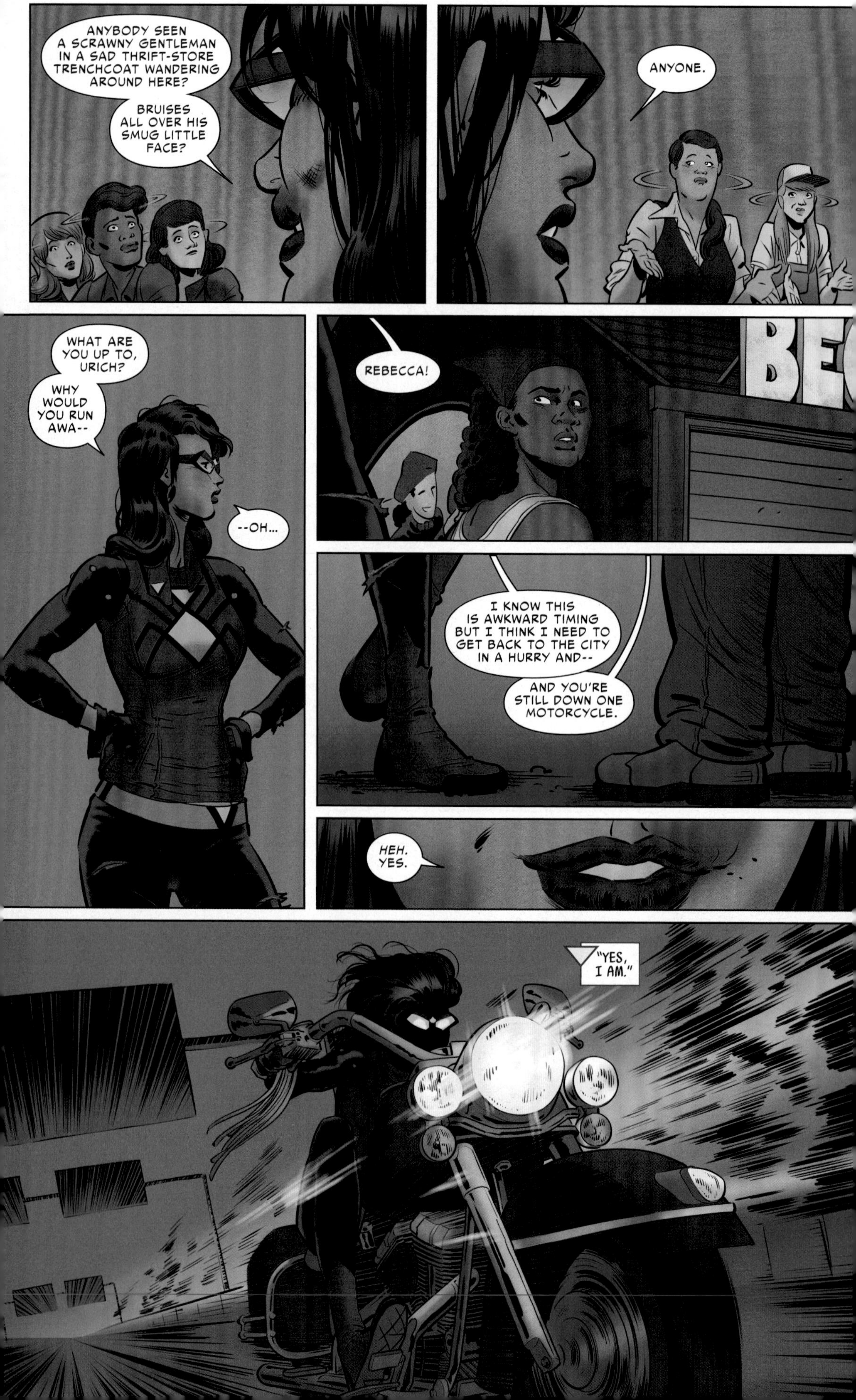
ANYBODY SEEN A SCRAWNY GENTLEMAN IN A SAD THRIFT-STORE TRENCHCOAT WANDERING AROUND HERE?
BRUISES ALL OVER HIS SMUG LITTLE FACE?
ANYONE.
WHAT ARE YOU UP TO, URICH?
WHY WOULD YOU RUN AWA--
--OH...
REBECCA!
I KNOW THIS IS AWKWARD TIMING BUT I THINK I NEED TO GET BACK TO THE CITY IN A HURRY AND--
AND YOU'RE STILL DOWN ONE MOTORCYCLE.
HEH. YES.
"YES, I AM."

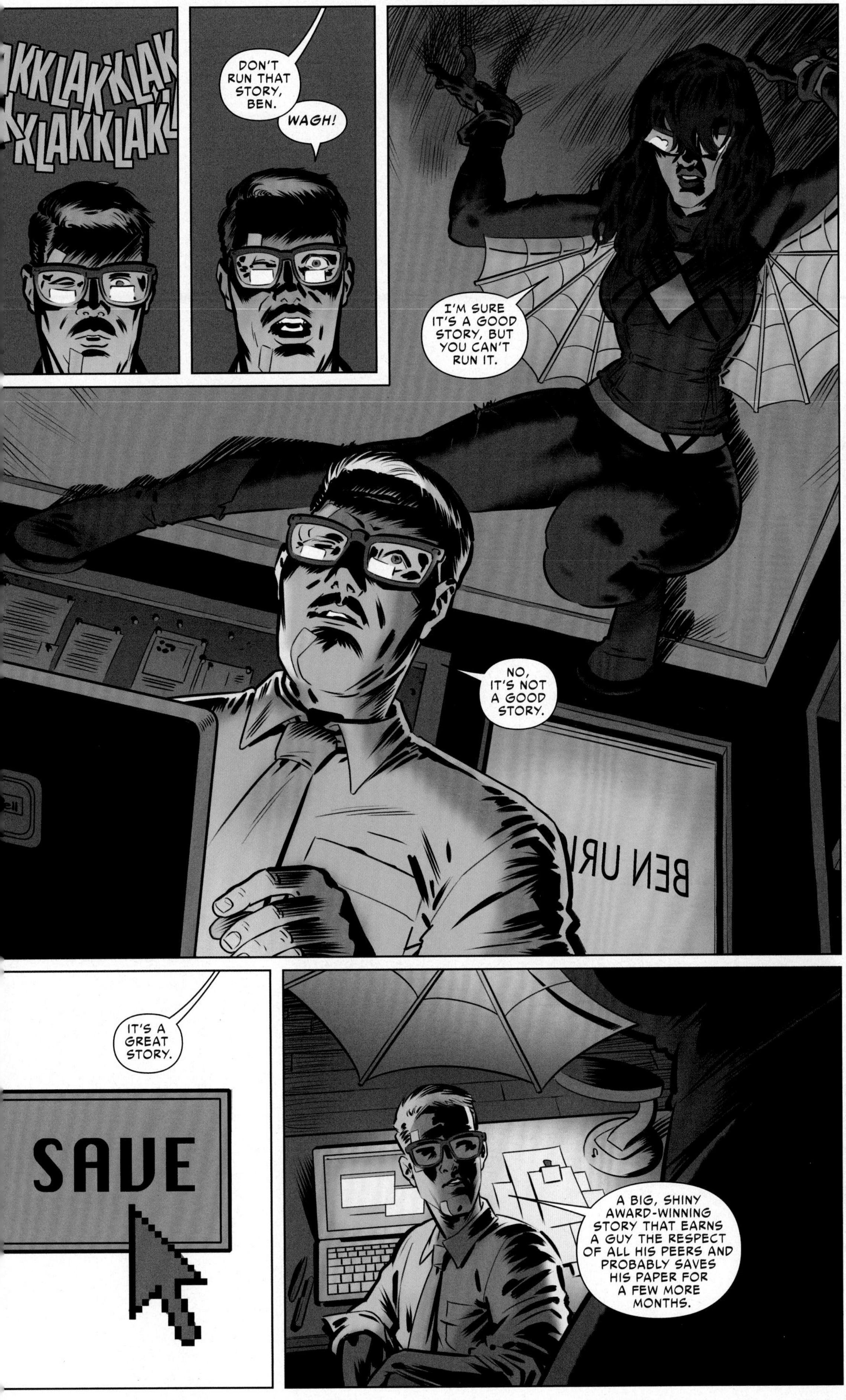
KLAKKLAKKLAK
KLAKKLAKKLAK
DON'T RUN THAT STORY, BEN.
WAGH!
I'M SURE IT'S A GOOD STORY, BUT YOU CAN'T RUN IT.
NO, IT'S NOT A GOOD STORY.
BEN URI
IT'S A GREAT STORY.
SAVE
A BIG, SHINY AWARD-WINNING STORY THAT EARNS A GUY THE RESPECT OF ALL HIS PEERS AND PROBABLY SAVES HIS PAPER FOR A FEW MORE MONTHS.

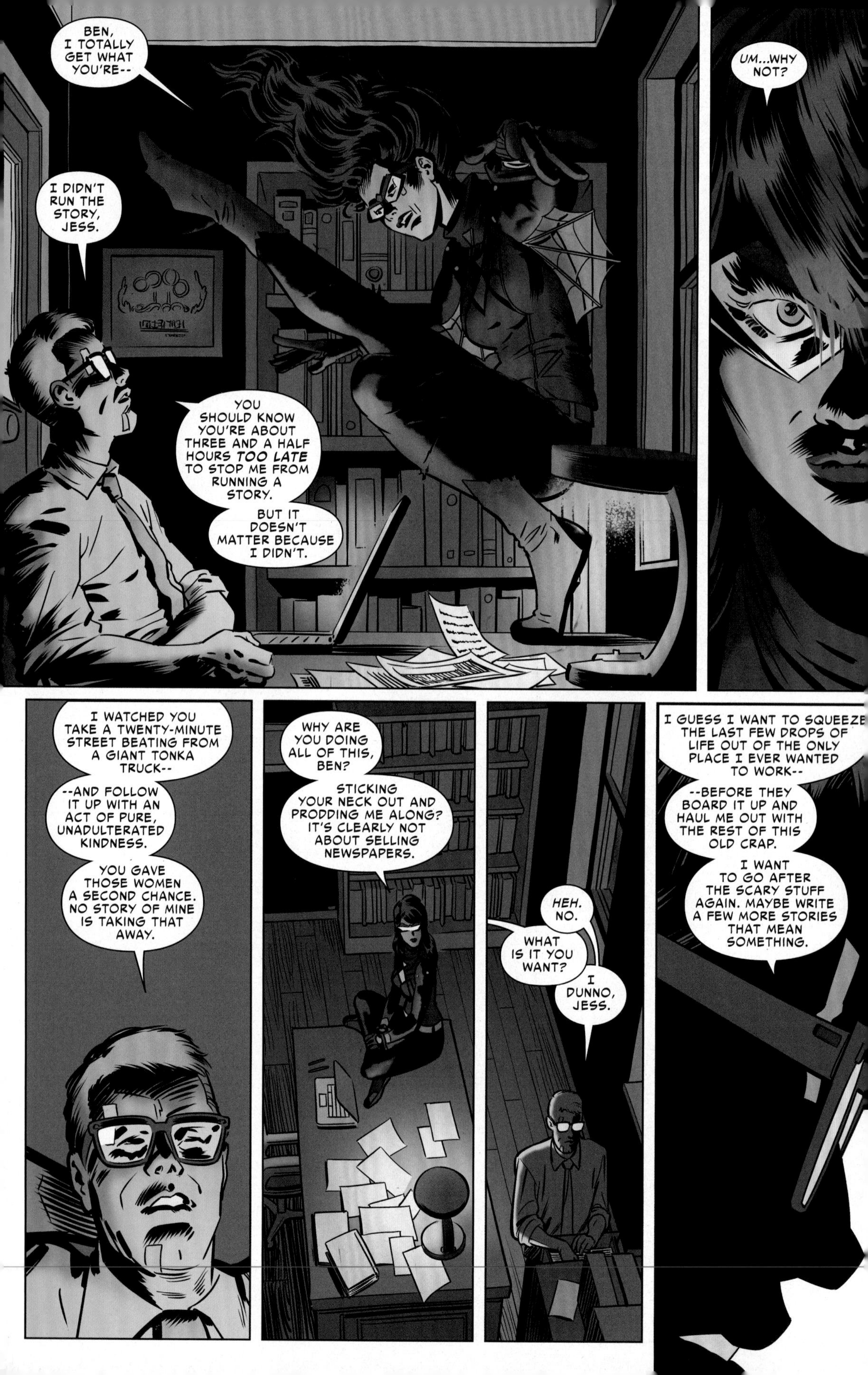

BEN, I TOTALLY GET WHAT YOU'RE--
I DIDN'T RUN THE STORY, JESS.
YOU SHOULD KNOW YOU'RE ABOUT THREE AND A HALF HOURS *TOO LATE* TO STOP ME FROM RUNNING A STORY.
BUT IT DOESN'T MATTER BECAUSE I DIDN'T.
UM...WHY NOT?
I WATCHED YOU TAKE A TWENTY-MINUTE STREET BEATING FROM A GIANT TONKA TRUCK--
--AND FOLLOW IT UP WITH AN ACT OF PURE, UNADULTERATED KINDNESS.
YOU GAVE THOSE WOMEN A SECOND CHANCE. NO STORY OF MINE IS TAKING THAT AWAY.
WHY ARE YOU DOING ALL OF THIS, BEN?
STICKING YOUR NECK OUT AND PRODDING ME ALONG? IT'S CLEARLY NOT ABOUT SELLING NEWSPAPERS.
HEH. NO.
WHAT IS IT YOU WANT?
I DUNNO, JESS.
I GUESS I WANT TO SQUEEZE THE LAST FEW DROPS OF LIFE OUT OF THE ONLY PLACE I EVER WANTED TO WORK--
--BEFORE THEY BOARD IT UP AND HAUL ME OUT WITH THE REST OF THIS OLD CRAP.
I WANT TO GO AFTER THE SCARY STUFF AGAIN. MAYBE WRITE A FEW MORE STORIES THAT MEAN SOMETHING.

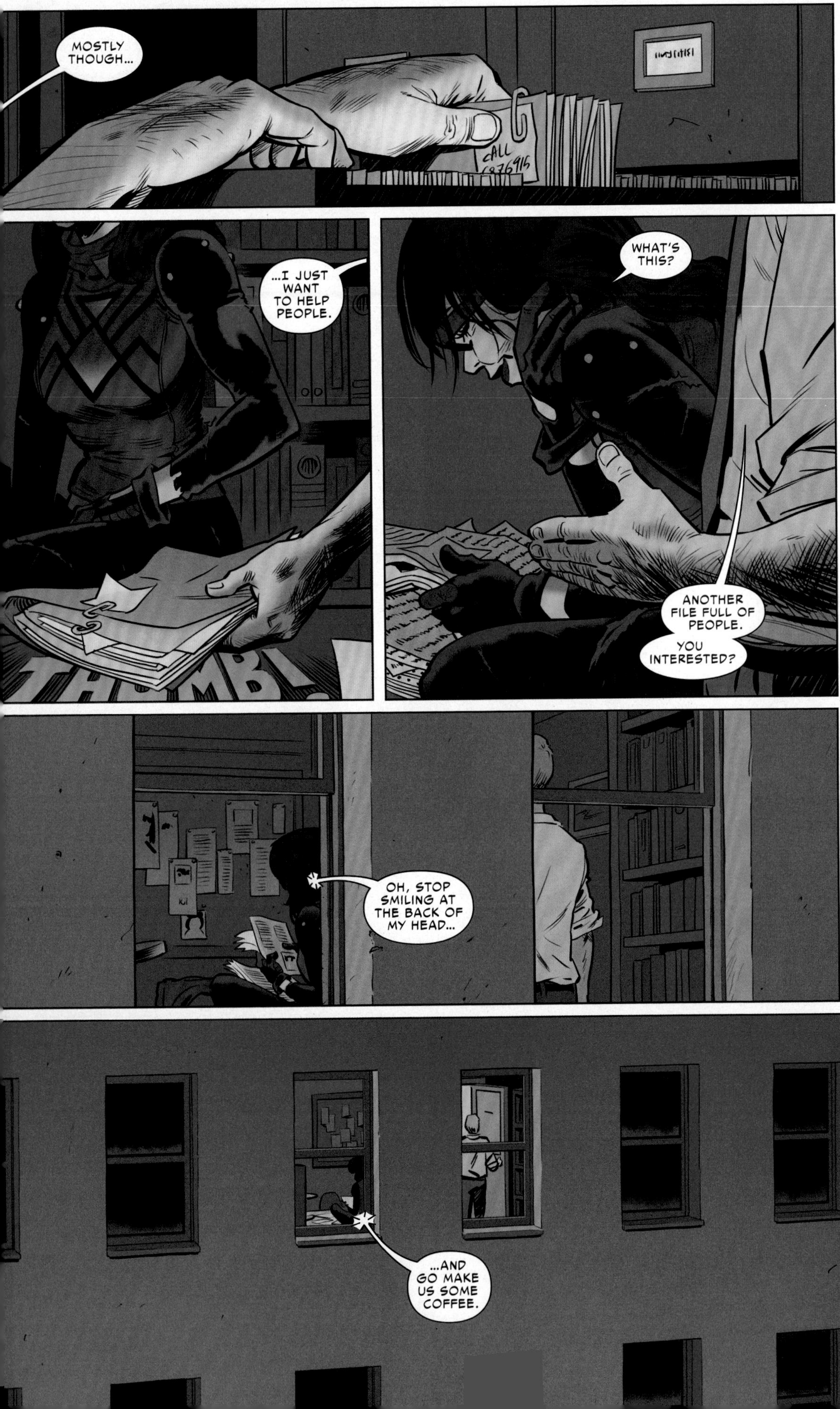
MOSTLY THOUGH...
CALL
...I JUST WANT TO HELP PEOPLE.
THUMB!
WHAT'S THIS?
ANOTHER FILE FULL OF PEOPLE.
YOU INTERESTED?
OH, STOP SMILING AT THE BACK OF MY HEAD...
...AND GO MAKE US SOME COFFEE.

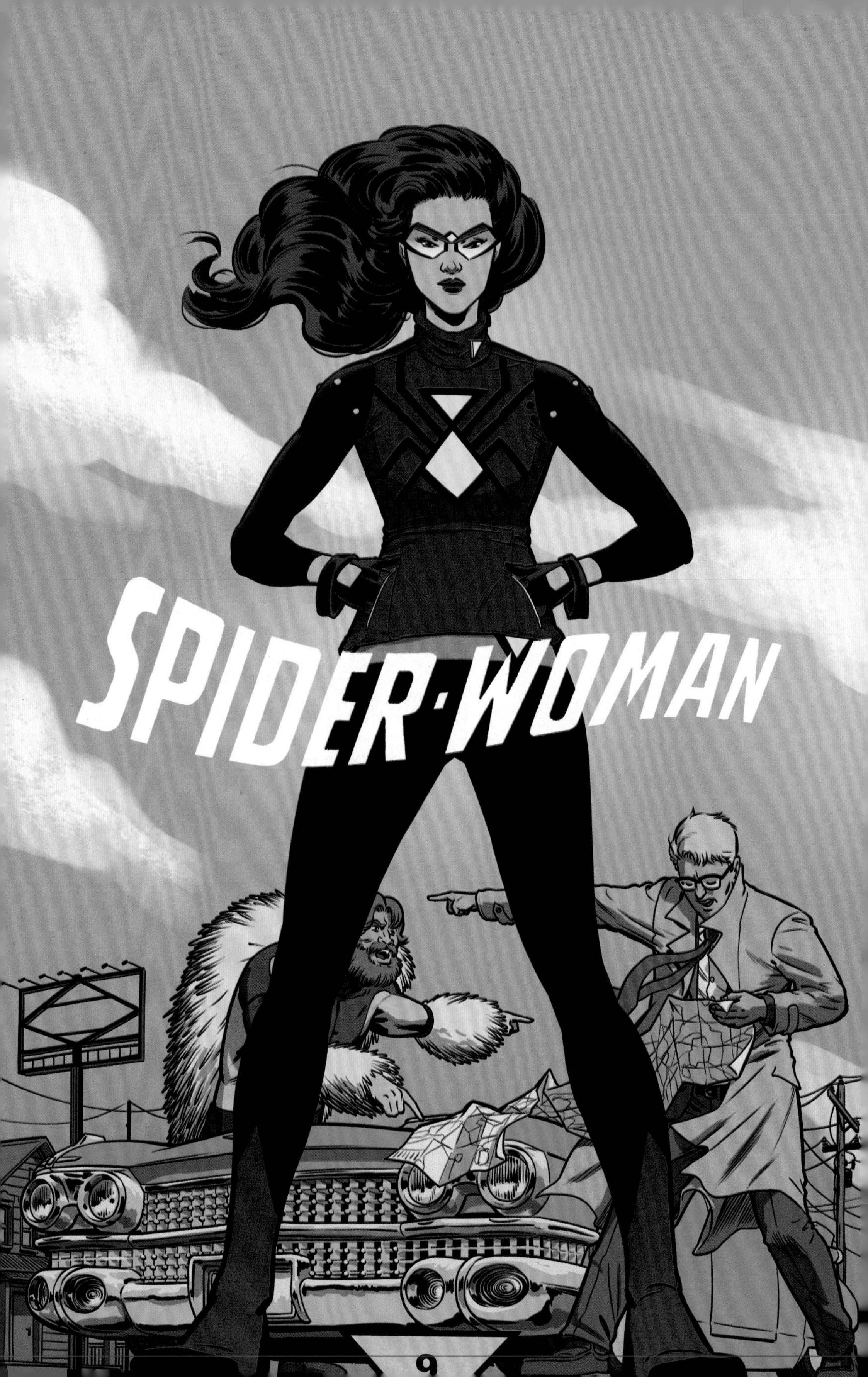
SPIDER-WOMAN
9

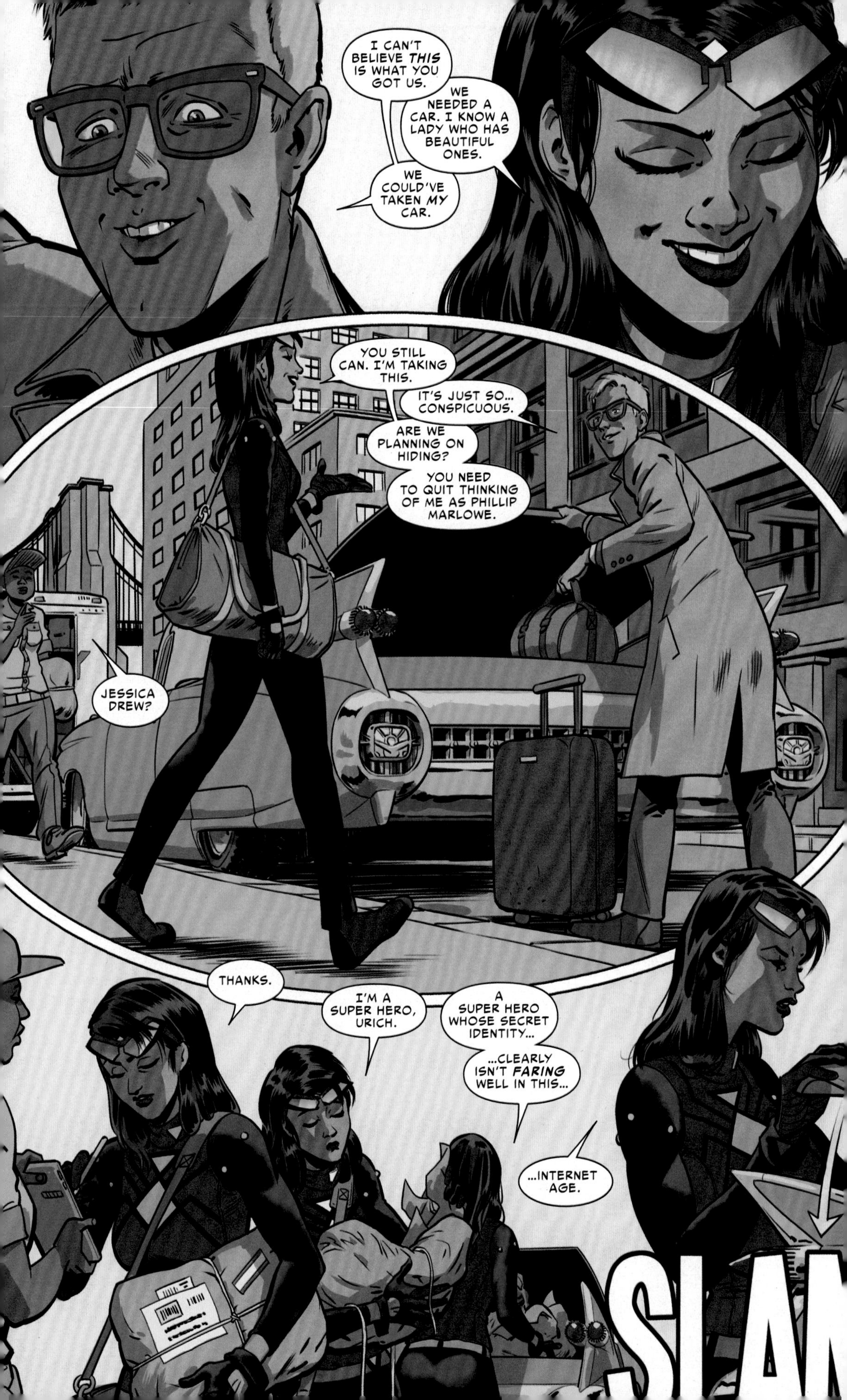
I CAN'T BELIEVE *THIS* IS WHAT YOU GOT US.
WE NEEDED A CAR. I KNOW A LADY WHO HAS BEAUTIFUL ONES.
WE COULD'VE TAKEN *MY* CAR.
YOU STILL CAN. I'M TAKING THIS.
IT'S JUST SO... CONSPICUOUS.
ARE WE PLANNING ON HIDING?
YOU NEED TO QUIT THINKING OF ME AS PHILLIP MARLOWE.
JESSICA DREW?
THANKS.
I'M A SUPER HERO, URICH.
A SUPER HERO WHOSE SECRET IDENTITY...
...CLEARLY ISN'T *FARING* WELL IN THIS...
...INTERNET AGE.
SLAM

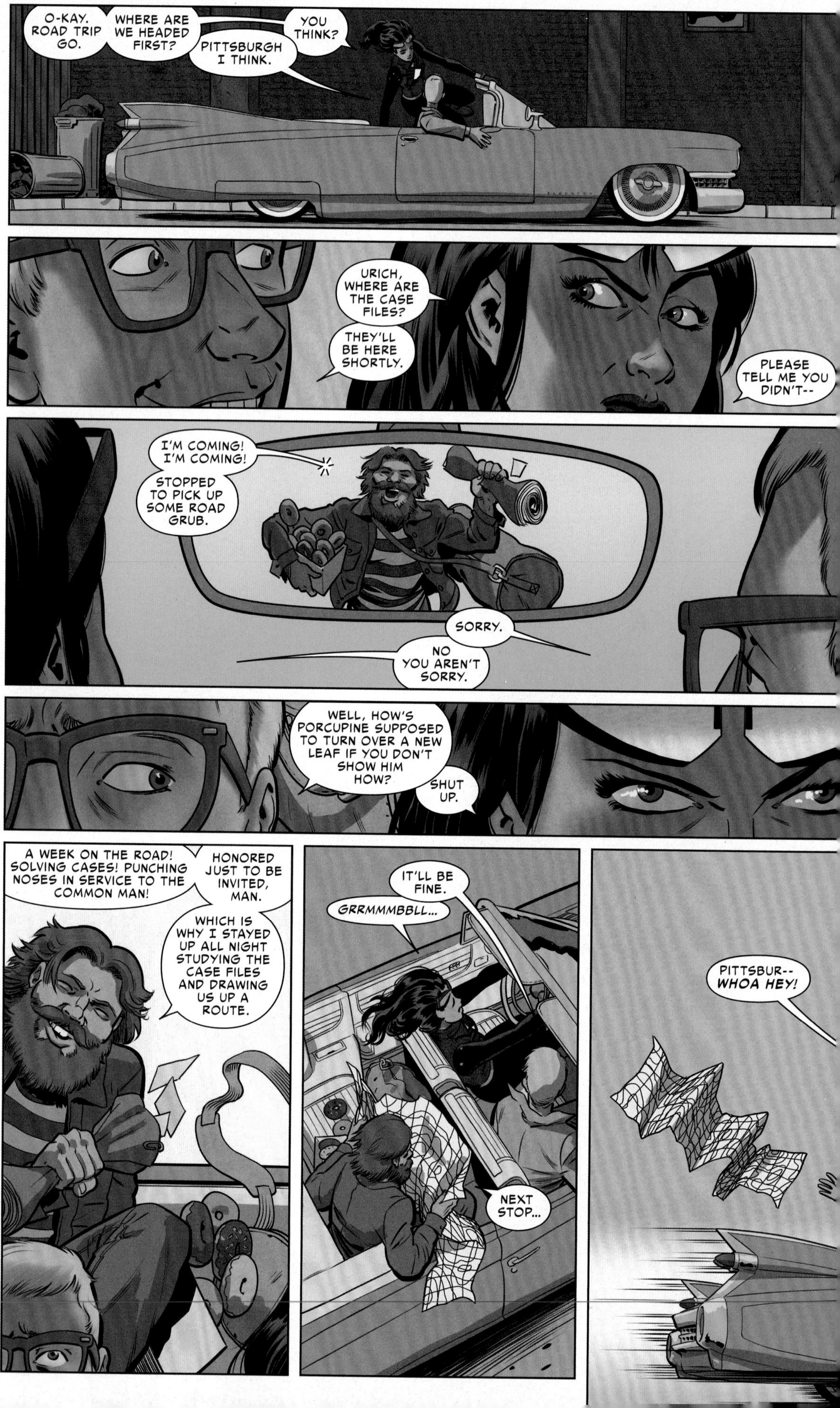
O-KAY. ROAD TRIP GO.
WHERE ARE WE HEADED FIRST?
PITTSBURGH I THINK.
YOU THINK?
URICH, WHERE ARE THE CASE FILES?
THEY'LL BE HERE SHORTLY.
PLEASE TELL ME YOU DIDN'T--
I'M COMING! I'M COMING!
STOPPED TO PICK UP SOME ROAD GRUB.
SORRY.
NO YOU AREN'T SORRY.
WELL, HOW'S PORCUPINE SUPPOSED TO TURN OVER A NEW LEAF IF YOU DON'T SHOW HIM HOW?
SHUT UP.
A WEEK ON THE ROAD! SOLVING CASES! PUNCHING NOSES IN SERVICE TO THE COMMON MAN!
HONORED JUST TO BE INVITED, MAN.
WHICH IS WHY I STAYED UP ALL NIGHT STUDYING THE CASE FILES AND DRAWING US UP A ROUTE.
IT'LL BE FINE.
GRRMMMBBLL...
NEXT STOP...
PITTSBUR-- WHOA HEY!

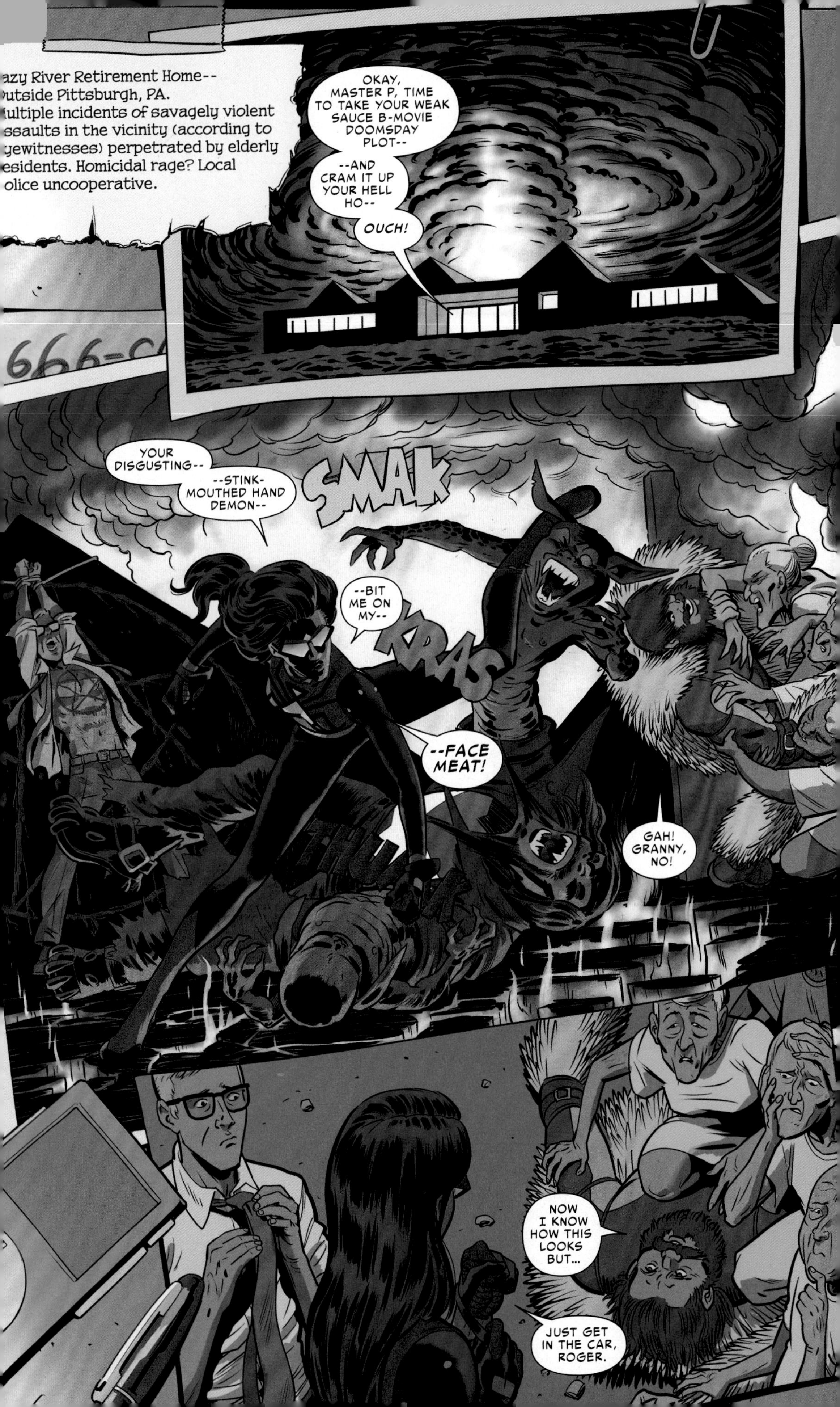
azy River Retirement Home--
utside Pittsburgh, PA.
ultiple incidents of savagely violent ssaults in the vicinity (according to yewitnesses) perpetrated by elderly esidents. Homicidal rage? Local olice uncooperative.
OKAY, MASTER P, TIME TO TAKE YOUR WEAK SAUCE B-MOVIE DOOMSDAY PLOT--
--AND CRAM IT UP YOUR HELL HO--
OUCH!
666-C
YOUR DISGUSTING--
--STINK-MOUTHED HAND DEMON--
SMAK
--BIT ME ON MY--
KRAS
--FACE MEAT!
GAH! GRANNY, NO!
NOW I KNOW HOW THIS LOOKS BUT...
JUST GET IN THE CAR, ROGER.

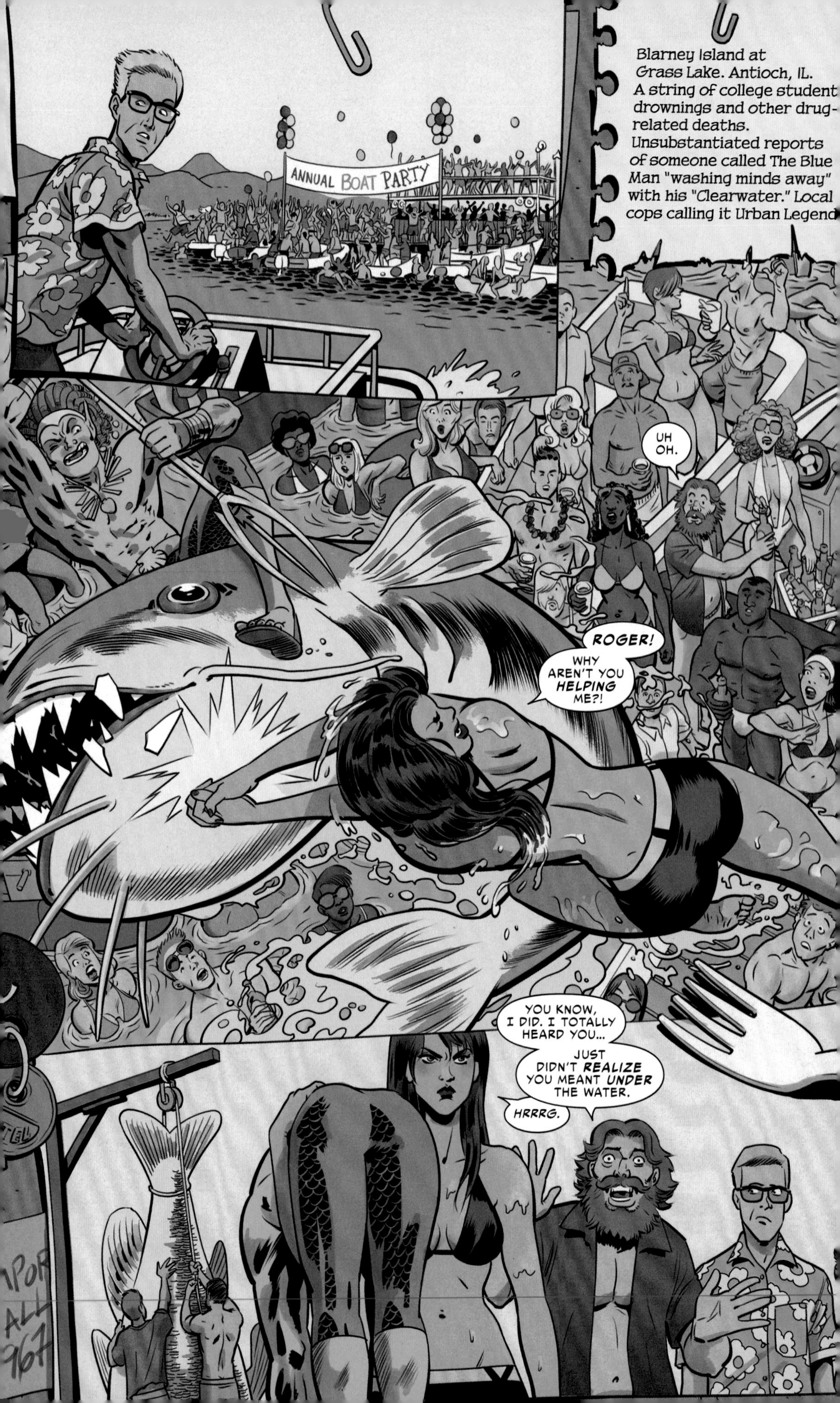

Blarney Island at Grass Lake. Antioch, IL. A string of college student drownings and other drug-related deaths. Unsubstantiated reports of someone called The Blue Man "washing minds away" with his "Clearwater." Local cops calling it Urban Legend
ANNUAL BOAT PARTY
UH OH.
ROGER!
WHY AREN'T YOU HELPING ME?!
YOU KNOW, I DID. I TOTALLY HEARD YOU...
JUST DIDN'T REALIZE YOU MEANT UNDER THE WATER.
HRRRG.

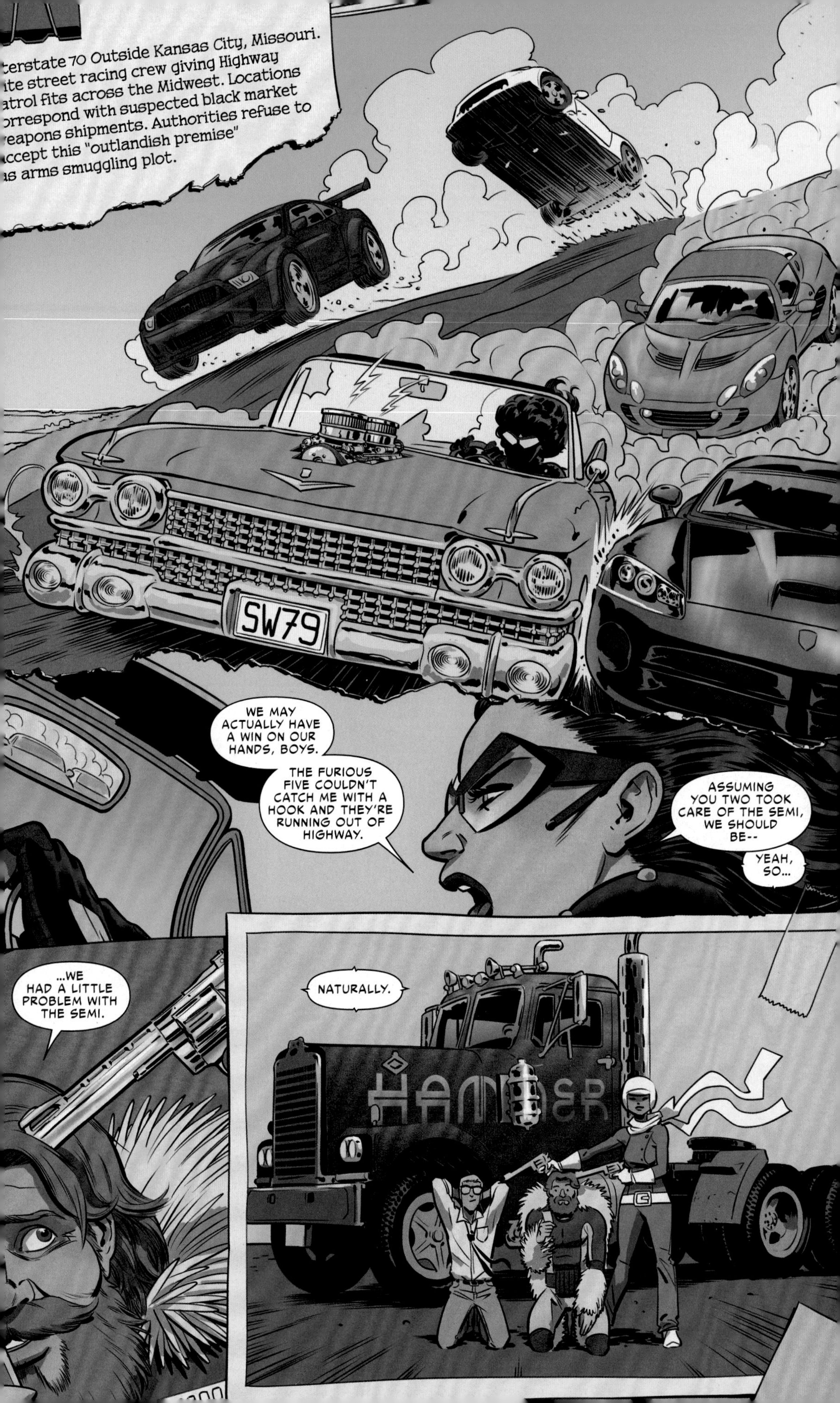

terstate 70 Outside Kansas City, Missouri. ite street racing crew giving Highway atrol fits across the Midwest. Locations orrespond with suspected black market eapons shipments. Authorities refuse to ccept this "outlandish premise" as arms smuggling plot.
SW79
WE MAY ACTUALLY HAVE A WIN ON OUR HANDS, BOYS.
THE FURIOUS FIVE COULDN'T CATCH ME WITH A HOOK AND THEY'RE RUNNING OUT OF HIGHWAY.
ASSUMING YOU TWO TOOK CARE OF THE SEMI, WE SHOULD BE--
YEAH, SO...
...WE HAD A LITTLE PROBLEM WITH THE SEMI.
NATURALLY.

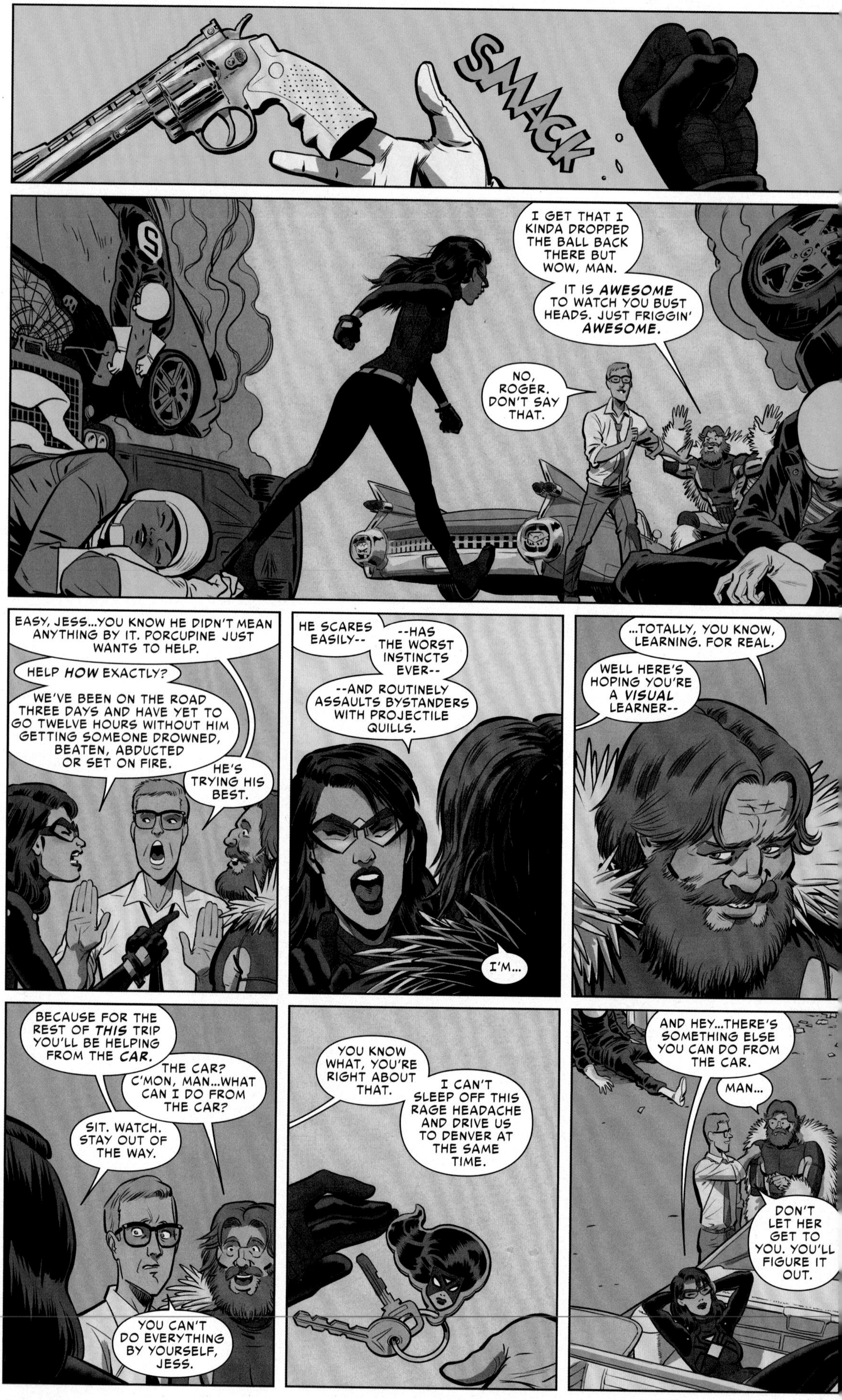
SMACK
I GET THAT I KINDA DROPPED THE BALL BACK THERE BUT WOW, MAN.
IT IS AWESOME TO WATCH YOU BUST HEADS. JUST FRIGGIN' AWESOME.
NO, ROGER. DON'T SAY THAT.
EASY, JESS...YOU KNOW HE DIDN'T MEAN ANYTHING BY IT. PORCUPINE JUST WANTS TO HELP.
HELP HOW EXACTLY?
WE'VE BEEN ON THE ROAD THREE DAYS AND HAVE YET TO GO TWELVE HOURS WITHOUT HIM GETTING SOMEONE DROWNED, BEATEN, ABDUCTED OR SET ON FIRE.
HE'S TRYING HIS BEST.
HE SCARES EASILY--
--HAS THE WORST INSTINCTS EVER--
--AND ROUTINELY ASSAULTS BYSTANDERS WITH PROJECTILE QUILLS.
I'M...
...TOTALLY, YOU KNOW, LEARNING. FOR REAL.
WELL HERE'S HOPING YOU'RE A VISUAL LEARNER--
BECAUSE FOR THE REST OF THIS TRIP YOU'LL BE HELPING FROM THE CAR.
THE CAR? C'MON, MAN...WHAT CAN I DO FROM THE CAR?
SIT. WATCH. STAY OUT OF THE WAY.
YOU CAN'T DO EVERYTHING BY YOURSELF, JESS.
YOU KNOW WHAT, YOU'RE RIGHT ABOUT THAT.
I CAN'T SLEEP OFF THIS RAGE HEADACHE AND DRIVE US TO DENVER AT THE SAME TIME.
AND HEY...THERE'S SOMETHING ELSE YOU CAN DO FROM THE CAR.
MAN...
DON'T LET HER GET TO YOU. YOU'LL FIGURE IT OUT.

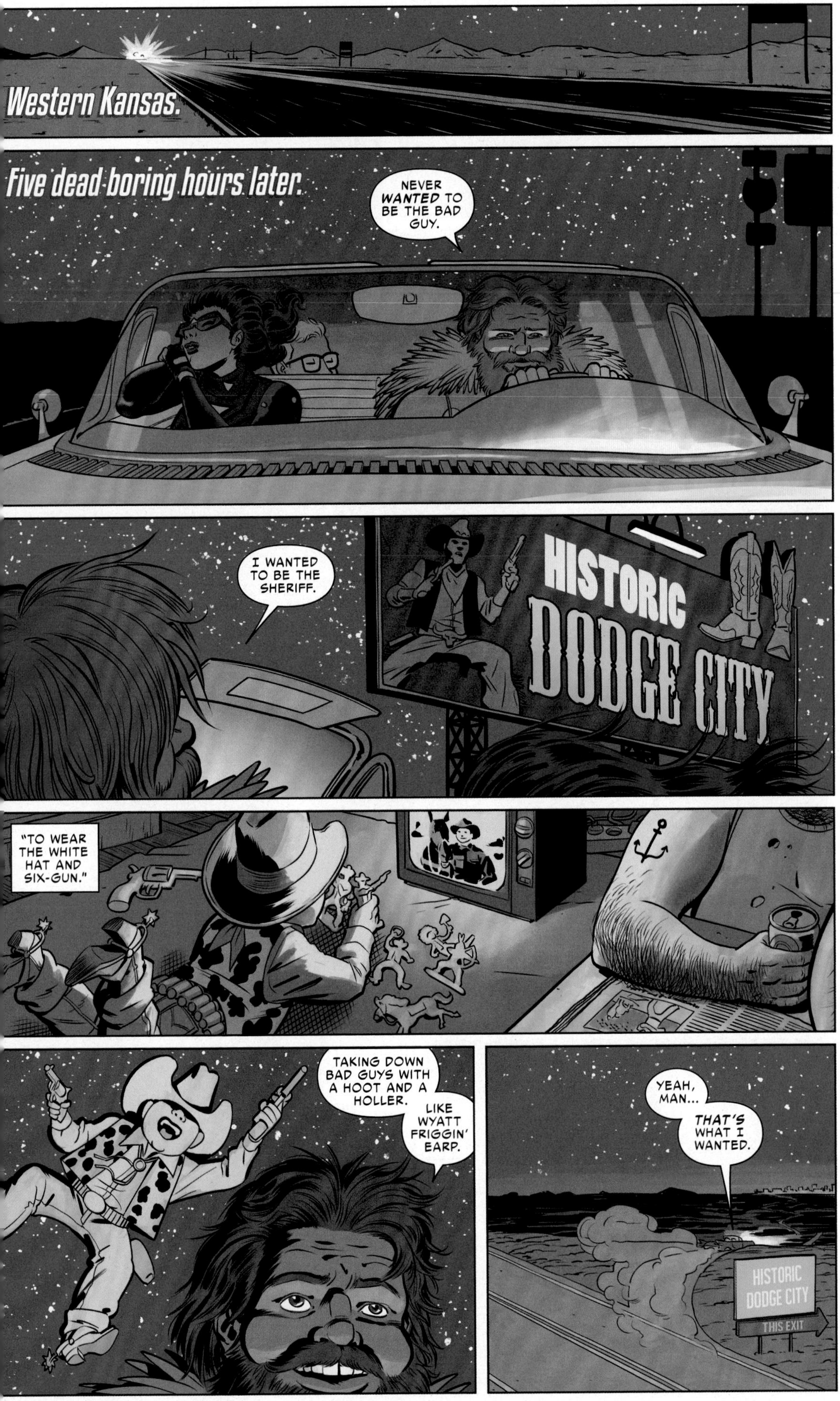
Western Kansas.
Five dead-boring hours later.
NEVER WANTED TO BE THE BAD GUY.
I WANTED TO BE THE SHERIFF.
HISTORIC DODGE CITY
"TO WEAR THE WHITE HAT AND SIX-GUN."
TAKING DOWN BAD GUYS WITH A HOOT AND A HOLLER.
LIKE WYATT FRIGGIN' EARP.
YEAH, MAN...
THAT'S WHAT I WANTED.
HISTORIC DODGE CITY
THIS EXIT

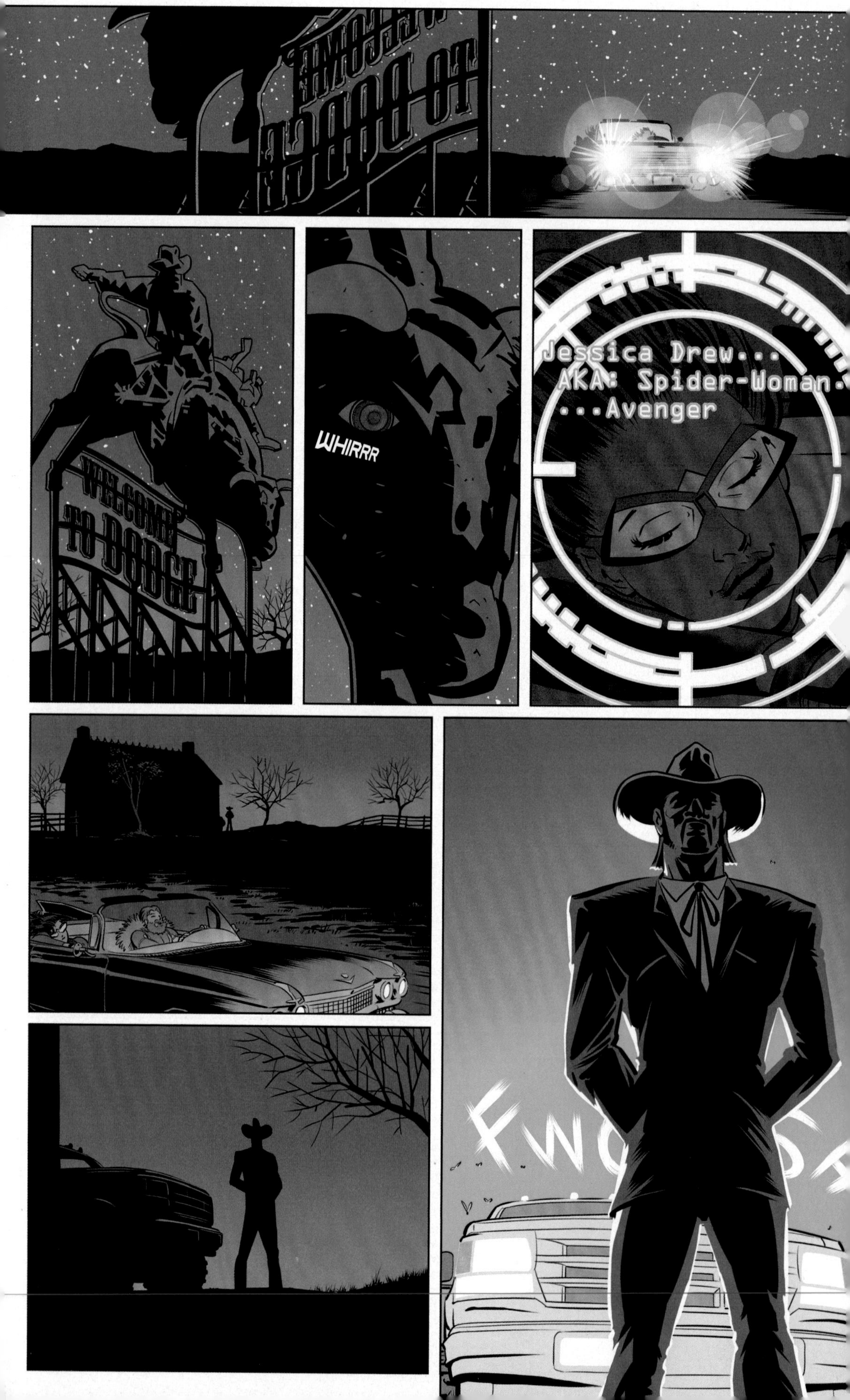
WELCOME TO DODGE
WHIRRR
Jessica Drew...
AKA: Spider-Woman...
...Avenger
FWO

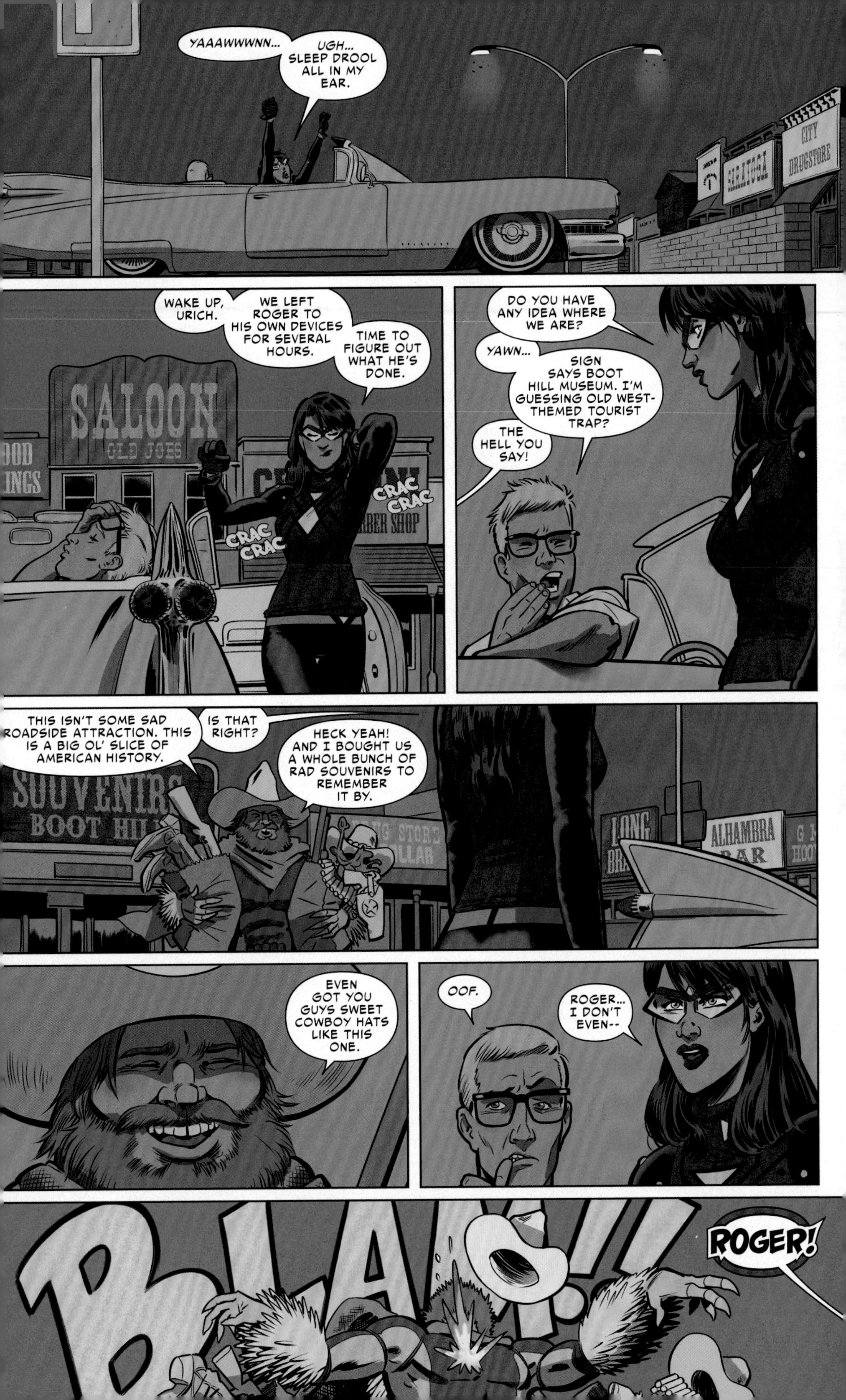
YAAAWWWNN...
UGH... SLEEP DROOL ALL IN MY EAR.
SARATOGA
CITY DRUGSTORE
WAKE UP, URICH.
WE LEFT ROGER TO HIS OWN DEVICES FOR SEVERAL HOURS.
TIME TO FIGURE OUT WHAT HE'S DONE.
SALOON
OLD JOES
BARBER SHOP
CRAC CRAC
CRAC CRAC
DO YOU HAVE ANY IDEA WHERE WE ARE?
YAWN...
SIGN SAYS BOOT HILL MUSEUM. I'M GUESSING OLD WEST-THEMED TOURIST TRAP?
THE HELL YOU SAY!
THIS ISN'T SOME SAD ROADSIDE ATTRACTION. THIS IS A BIG OL' SLICE OF AMERICAN HISTORY.
IS THAT RIGHT?
HECK YEAH! AND I BOUGHT US A WHOLE BUNCH OF RAD SOUVENIRS TO REMEMBER IT BY.
SOUVENIRS
BOOT HILL
ALHAMBRA
BAR
EVEN GOT YOU GUYS SWEET COWBOY HATS LIKE THIS ONE.
OOF.
ROGER... I DON'T EVEN--
ROGER!

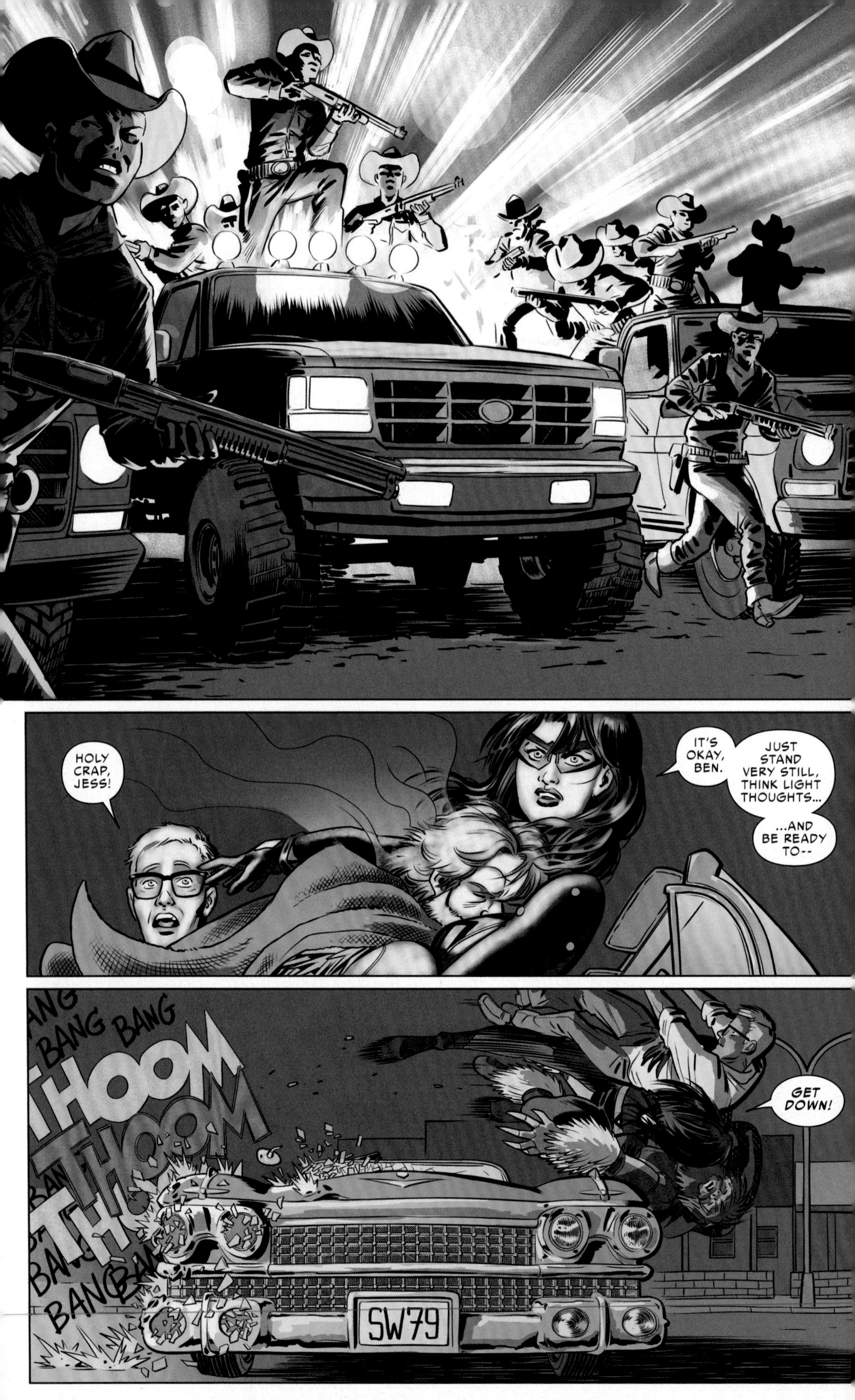
HOLY CRAP, JESS!
IT'S OKAY, BEN.
JUST STAND VERY STILL, THINK LIGHT THOUGHTS...
...AND BE READY TO--
BANG BANG BANG
THOOM
GET DOWN!
SW79

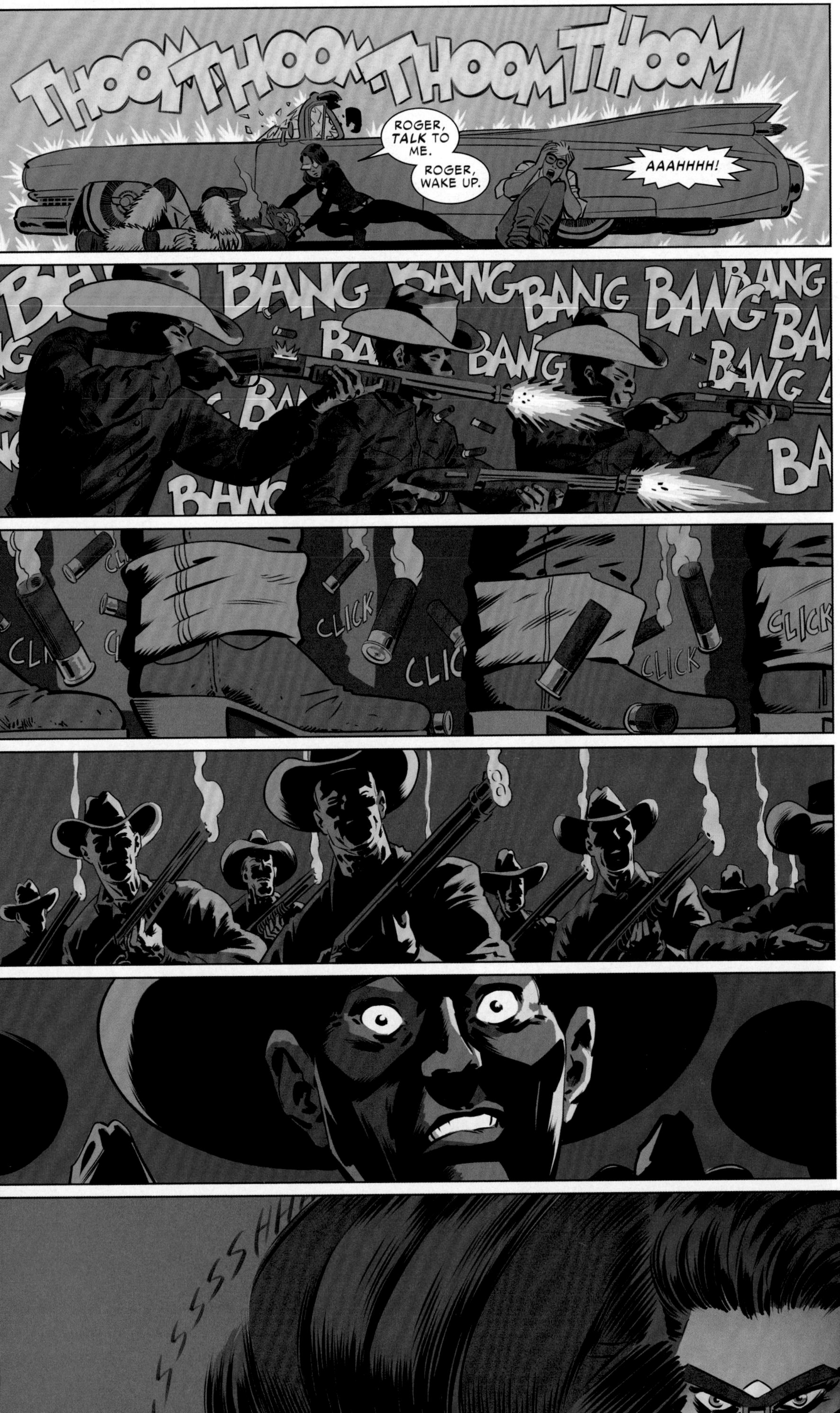

THOOM THOOM THOOM THOOM
ROGER, TALK TO ME.
ROGER, WAKE UP.
AAAHHHH!
BANG BANG BANG BANG BANG BANG BANG BANG BANG
CLICK CLICK CLICK CLICK

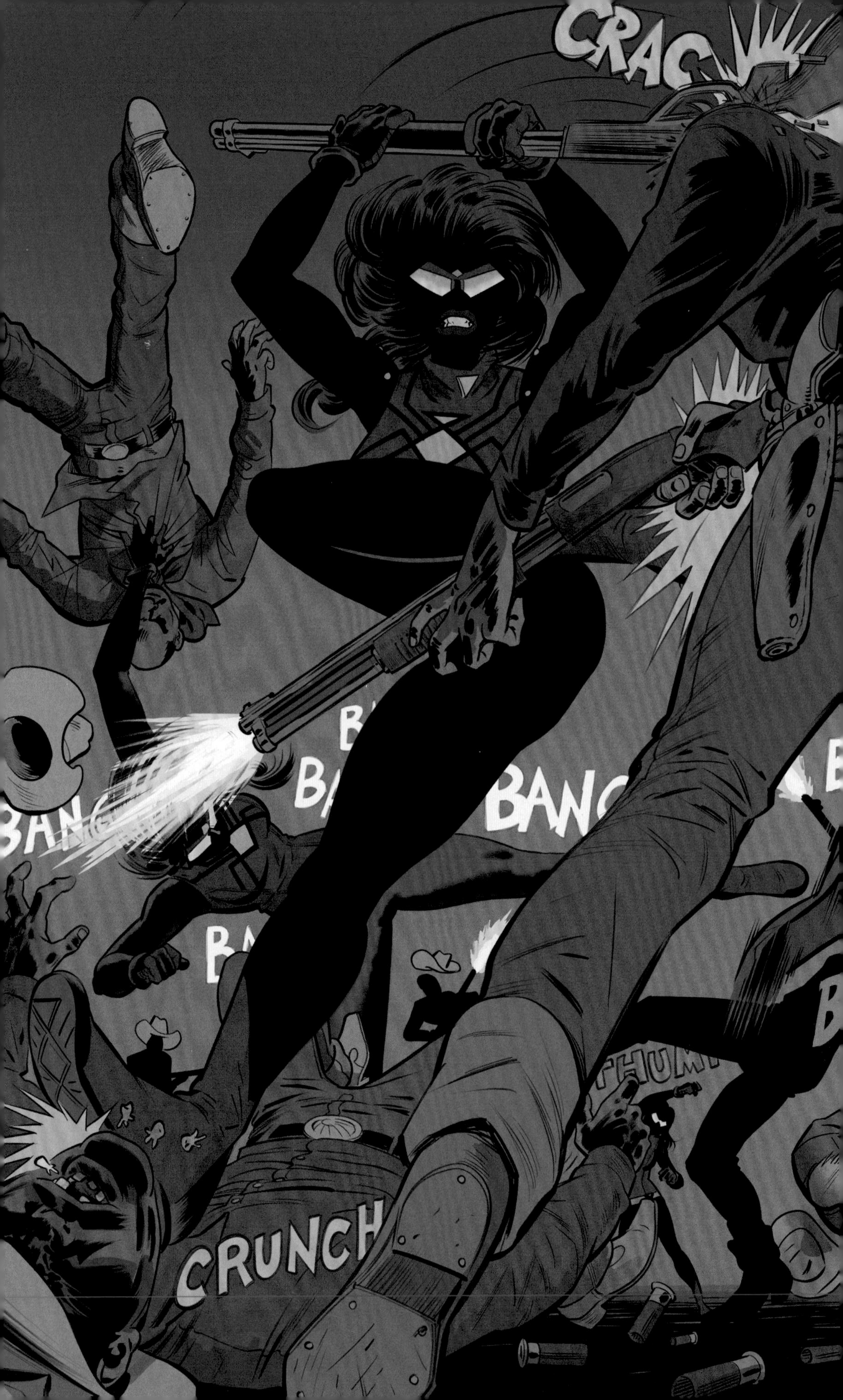

CRAC
BA
BANG
BA
THUM
CRUNCH

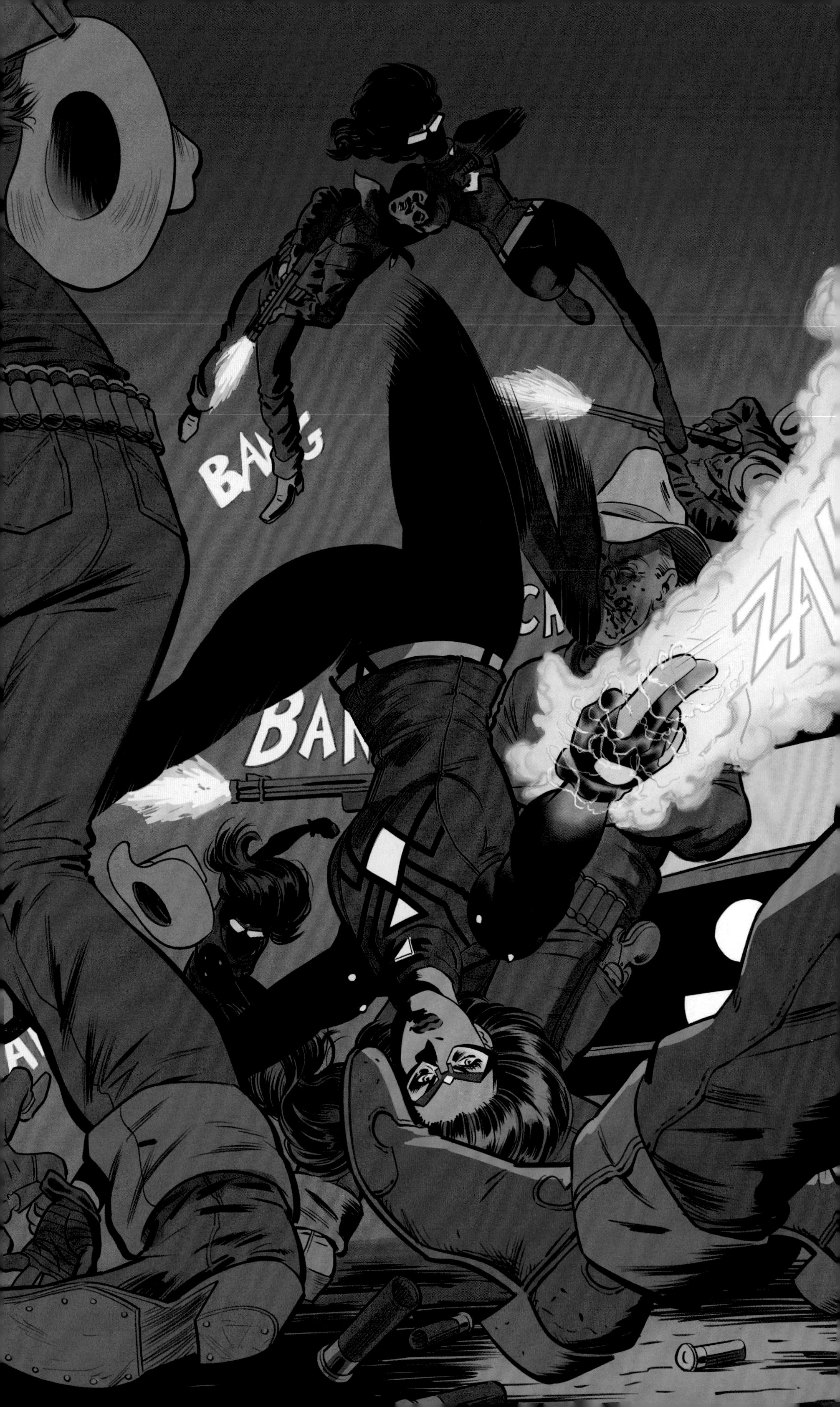

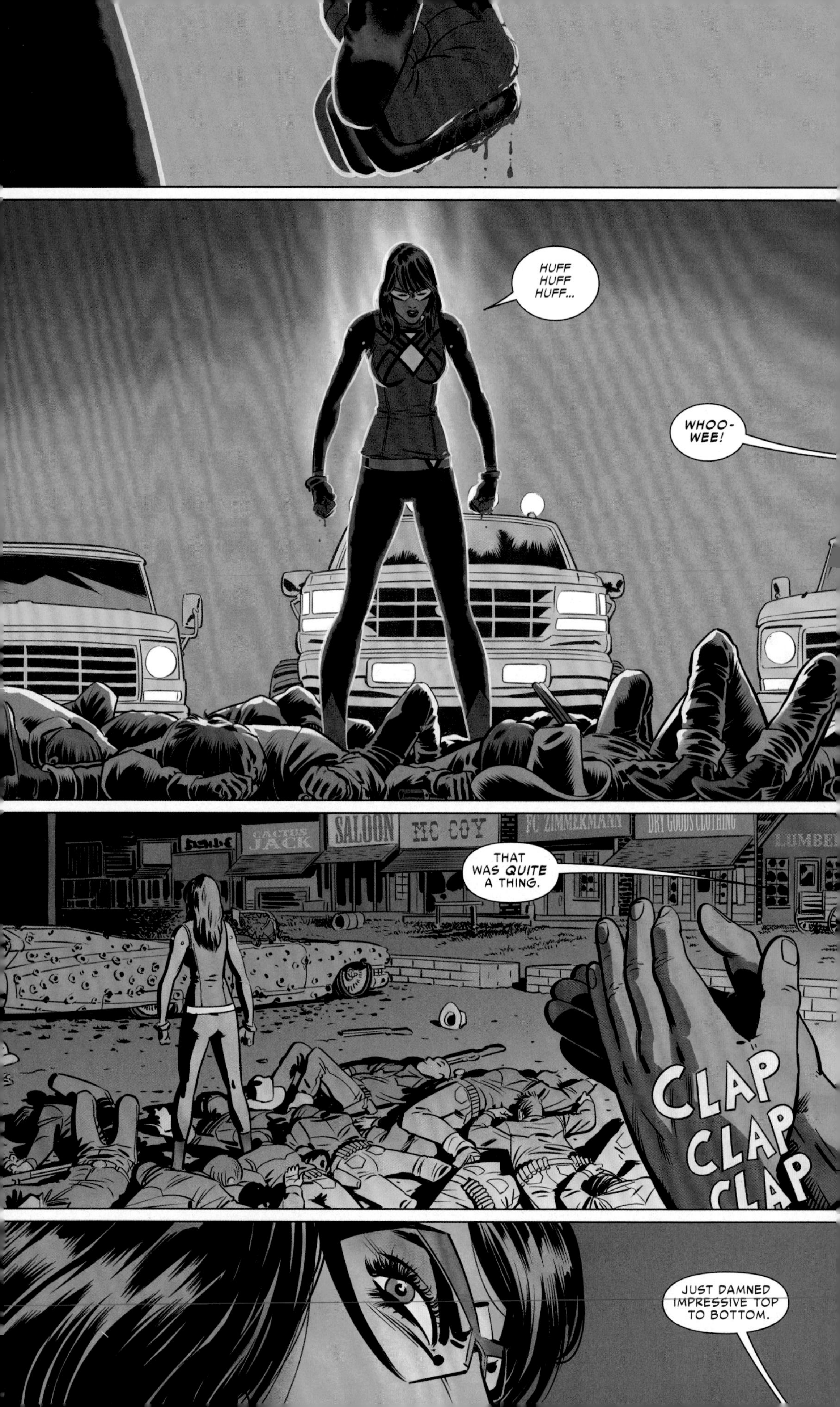
HUFF HUFF HUFF...
WHOO-WEE!
SALOON
MC COY
FC ZIMMERMANN
DRY GOODS CLOTHING
THAT WAS QUITE A THING.
CLAP CLAP CLAP CLAP
JUST DAMNED IMPRESSIVE TOP TO BOTTOM.

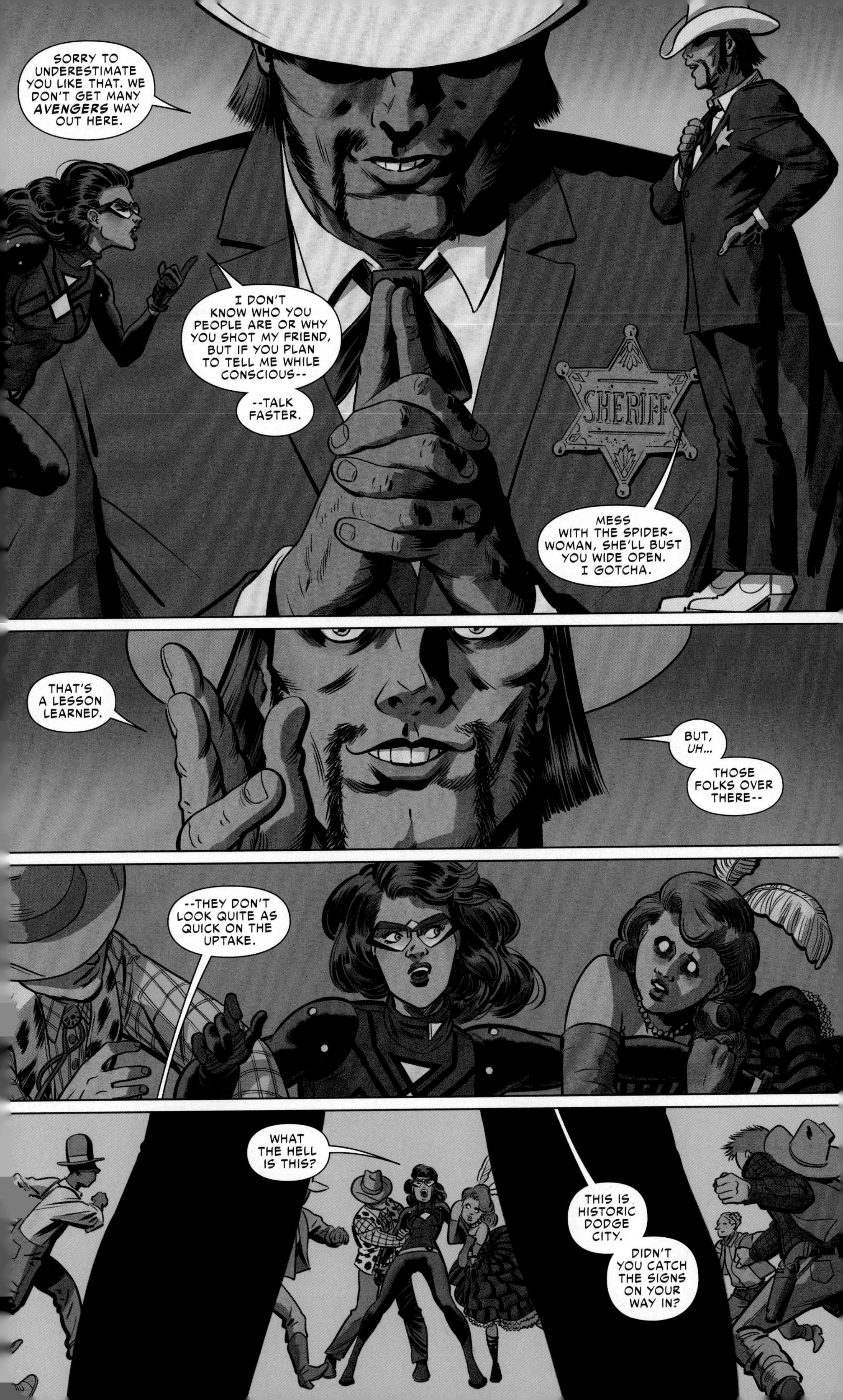
SORRY TO UNDERESTIMATE YOU LIKE THAT. WE DON'T GET MANY AVENGERS WAY OUT HERE.
I DON'T KNOW WHO YOU PEOPLE ARE OR WHY YOU SHOT MY FRIEND, BUT IF YOU PLAN TO TELL ME WHILE CONSCIOUS--
--TALK FASTER.
SHERIFF
MESS WITH THE SPIDER-WOMAN, SHE'LL BUST YOU WIDE OPEN. I GOTCHA.
THAT'S A LESSON LEARNED.
BUT, UH...
THOSE FOLKS OVER THERE--
--THEY DON'T LOOK QUITE AS QUICK ON THE UPTAKE.
WHAT THE HELL IS THIS?
THIS IS HISTORIC DODGE CITY.
DIDN'T YOU CATCH THE SIGNS ON YOUR WAY IN?

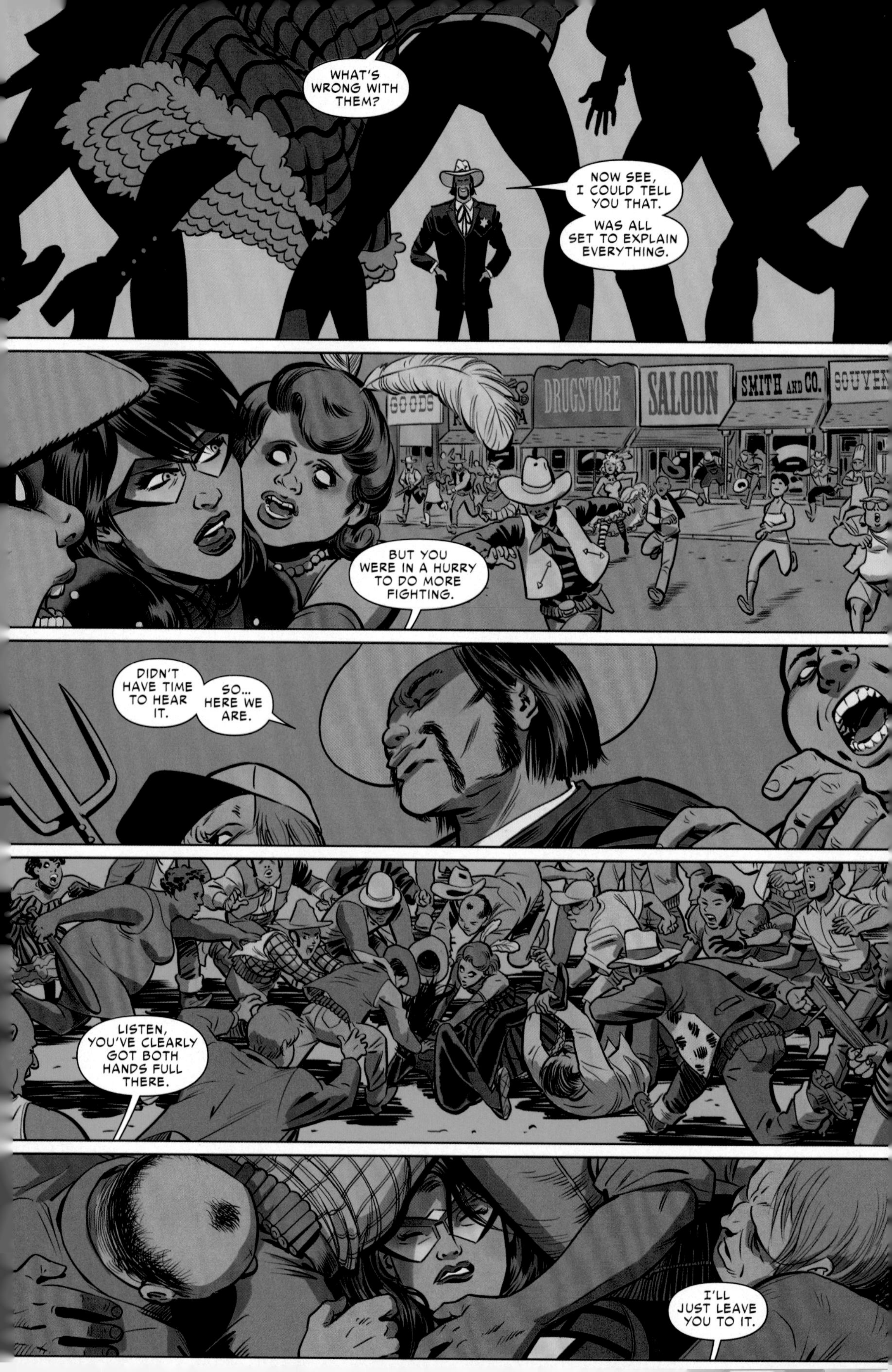
WHAT'S WRONG WITH THEM?
NOW SEE, I COULD TELL YOU THAT.
WAS ALL SET TO EXPLAIN EVERYTHING.
GOODS
DRUGSTORE
SALOON
SMITH AND CO.
BUT YOU WERE IN A HURRY TO DO MORE FIGHTING.
DIDN'T HAVE TIME TO HEAR IT.
SO... HERE WE ARE.
LISTEN, YOU'VE CLEARLY GOT BOTH HANDS FULL THERE.
I'LL JUST LEAVE YOU TO IT.

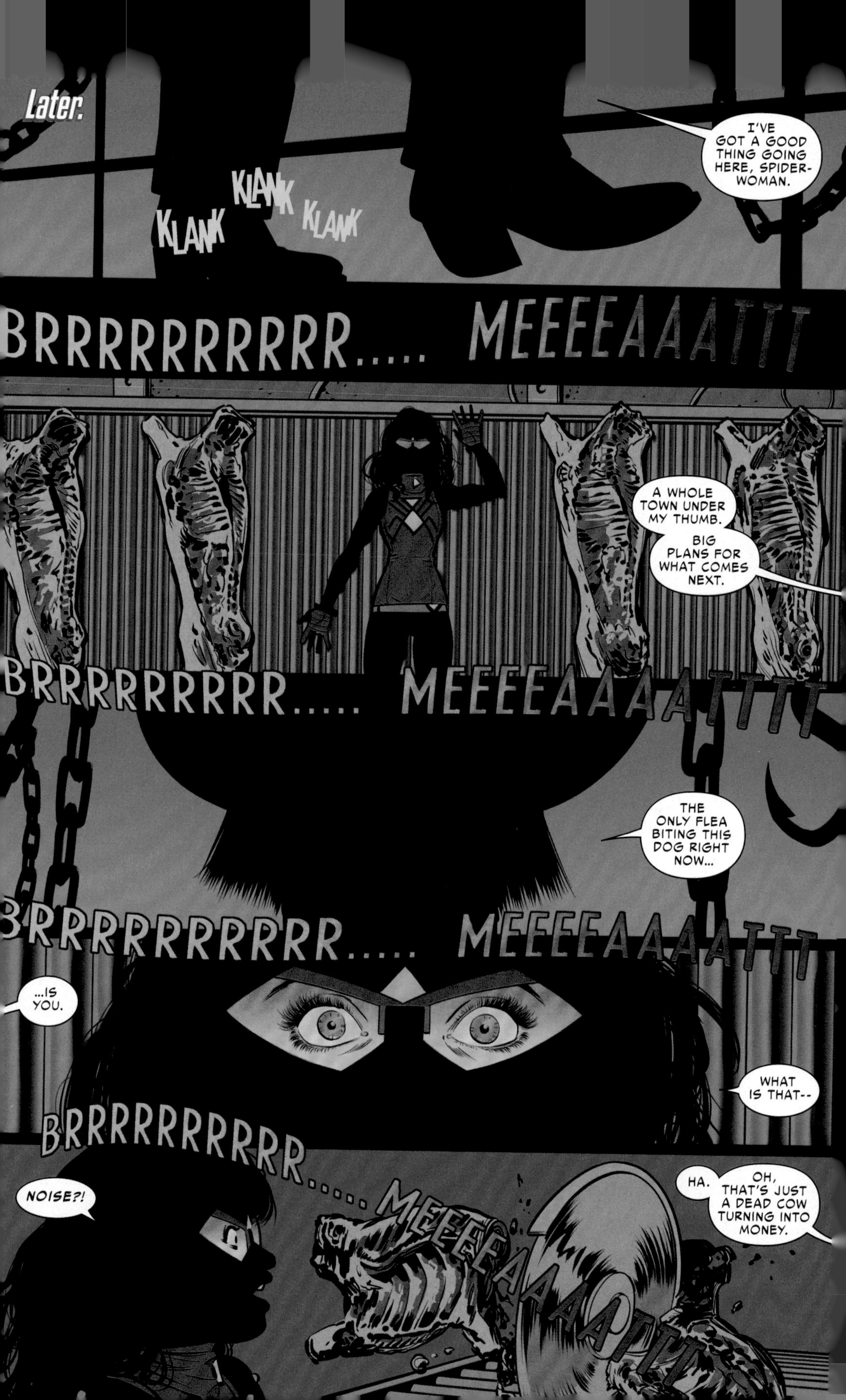

Later:
KLANK
KLANK
KLANK
I'VE GOT A GOOD THING GOING HERE, SPIDER-WOMAN.
BRRRRRRRRRR..... MEEEEAAATTT
A WHOLE TOWN UNDER MY THUMB.
BIG PLANS FOR WHAT COMES NEXT.
BRRRRRRRRRR..... MEEEEAAAATTTT
THE ONLY FLEA BITING THIS DOG RIGHT NOW...
BRRRRRRRRRRR..... MEEEEAAAATTT
...IS YOU.
WHAT IS THAT--
BRRRRRRRRRR......
NOISE?!
MEEEEAAAATTT
HA.
OH, THAT'S JUST A DEAD COW TURNING INTO MONEY.

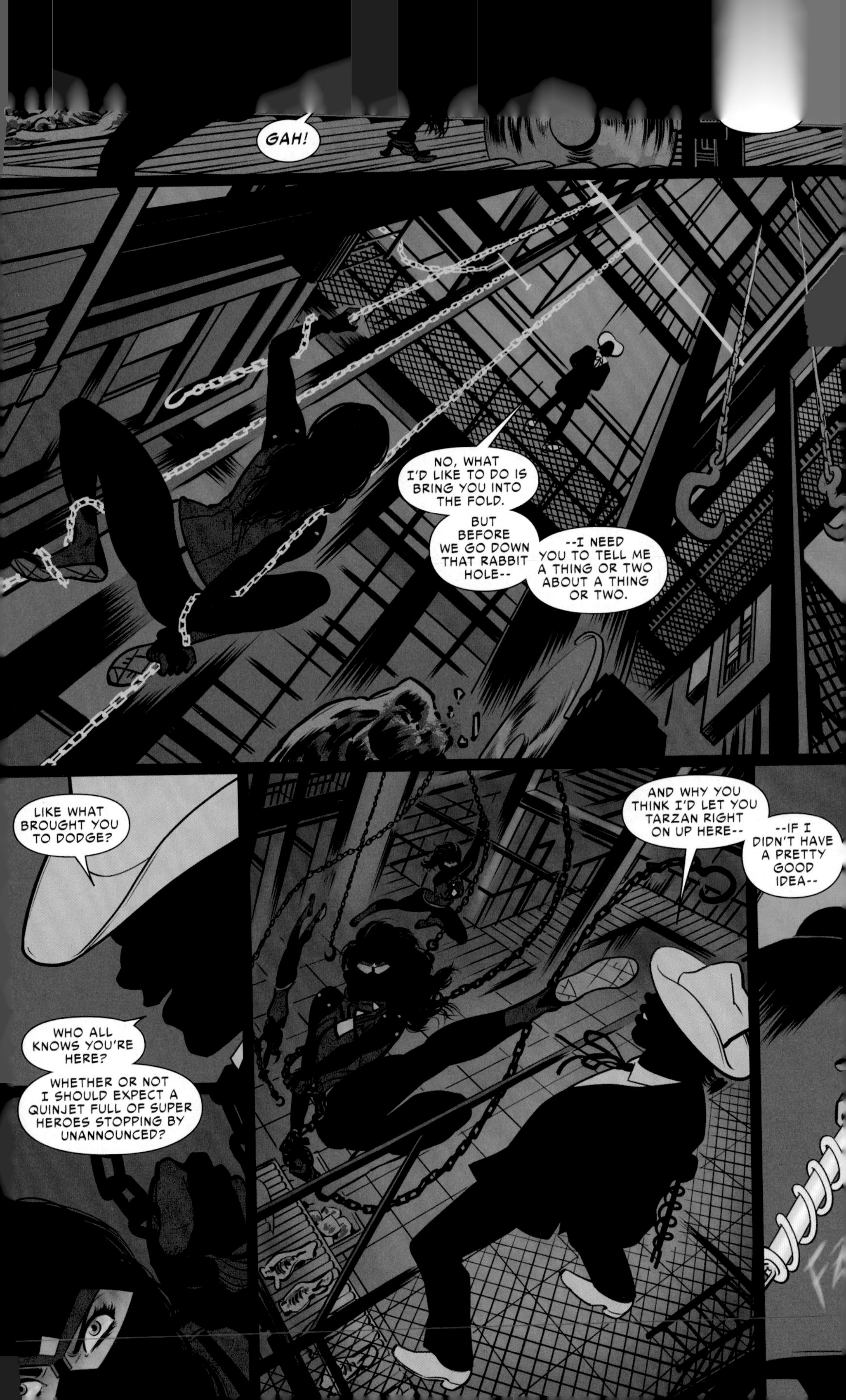
GAH!
NO, WHAT I'D LIKE TO DO IS BRING YOU INTO THE FOLD.
BUT BEFORE WE GO DOWN THAT RABBIT HOLE--
--I NEED YOU TO TELL ME A THING OR TWO ABOUT A THING OR TWO.
LIKE WHAT BROUGHT YOU TO DODGE?
WHO ALL KNOWS YOU'RE HERE?
WHETHER OR NOT I SHOULD EXPECT A QUINJET FULL OF SUPER HEROES STOPPING BY UNANNOUNCED?
AND WHY YOU THINK I'D LET YOU TARZAN RIGHT ON UP HERE--
--IF I DIDN'T HAVE A PRETTY GOOD IDEA--

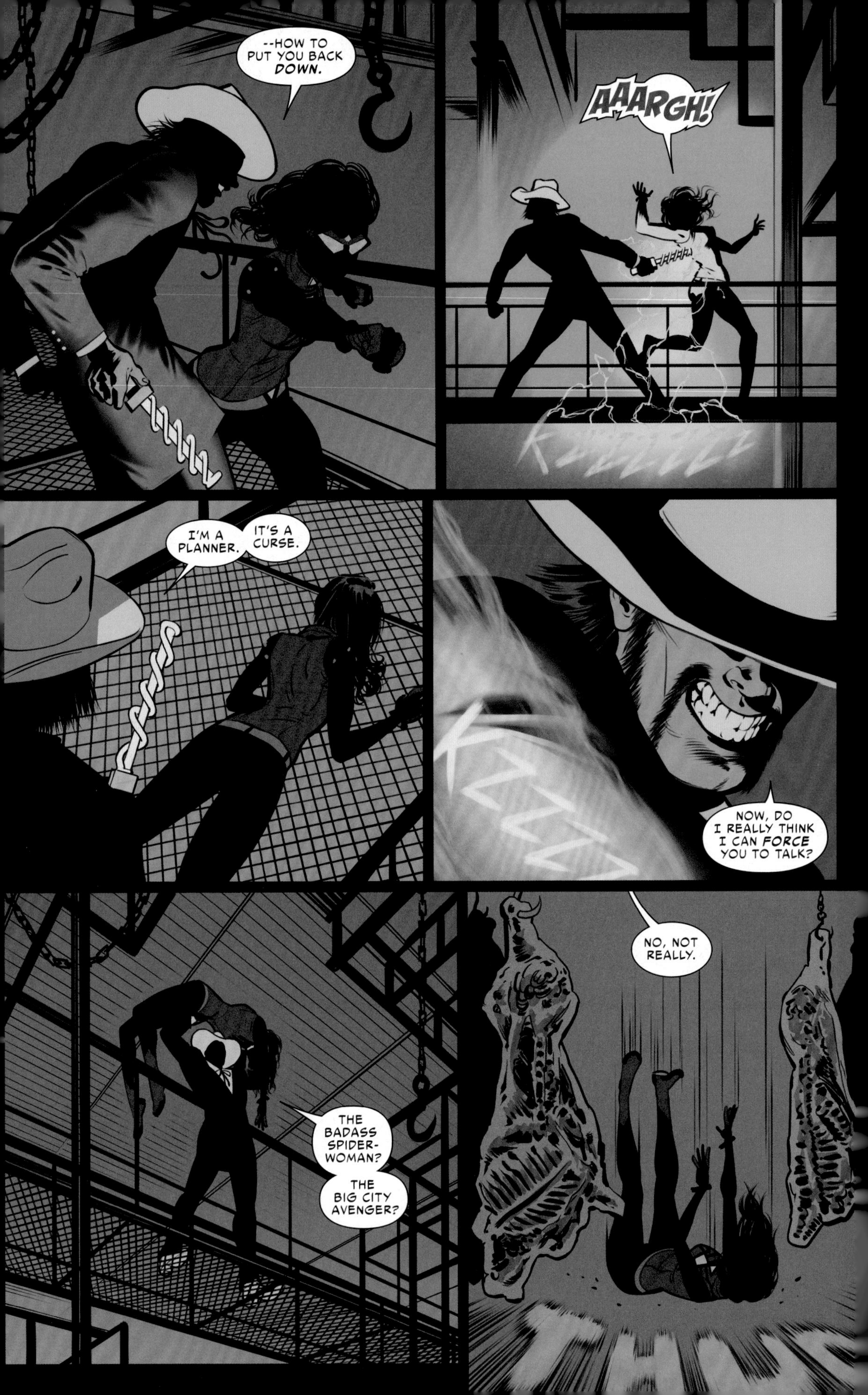
--HOW TO PUT YOU BACK DOWN.
AAARGH!
KZZZZZZZ
I'M A PLANNER.
IT'S A CURSE.
NOW, DO I REALLY THINK I CAN FORCE YOU TO TALK?
NO, NOT REALLY.
THE BADASS SPIDER-WOMAN?
THE BIG CITY AVENGER?

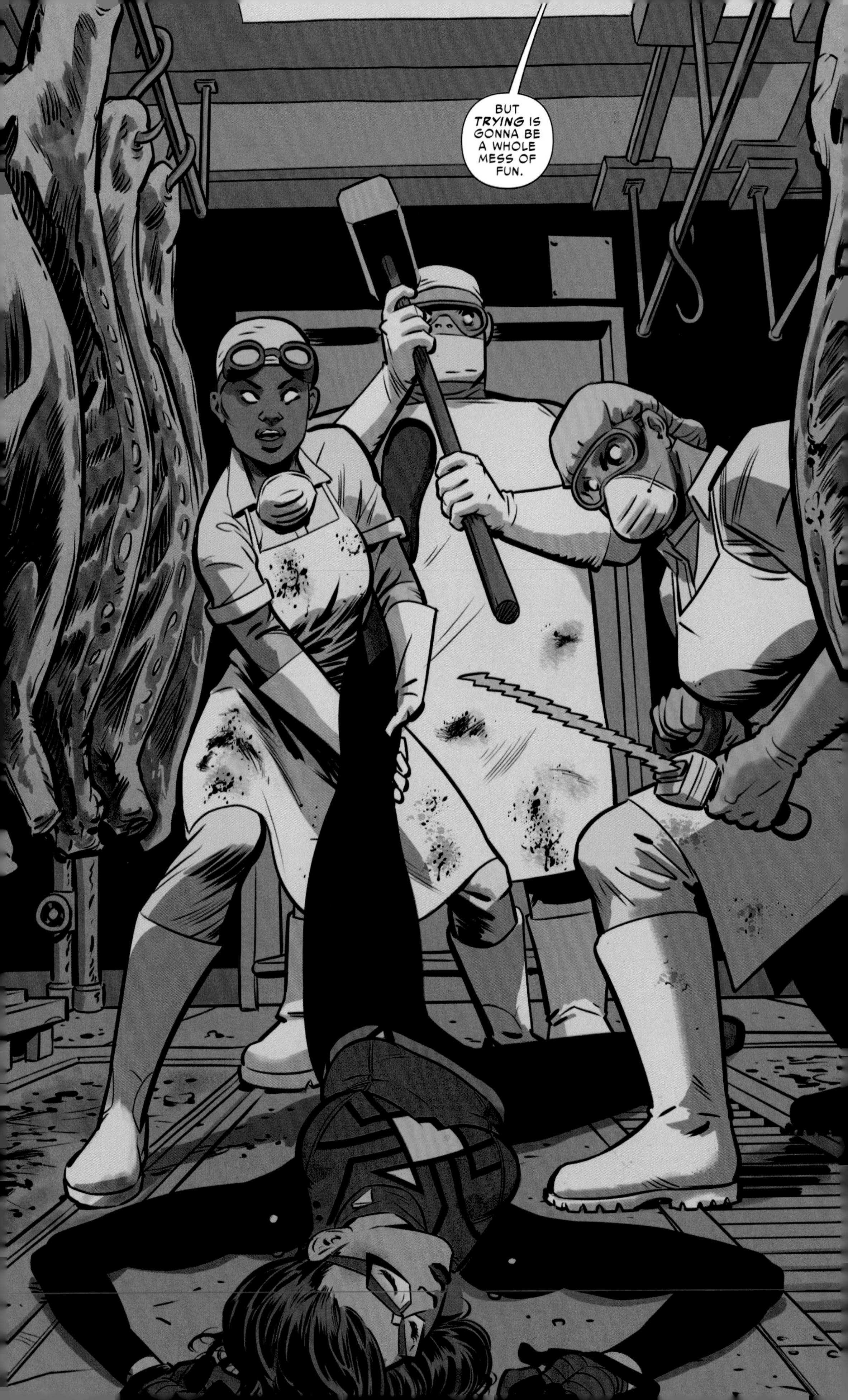
BUT *TRYING* IS GONNA BE A WHOLE MESS OF FUN.

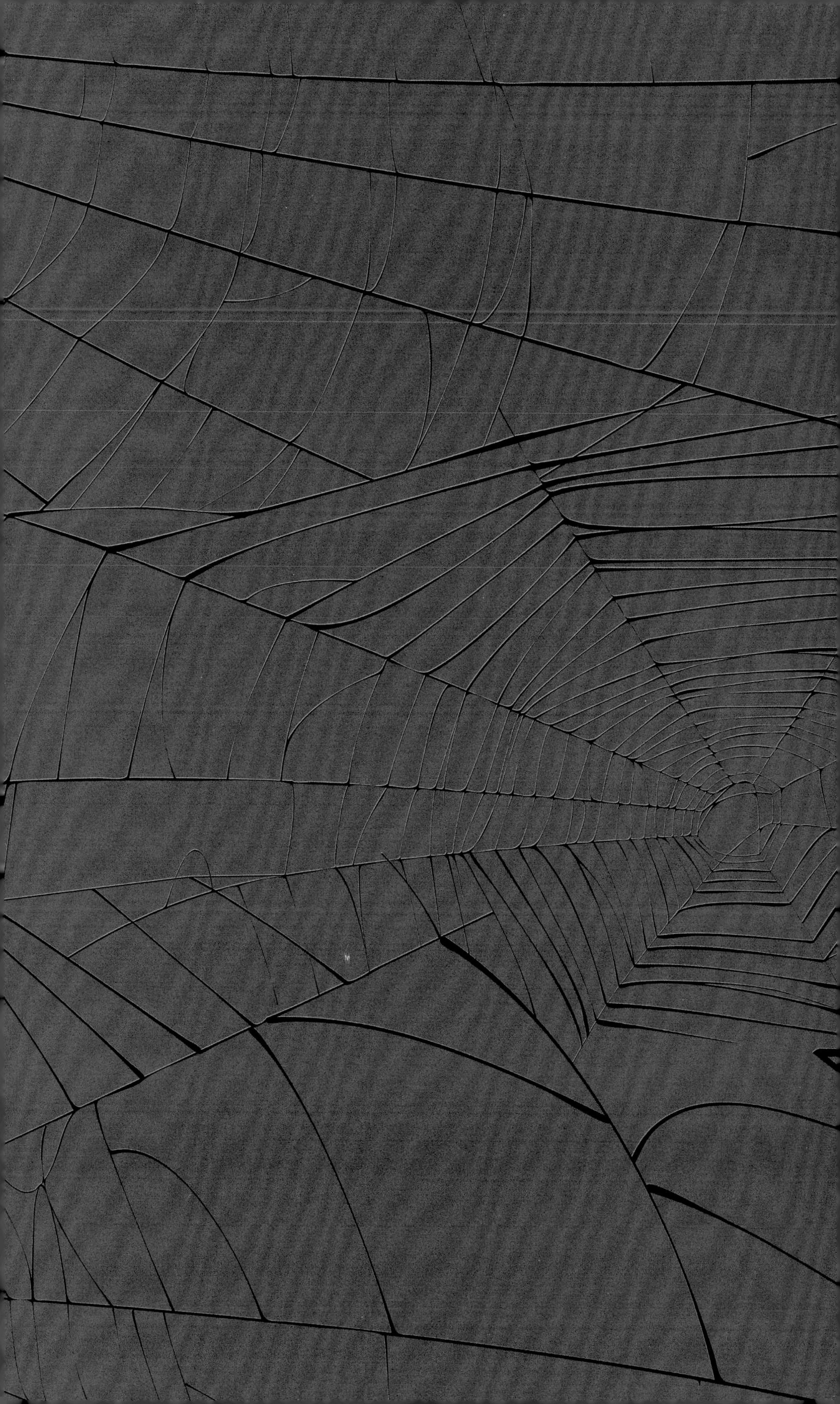

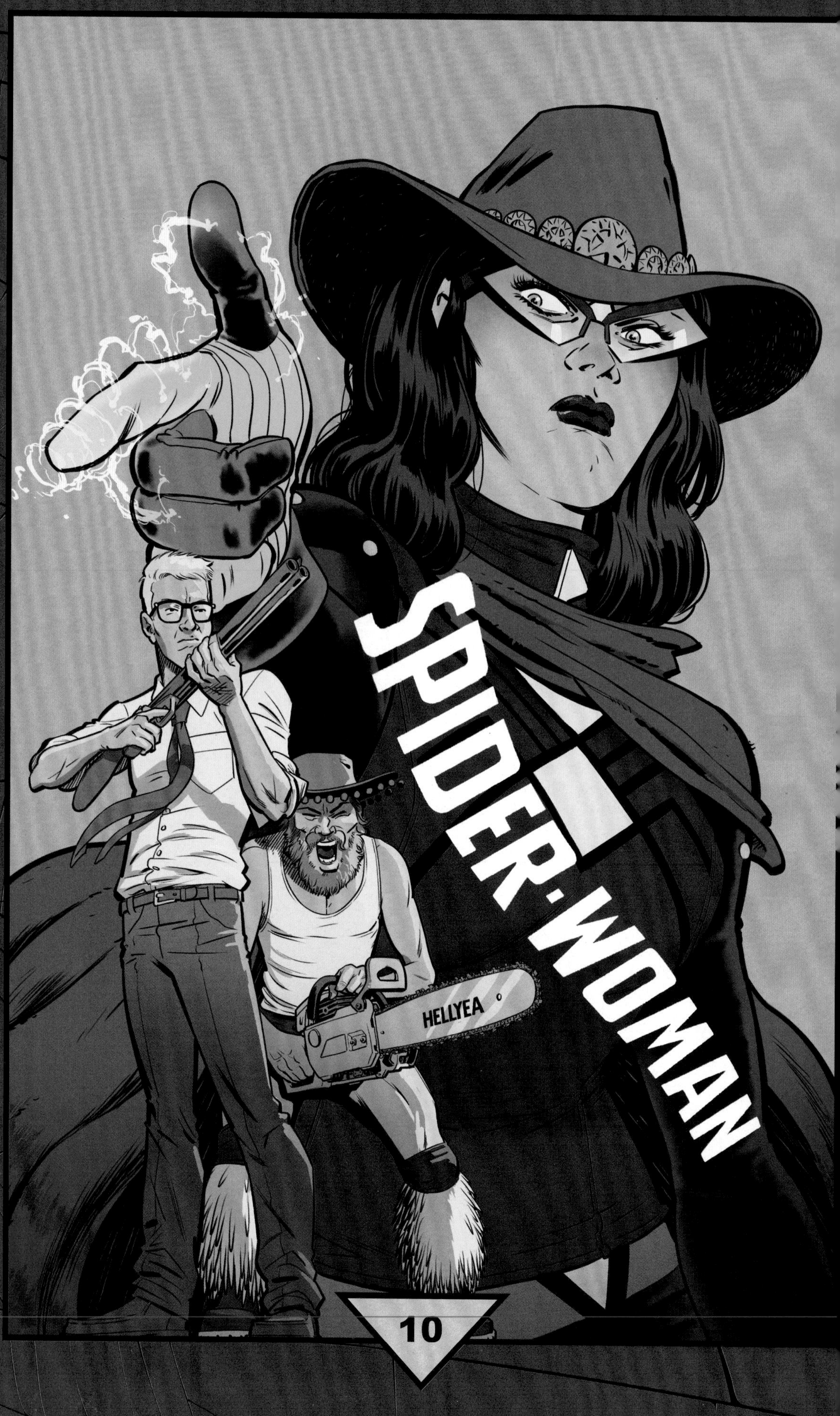
SPIDER-WOMAN
HELLYEA
10

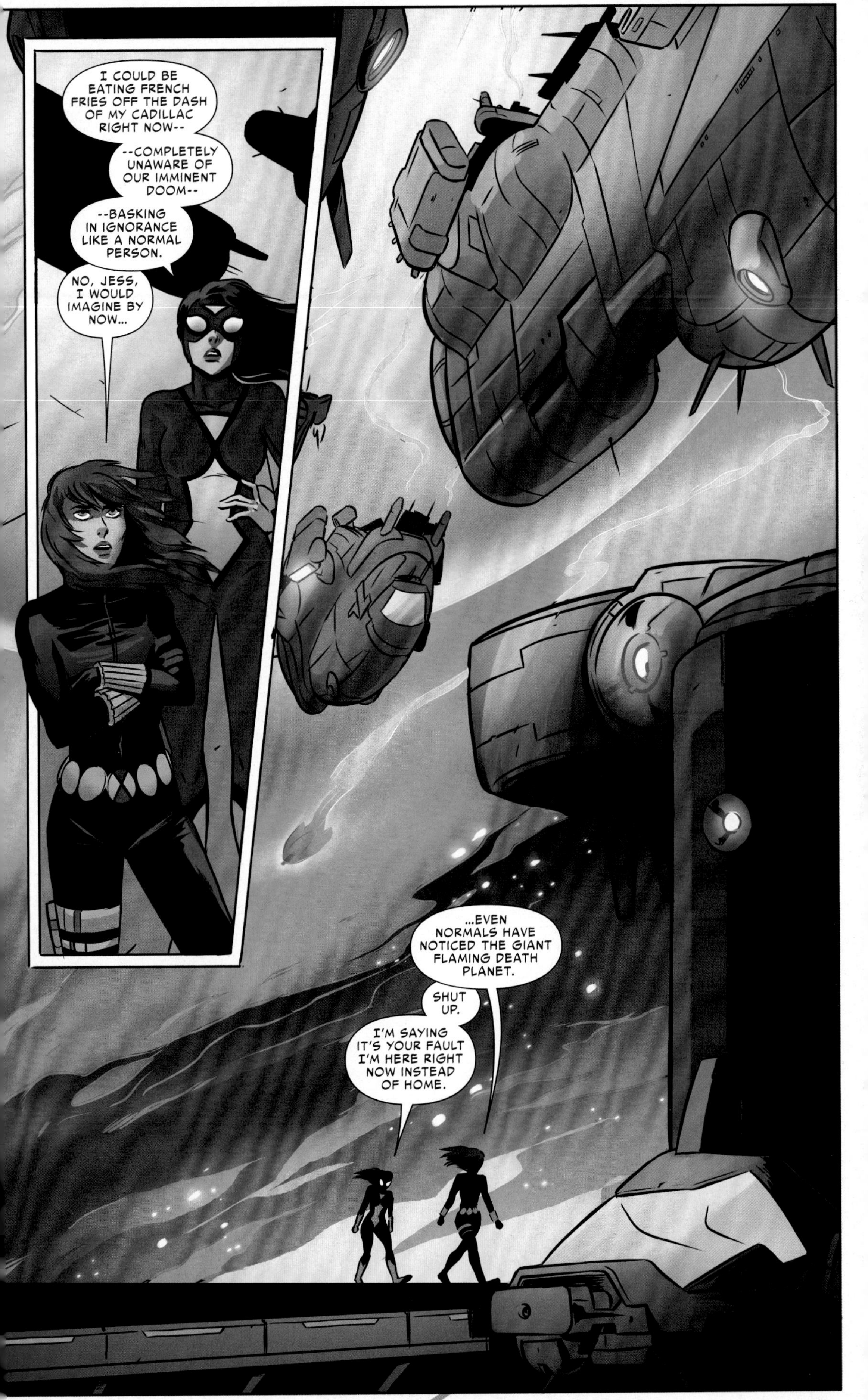
I COULD BE EATING FRENCH FRIES OFF THE DASH OF MY CADILLAC RIGHT NOW--
--COMPLETELY UNAWARE OF OUR IMMINENT DOOM--
--BASKING IN IGNORANCE LIKE A NORMAL PERSON.
NO, JESS, I WOULD IMAGINE BY NOW...
...EVEN NORMALS HAVE NOTICED THE GIANT FLAMING DEATH PLANET.
SHUT UP.
I'M SAYING IT'S YOUR FAULT I'M HERE RIGHT NOW INSTEAD OF HOME.

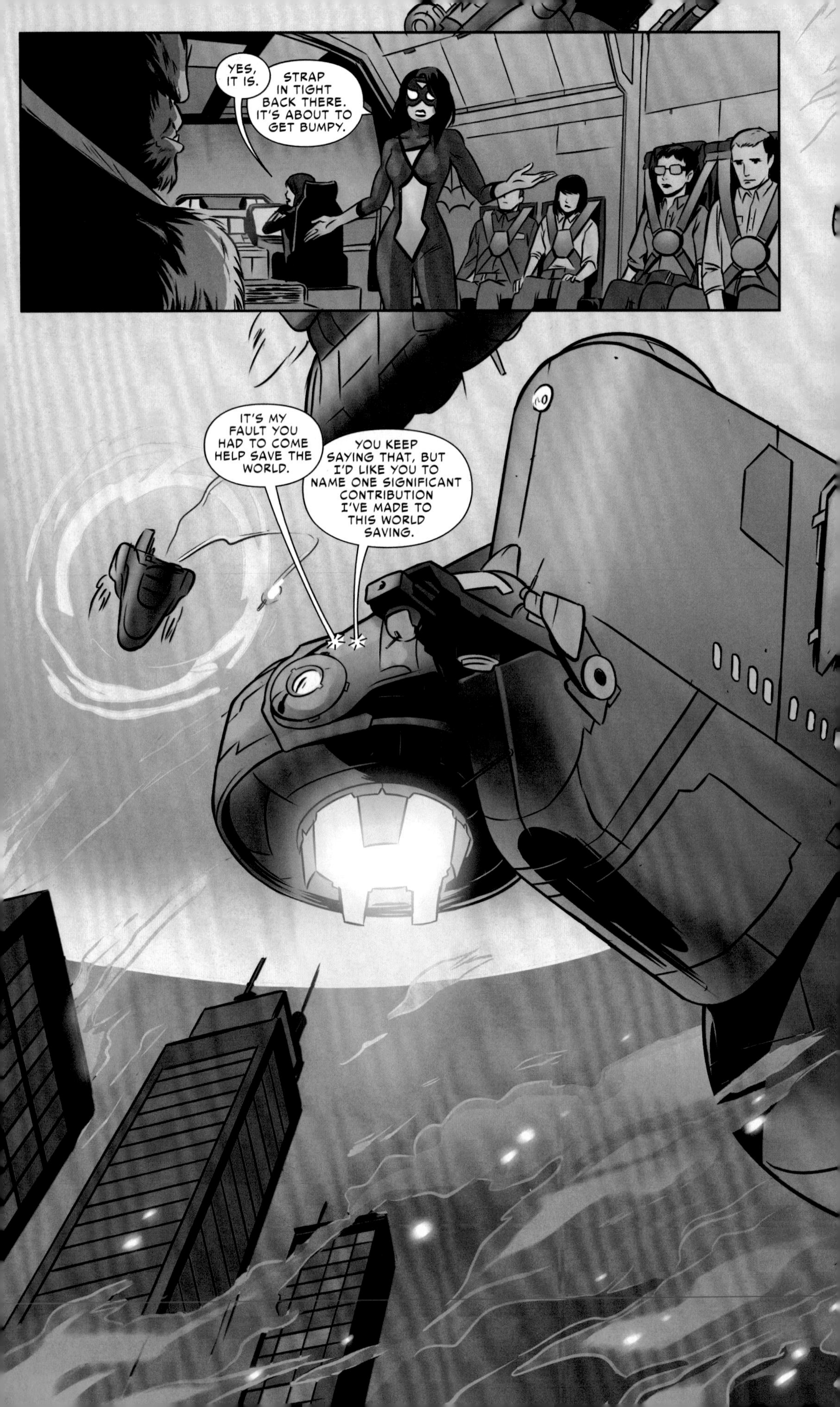
YES, IT IS.
STRAP IN TIGHT BACK THERE. IT'S ABOUT TO GET BUMPY.
IT'S MY FAULT YOU HAD TO COME HELP SAVE THE WORLD.
YOU KEEP SAYING THAT, BUT I'D LIKE YOU TO NAME ONE SIGNIFICANT CONTRIBUTION I'VE MADE TO THIS WORLD SAVING.

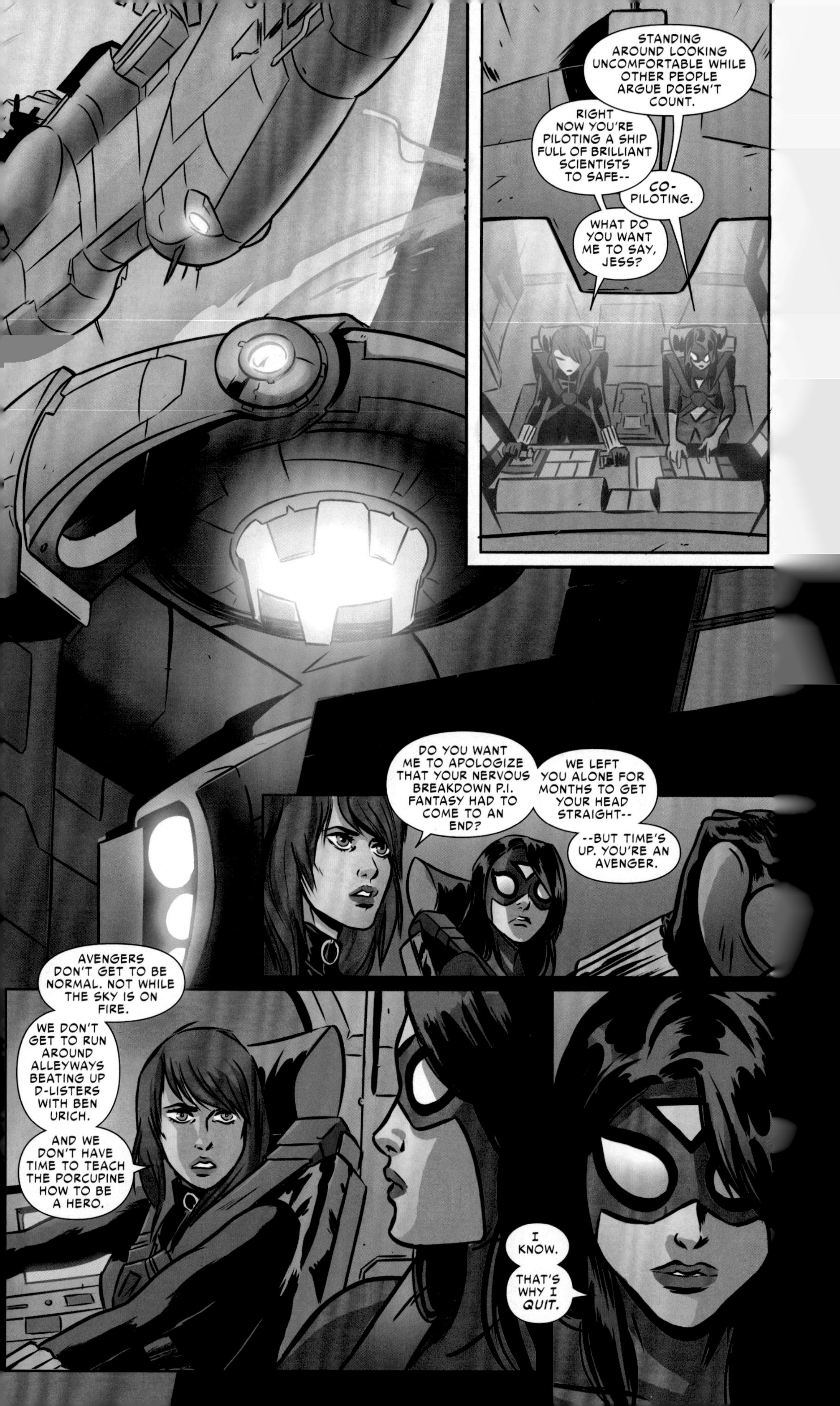
STANDING AROUND LOOKING UNCOMFORTABLE WHILE OTHER PEOPLE ARGUE DOESN'T COUNT.
RIGHT NOW YOU'RE PILOTING A SHIP FULL OF BRILLIANT SCIENTISTS TO SAFE--
CO-PILOTING.
WHAT DO YOU WANT ME TO SAY, JESS?
DO YOU WANT ME TO APOLOGIZE THAT YOUR NERVOUS BREAKDOWN P.I. FANTASY HAD TO COME TO AN END?
WE LEFT YOU ALONE FOR MONTHS TO GET YOUR HEAD STRAIGHT--
--BUT TIME'S UP. YOU'RE AN AVENGER.
AVENGERS DON'T GET TO BE NORMAL. NOT WHILE THE SKY IS ON FIRE.
WE DON'T GET TO RUN AROUND ALLEYWAYS BEATING UP D-LISTERS WITH BEN URICH.
AND WE DON'T HAVE TIME TO TEACH THE PORCUPINE HOW TO BE A HERO.
I KNOW.
THAT'S WHY I QUIT.

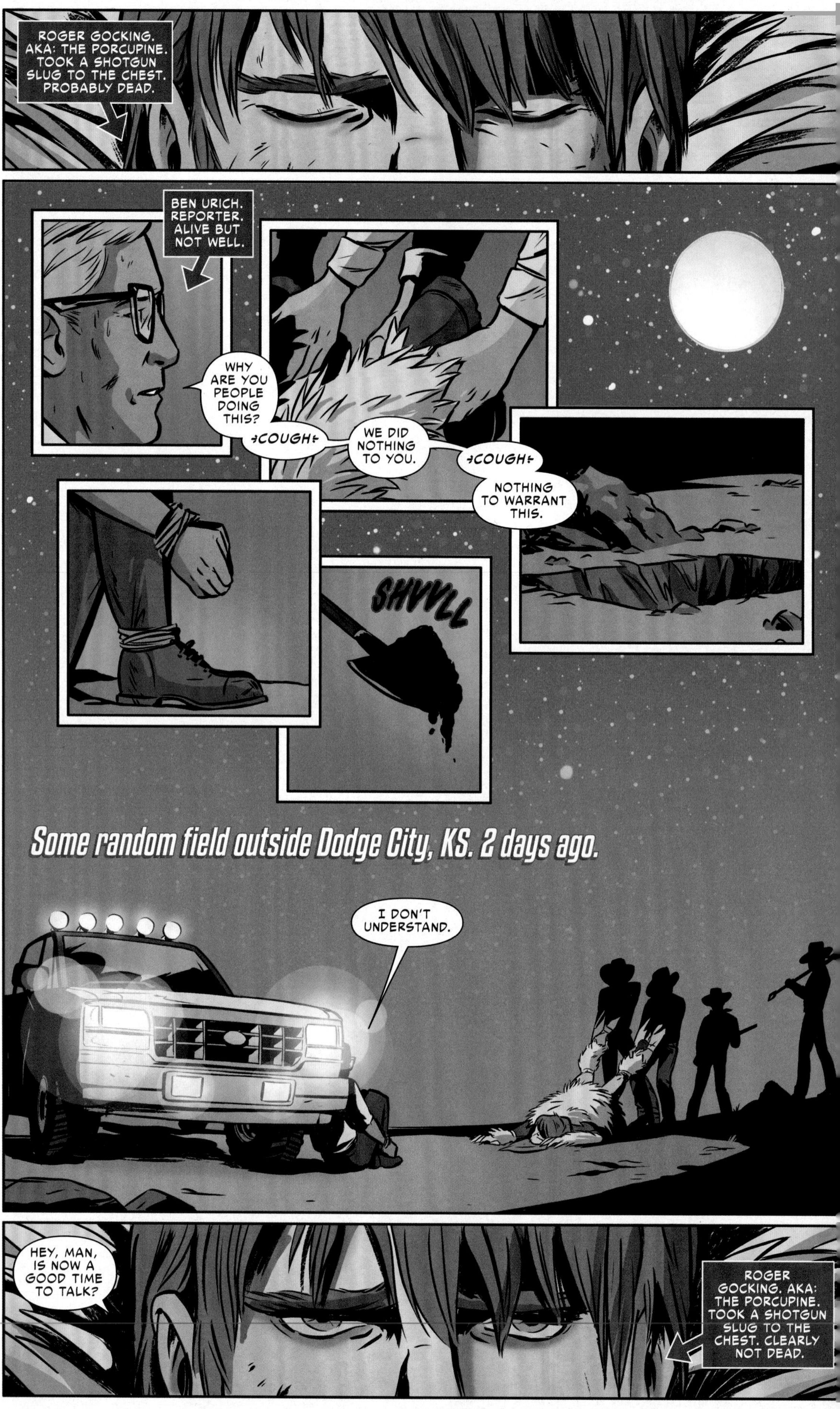
ROGER GOCKING. AKA: THE PORCUPINE. TOOK A SHOTGUN SLUG TO THE CHEST. PROBABLY DEAD.
BEN URICH. REPORTER. ALIVE BUT NOT WELL.
WHY ARE YOU PEOPLE DOING THIS?
COUGH
WE DID NOTHING TO YOU.
COUGH
NOTHING TO WARRANT THIS.
SHVVLL
Some random field outside Dodge City, KS. 2 days ago.
I DON'T UNDERSTAND.
HEY, MAN, IS NOW A GOOD TIME TO TALK?
ROGER GOCKING. AKA: THE PORCUPINE. TOOK A SHOTGUN SLUG TO THE CHEST. CLEARLY NOT DEAD.

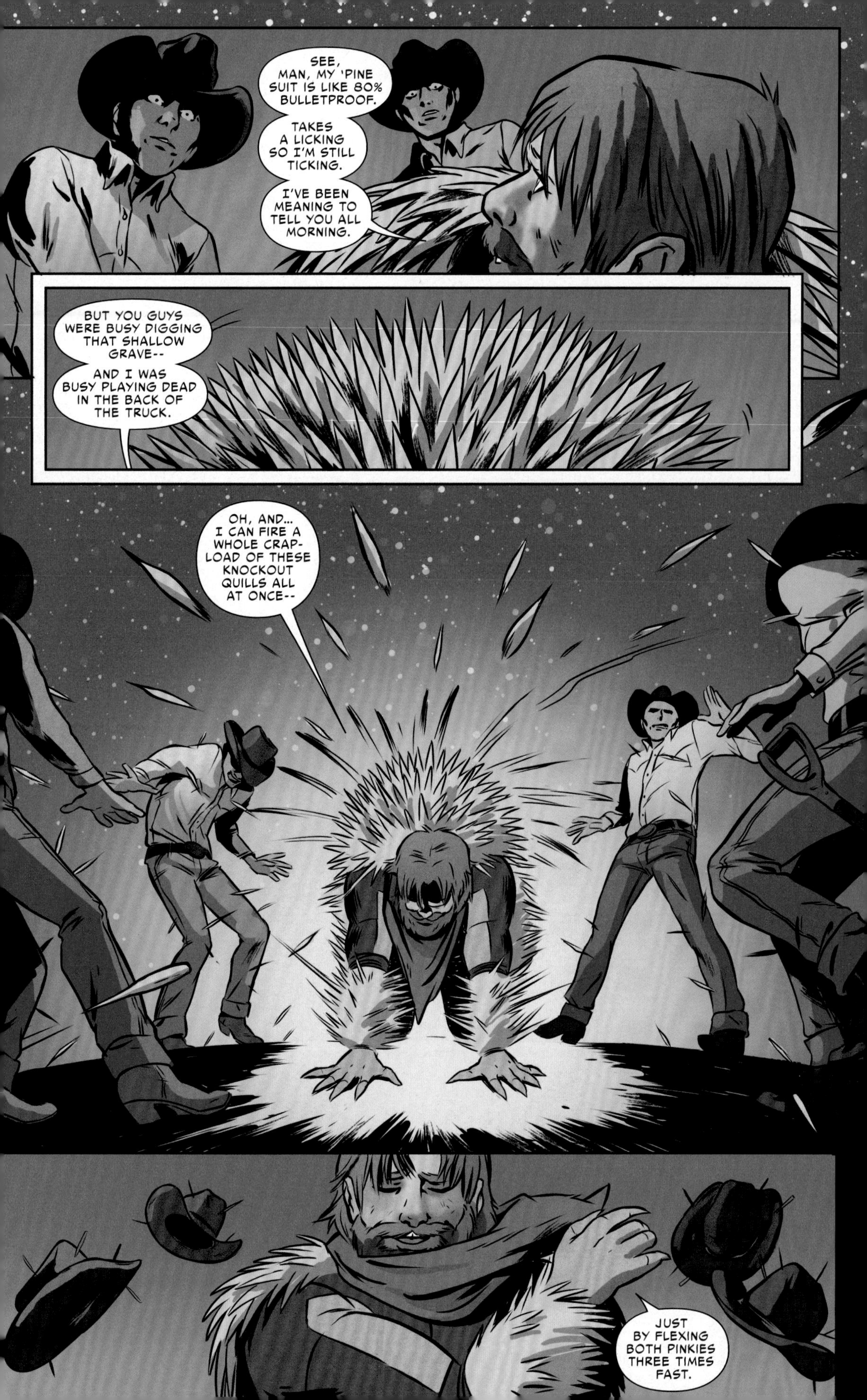
SEE, MAN, MY 'PINE SUIT IS LIKE 80% BULLETPROOF.
TAKES A LICKING SO I'M STILL TICKING.
I'VE BEEN MEANING TO TELL YOU ALL MORNING.
BUT YOU GUYS WERE BUSY DIGGING THAT SHALLOW GRAVE--
AND I WAS BUSY PLAYING DEAD IN THE BACK OF THE TRUCK.
OH, AND... I CAN FIRE A WHOLE CRAP-LOAD OF THESE KNOCKOUT QUILLS ALL AT ONCE--
JUST BY FLEXING BOTH PINKIES THREE TIMES FAST.

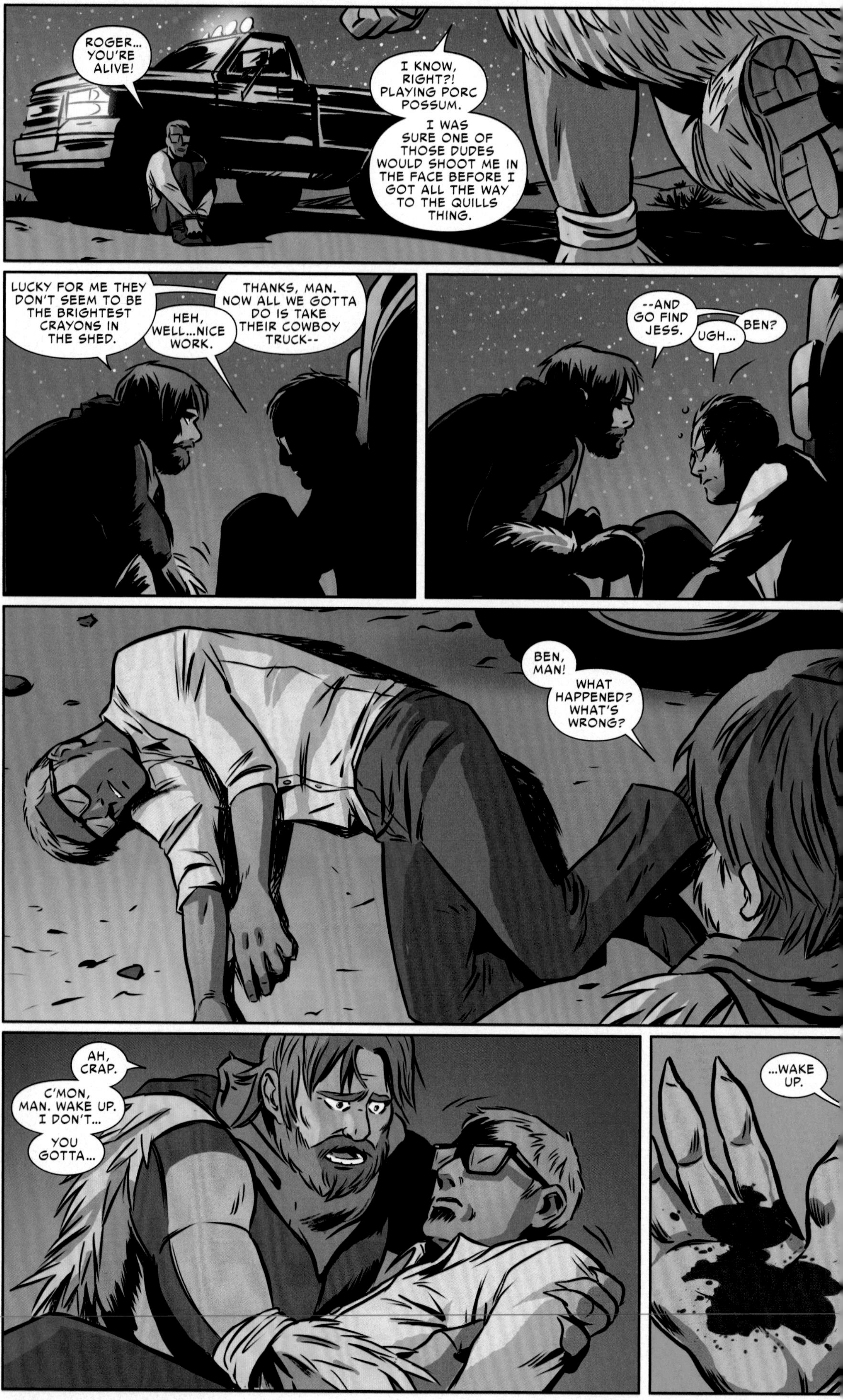

ROGER... YOU'RE ALIVE!
I KNOW, RIGHT?! PLAYING PORC POSSUM.
I WAS SURE ONE OF THOSE DUDES WOULD SHOOT ME IN THE FACE BEFORE I GOT ALL THE WAY TO THE QUILLS THING.
LUCKY FOR ME THEY DON'T SEEM TO BE THE BRIGHTEST CRAYONS IN THE SHED.
HEH, WELL...NICE WORK.
THANKS, MAN. NOW ALL WE GOTTA DO IS TAKE THEIR COWBOY TRUCK--
--AND GO FIND JESS.
UGH...
BEN?
BEN, MAN!
WHAT HAPPENED? WHAT'S WRONG?
AH, CRAP.
C'MON, MAN. WAKE UP. I DON'T...
YOU GOTTA...
...WAKE UP.

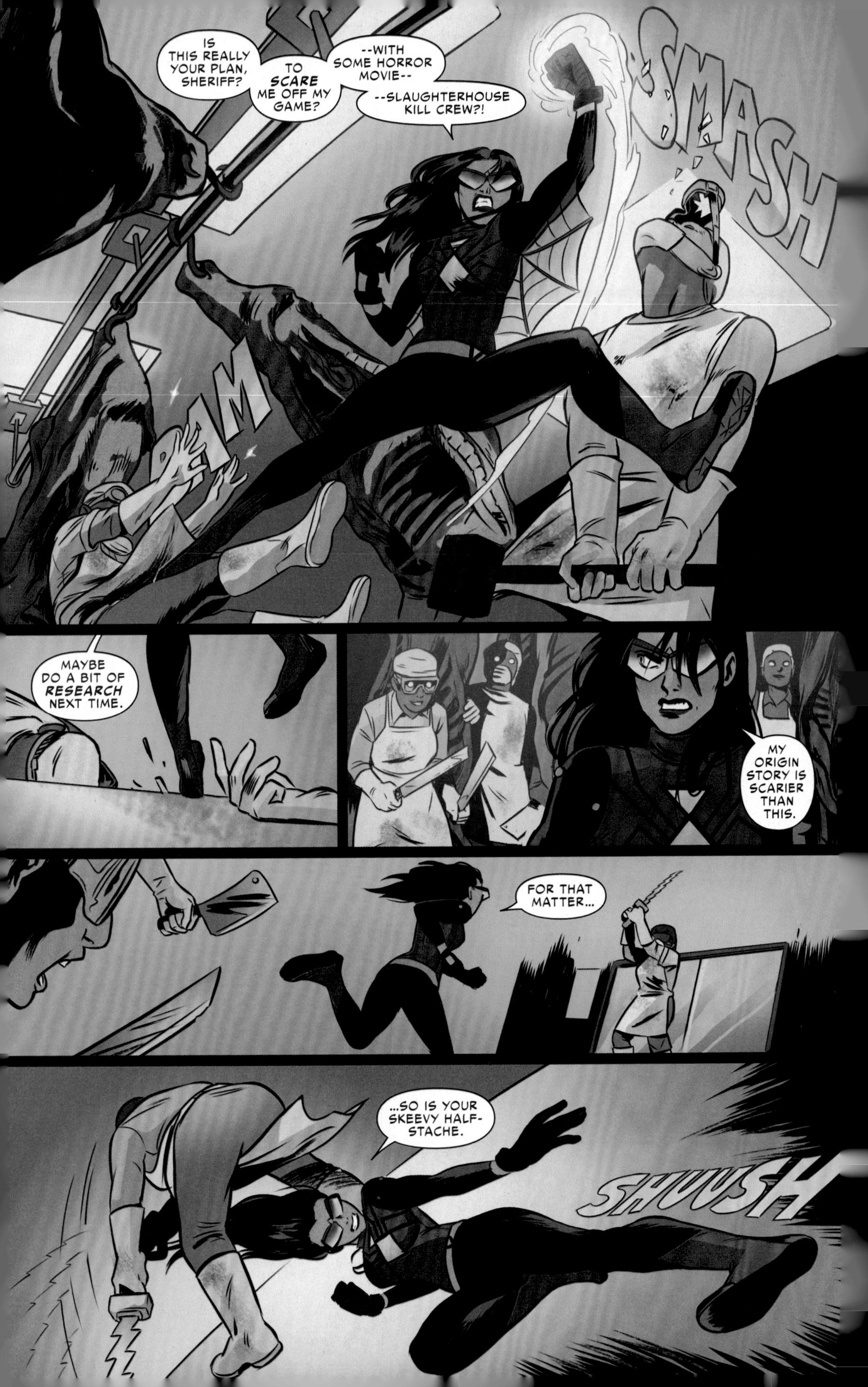
IS THIS REALLY YOUR PLAN, SHERIFF?
TO SCARE ME OFF MY GAME?
--WITH SOME HORROR MOVIE--
--SLAUGHTERHOUSE KILL CREW?!
SMASH
BAM
MAYBE DO A BIT OF RESEARCH NEXT TIME.
MY ORIGIN STORY IS SCARIER THAN THIS.
FOR THAT MATTER...
...SO IS YOUR SKEEVY HALF-STACHE.
SHUUSH

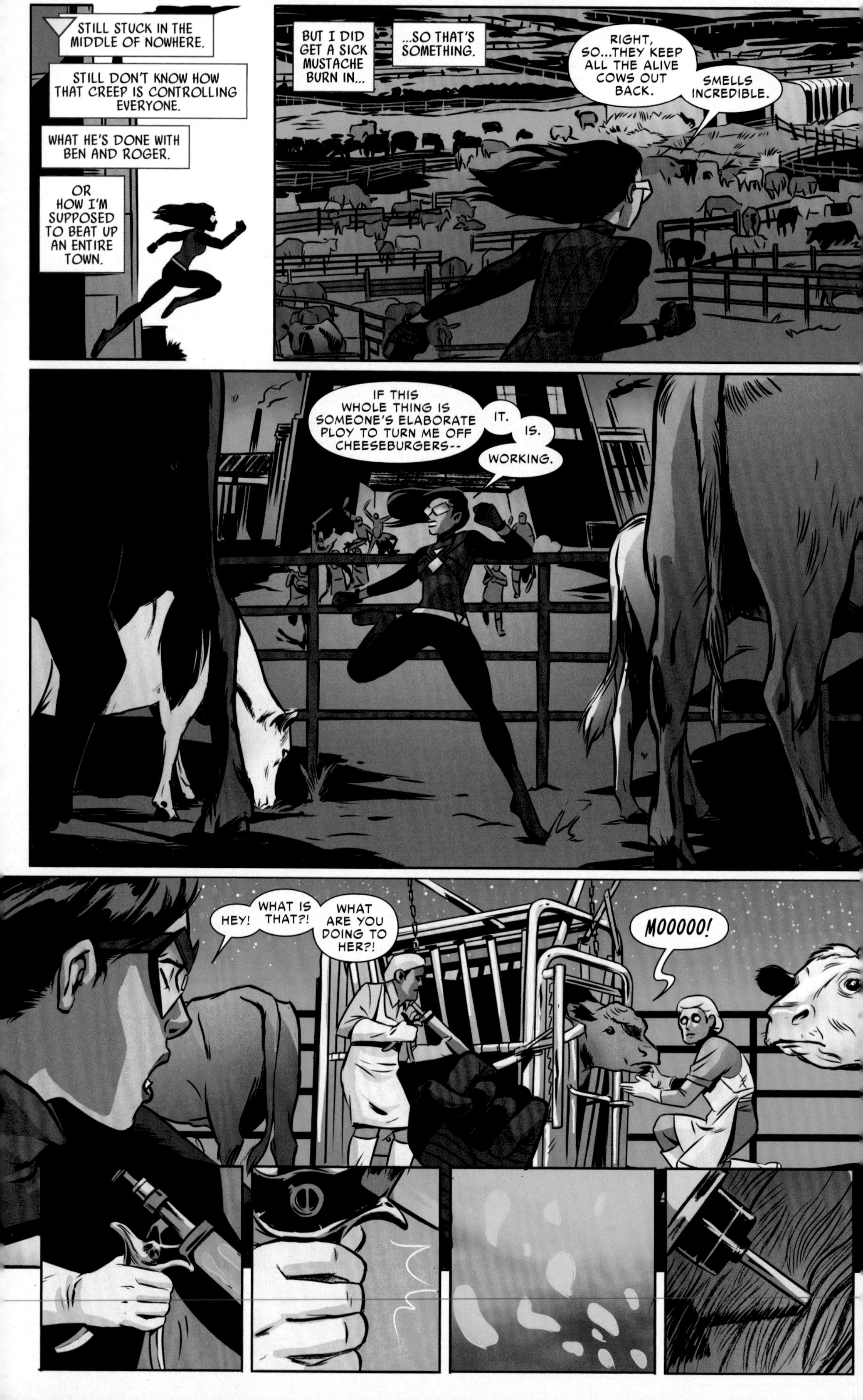
STILL STUCK IN THE MIDDLE OF NOWHERE.
STILL DON'T KNOW HOW THAT CREEP IS CONTROLLING EVERYONE.
WHAT HE'S DONE WITH BEN AND ROGER.
OR HOW I'M SUPPOSED TO BEAT UP AN ENTIRE TOWN.
BUT I DID GET A SICK MUSTACHE BURN IN...
...SO THAT'S SOMETHING.
RIGHT, SO...THEY KEEP ALL THE ALIVE COWS OUT BACK.
SMELLS INCREDIBLE.
IF THIS WHOLE THING IS SOMEONE'S ELABORATE PLOY TO TURN ME OFF CHEESEBURGERS--
IT.
IS.
WORKING.
HEY!
WHAT IS THAT?!
WHAT ARE YOU DOING TO HER?!
MOOOOO!

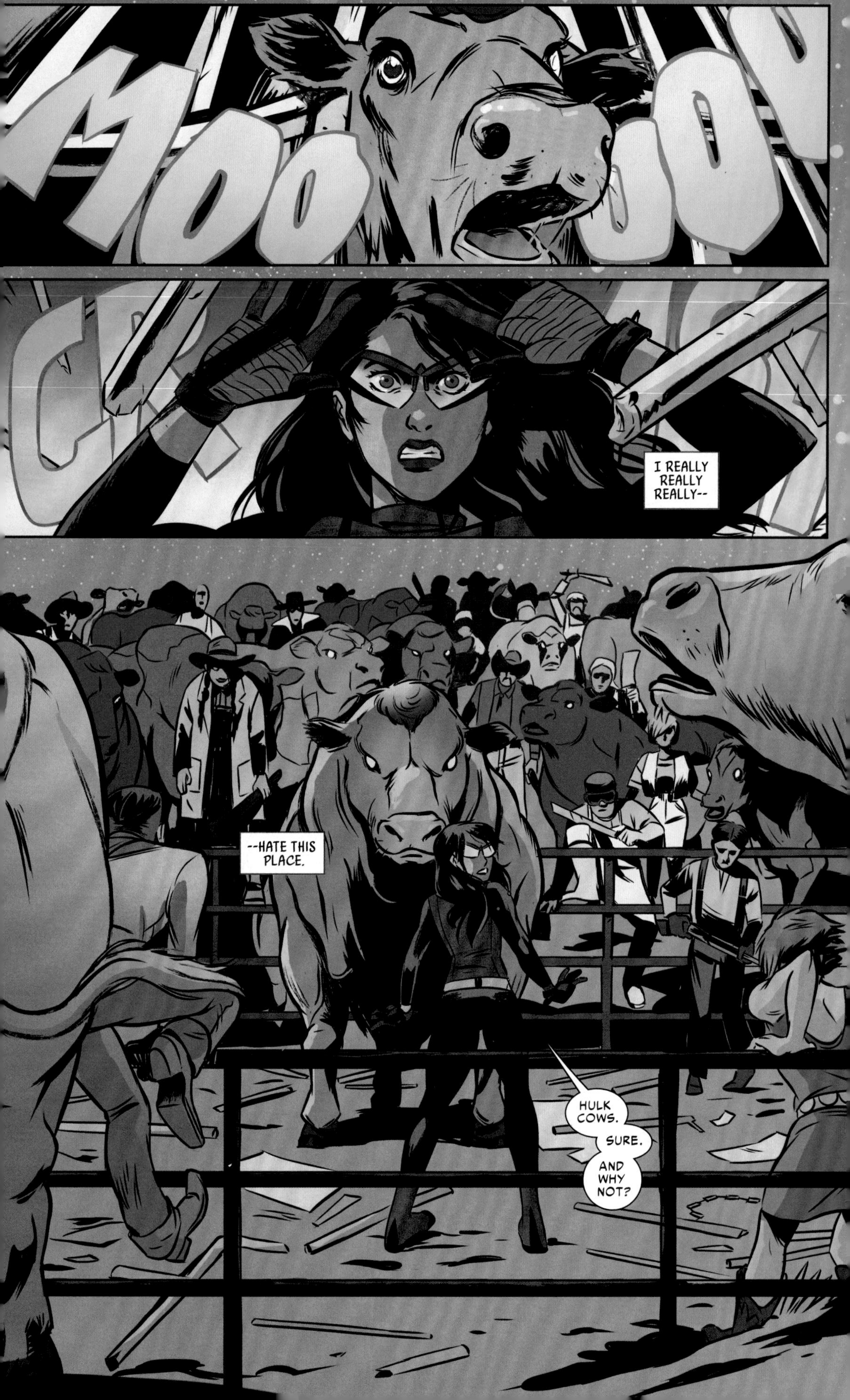
MOOOOO
I REALLY REALLY REALLY--
--HATE THIS PLACE.
HULK COWS.
SURE.
AND WHY NOT?

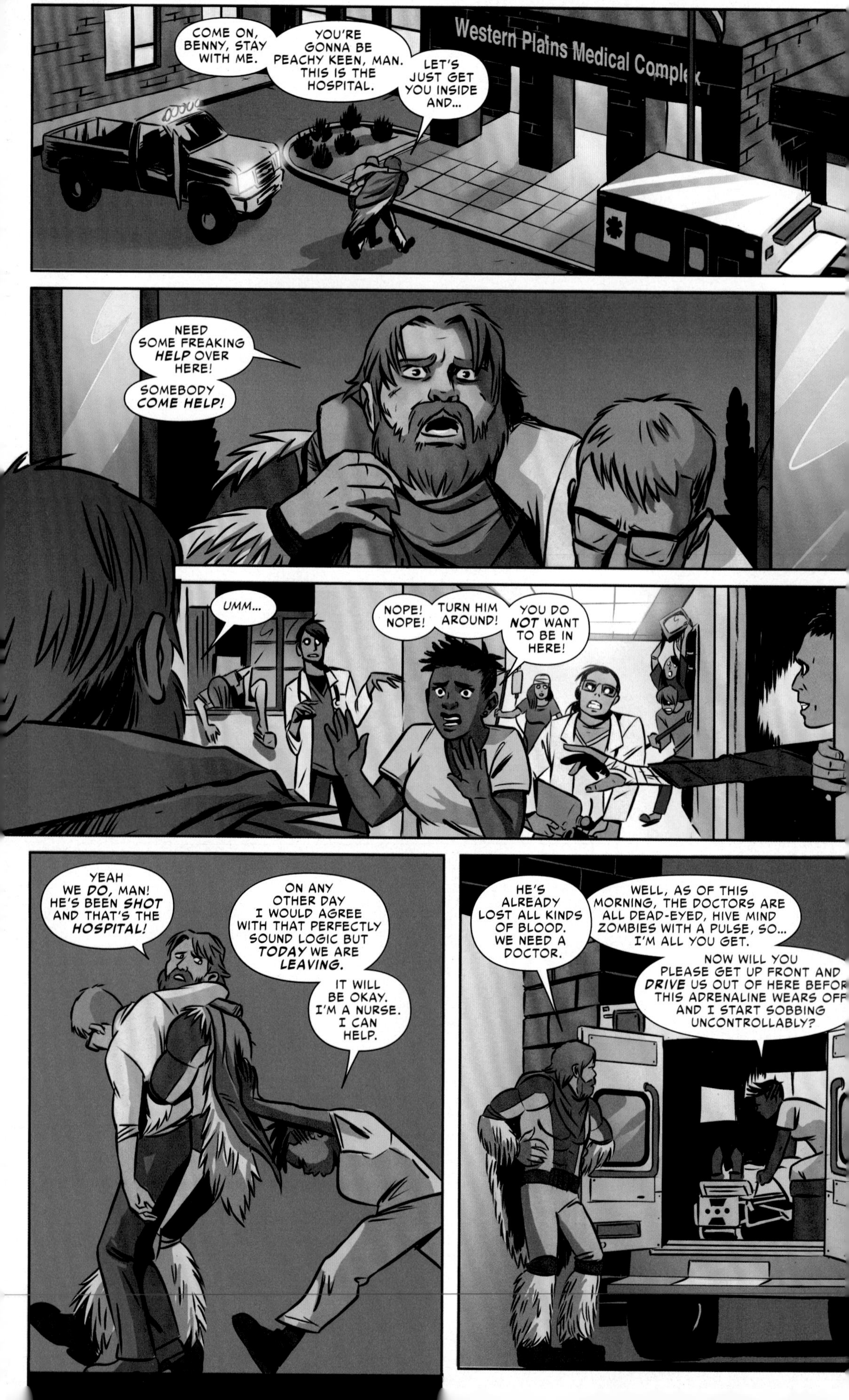
Western Plains Medical Complex
COME ON, BENNY, STAY WITH ME.
YOU'RE GONNA BE PEACHY KEEN, MAN. THIS IS THE HOSPITAL.
LET'S JUST GET YOU INSIDE AND...
NEED SOME FREAKING HELP OVER HERE!
SOMEBODY COME HELP!
UMM...
NOPE! NOPE!
TURN HIM AROUND!
YOU DO NOT WANT TO BE IN HERE!
YEAH WE DO, MAN! HE'S BEEN SHOT AND THAT'S THE HOSPITAL!
ON ANY OTHER DAY I WOULD AGREE WITH THAT PERFECTLY SOUND LOGIC BUT TODAY WE ARE LEAVING.
IT WILL BE OKAY. I'M A NURSE. I CAN HELP.
HE'S ALREADY LOST ALL KINDS OF BLOOD. WE NEED A DOCTOR.
WELL, AS OF THIS MORNING, THE DOCTORS ARE ALL DEAD-EYED, HIVE MIND ZOMBIES WITH A PULSE, SO... I'M ALL YOU GET.
NOW WILL YOU PLEASE GET UP FRONT AND DRIVE US OUT OF HERE BEFOR THIS ADRENALINE WEARS OFF AND I START SOBBING UNCONTROLLABLY?

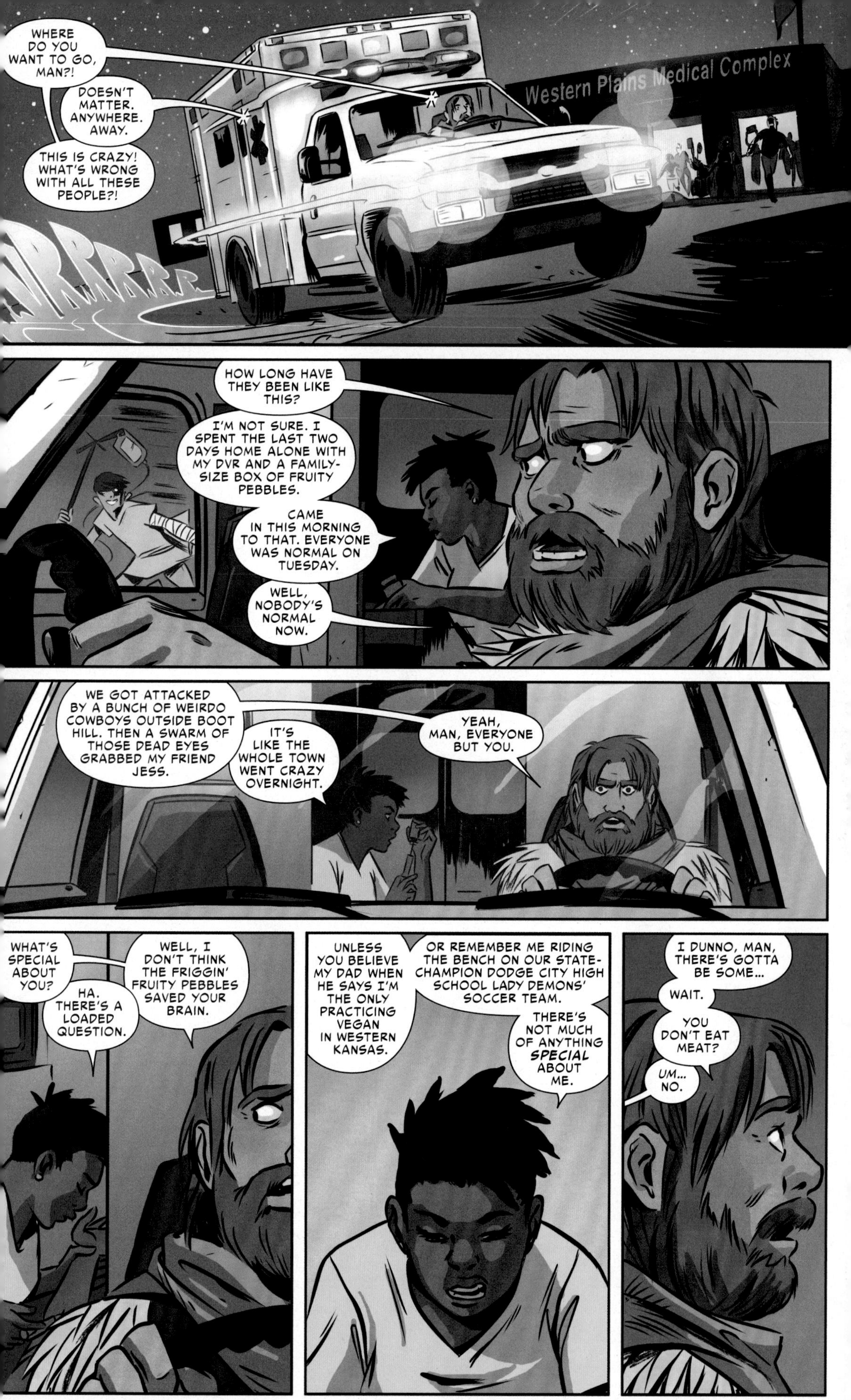
WHERE DO YOU WANT TO GO, MAN?!
DOESN'T MATTER. ANYWHERE. AWAY.
THIS IS CRAZY! WHAT'S WRONG WITH ALL THESE PEOPLE?!
Western Plains Medical Complex
RRRRRR
HOW LONG HAVE THEY BEEN LIKE THIS?
I'M NOT SURE. I SPENT THE LAST TWO DAYS HOME ALONE WITH MY DVR AND A FAMILY-SIZE BOX OF FRUITY PEBBLES.
CAME IN THIS MORNING TO THAT. EVERYONE WAS NORMAL ON TUESDAY.
WELL, NOBODY'S NORMAL NOW.
WE GOT ATTACKED BY A BUNCH OF WEIRDO COWBOYS OUTSIDE BOOT HILL. THEN A SWARM OF THOSE DEAD EYES GRABBED MY FRIEND JESS.
IT'S LIKE THE WHOLE TOWN WENT CRAZY OVERNIGHT.
YEAH, MAN, EVERYONE BUT YOU.
WHAT'S SPECIAL ABOUT YOU?
HA. THERE'S A LOADED QUESTION.
WELL, I DON'T THINK THE FRIGGIN' FRUITY PEBBLES SAVED YOUR BRAIN.
UNLESS YOU BELIEVE MY DAD WHEN HE SAYS I'M THE ONLY PRACTICING VEGAN IN WESTERN KANSAS.
OR REMEMBER ME RIDING THE BENCH ON OUR STATE-CHAMPION DODGE CITY HIGH SCHOOL LADY DEMONS' SOCCER TEAM.
THERE'S NOT MUCH OF ANYTHING SPECIAL ABOUT ME.
I DUNNO, MAN, THERE'S GOTTA BE SOME...
WAIT.
YOU DON'T EAT MEAT?
UM... NO.

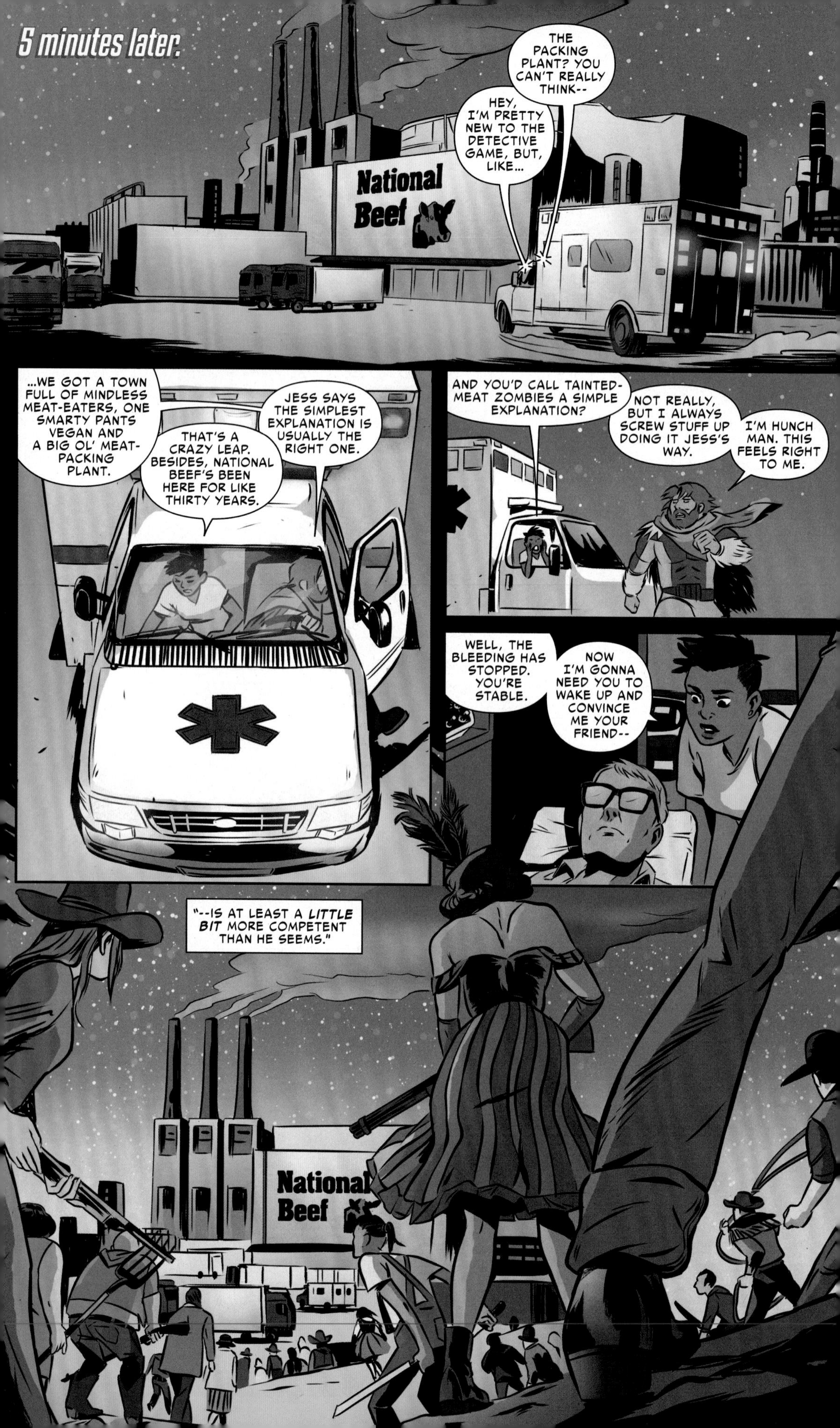
5 minutes later.
HEY, I'M PRETTY NEW TO THE DETECTIVE GAME, BUT, LIKE...
THE PACKING PLANT? YOU CAN'T REALLY THINK--
National Beef
...WE GOT A TOWN FULL OF MINDLESS MEAT-EATERS, ONE SMARTY PANTS VEGAN AND A BIG OL' MEAT-PACKING PLANT.
THAT'S A CRAZY LEAP. BESIDES, NATIONAL BEEF'S BEEN HERE FOR LIKE THIRTY YEARS.
JESS SAYS THE SIMPLEST EXPLANATION IS USUALLY THE RIGHT ONE.
AND YOU'D CALL TAINTED-MEAT ZOMBIES A SIMPLE EXPLANATION?
NOT REALLY, BUT I ALWAYS SCREW STUFF UP DOING IT JESS'S WAY.
I'M HUNCH MAN. THIS FEELS RIGHT TO ME.
WELL, THE BLEEDING HAS STOPPED. YOU'RE STABLE.
NOW I'M GONNA NEED YOU TO WAKE UP AND CONVINCE ME YOUR FRIEND--
"--IS AT LEAST A *LITTLE BIT* MORE COMPETENT THAN HE SEEMS."
National Beef

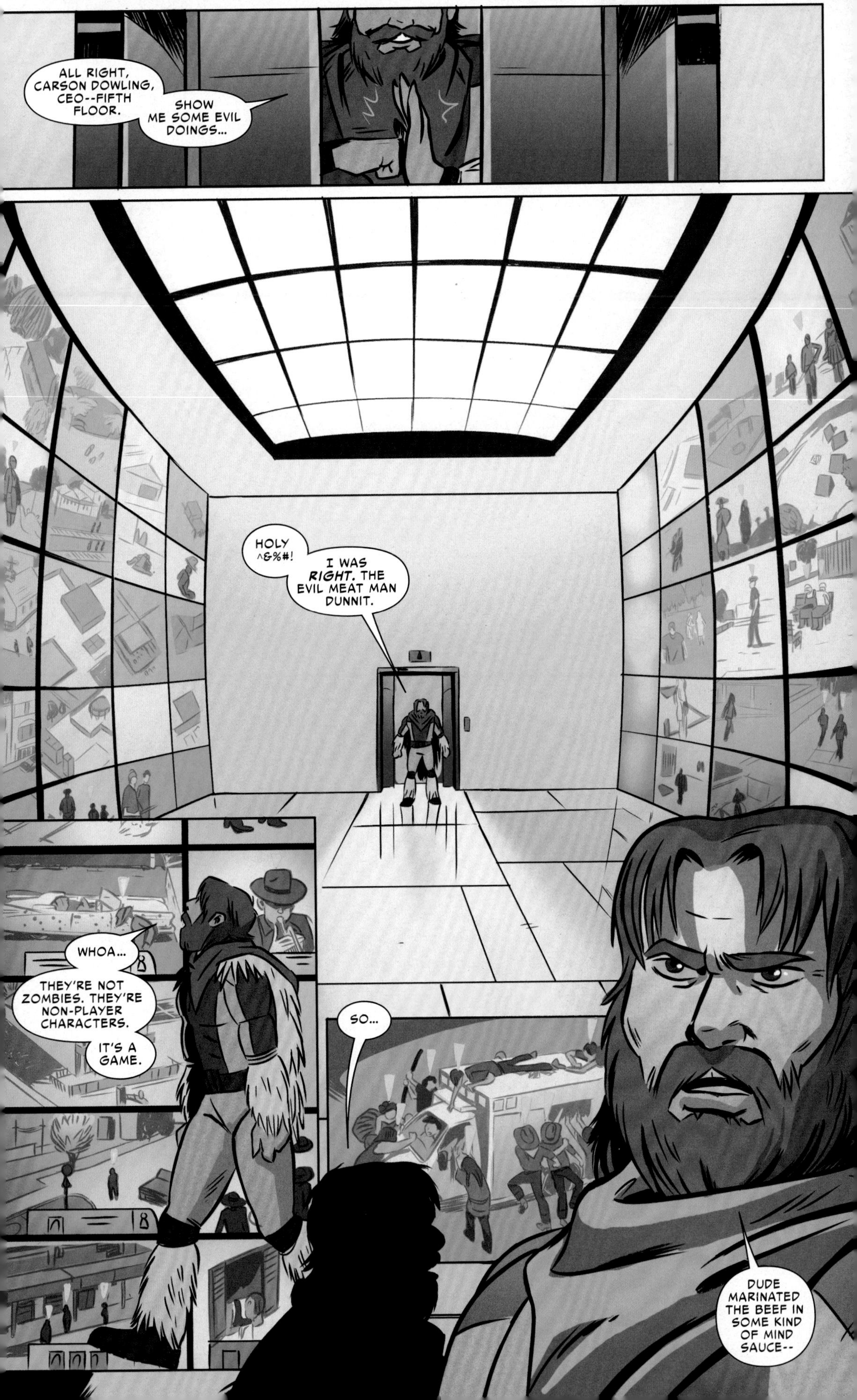
ALL RIGHT, CARSON DOWLING, CEO--FIFTH FLOOR.
SHOW ME SOME EVIL DOINGS...
HOLY ^&%#!
I WAS *RIGHT.* THE EVIL MEAT MAN DUNNIT.
WHOA...
THEY'RE NOT ZOMBIES. THEY'RE NON-PLAYER CHARACTERS.
IT'S A GAME.
SO...
DUDE MARINATED THE BEEF IN SOME KIND OF MIND SAUCE--

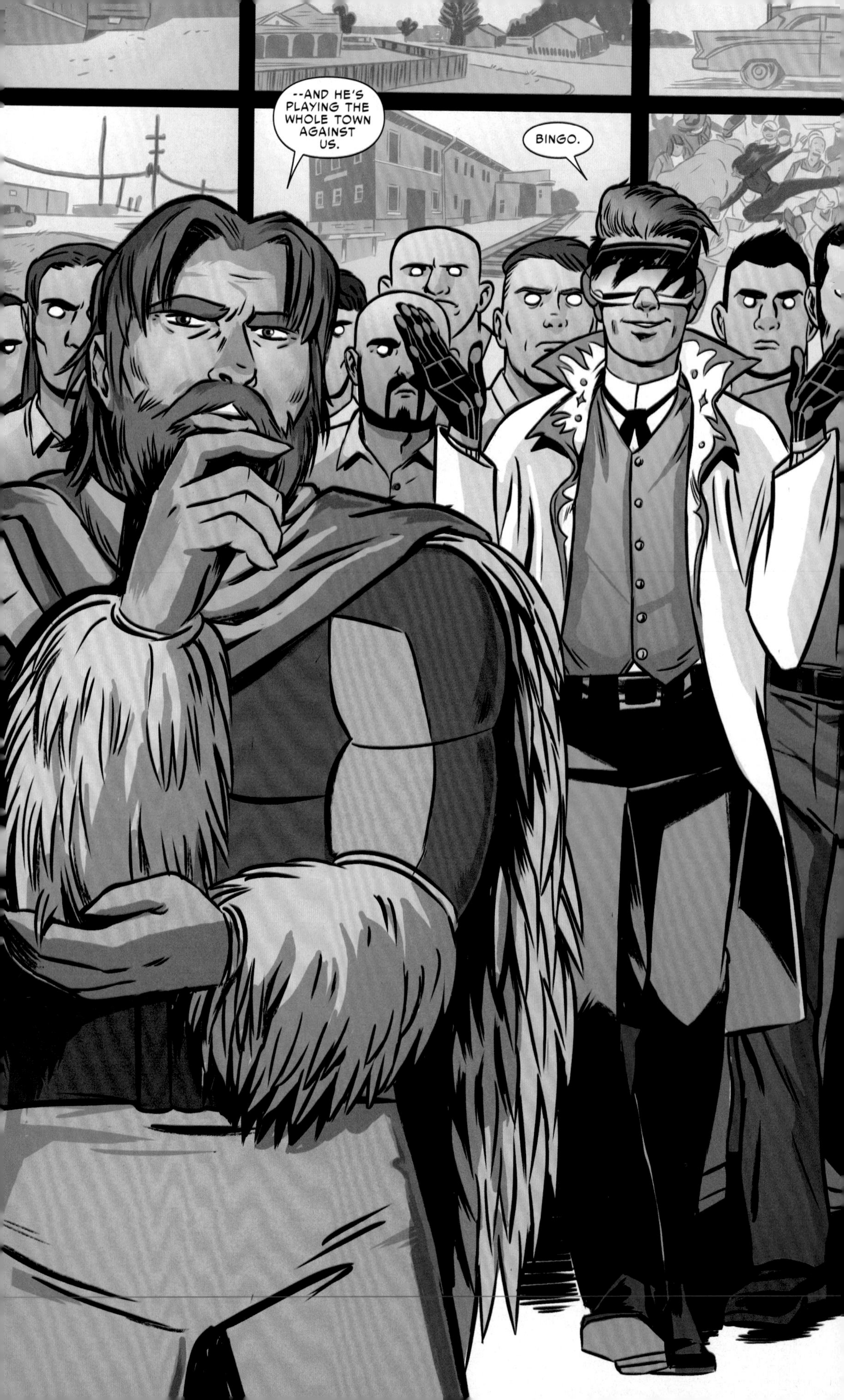
--AND HE'S PLAYING THE WHOLE TOWN AGAINST US.
BINGO.

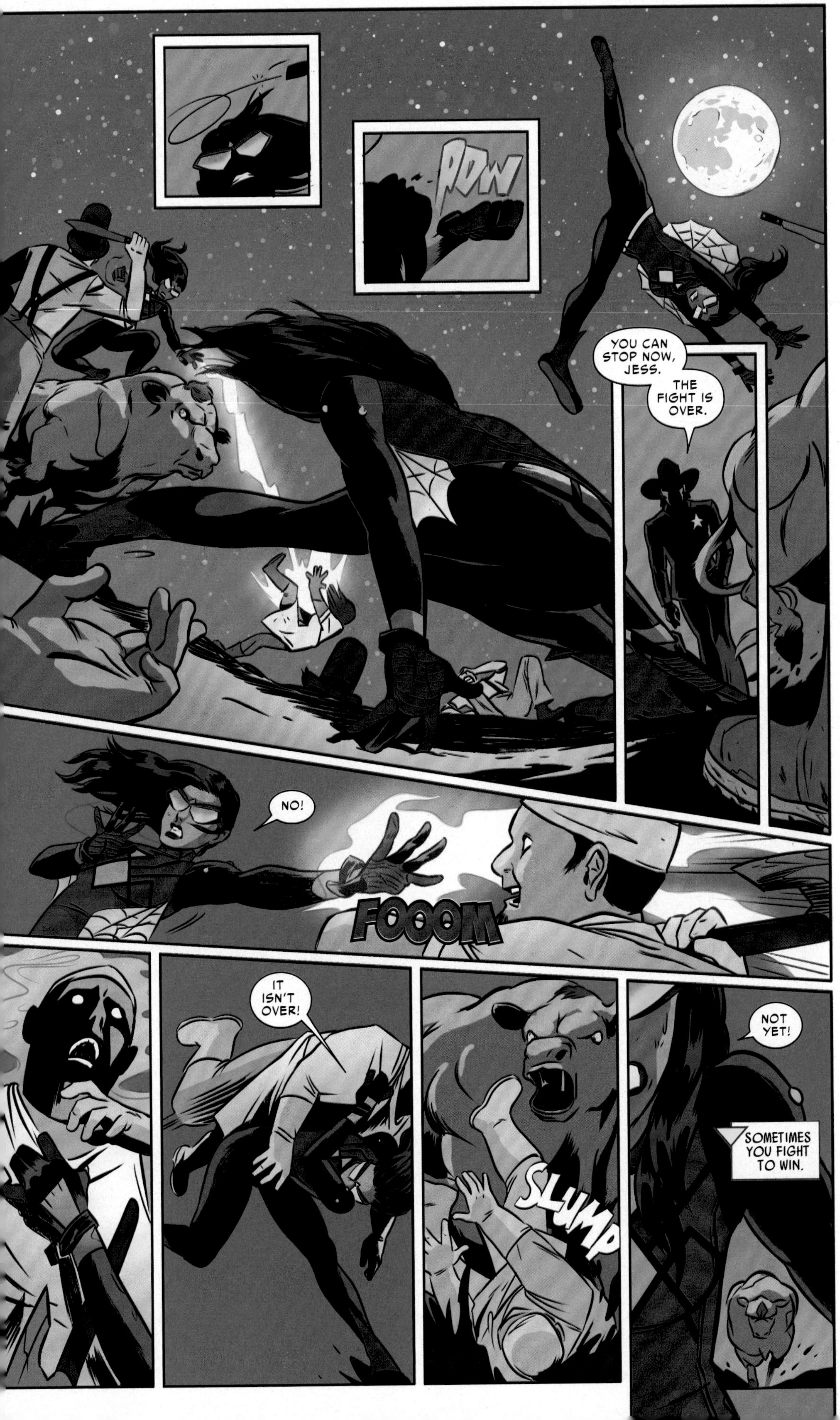
POW
YOU CAN STOP NOW, JESS.
THE FIGHT IS OVER.
NO!
FOOOM
IT ISN'T OVER!
SLUMP
NOT YET!
SOMETIMES YOU FIGHT TO WIN.

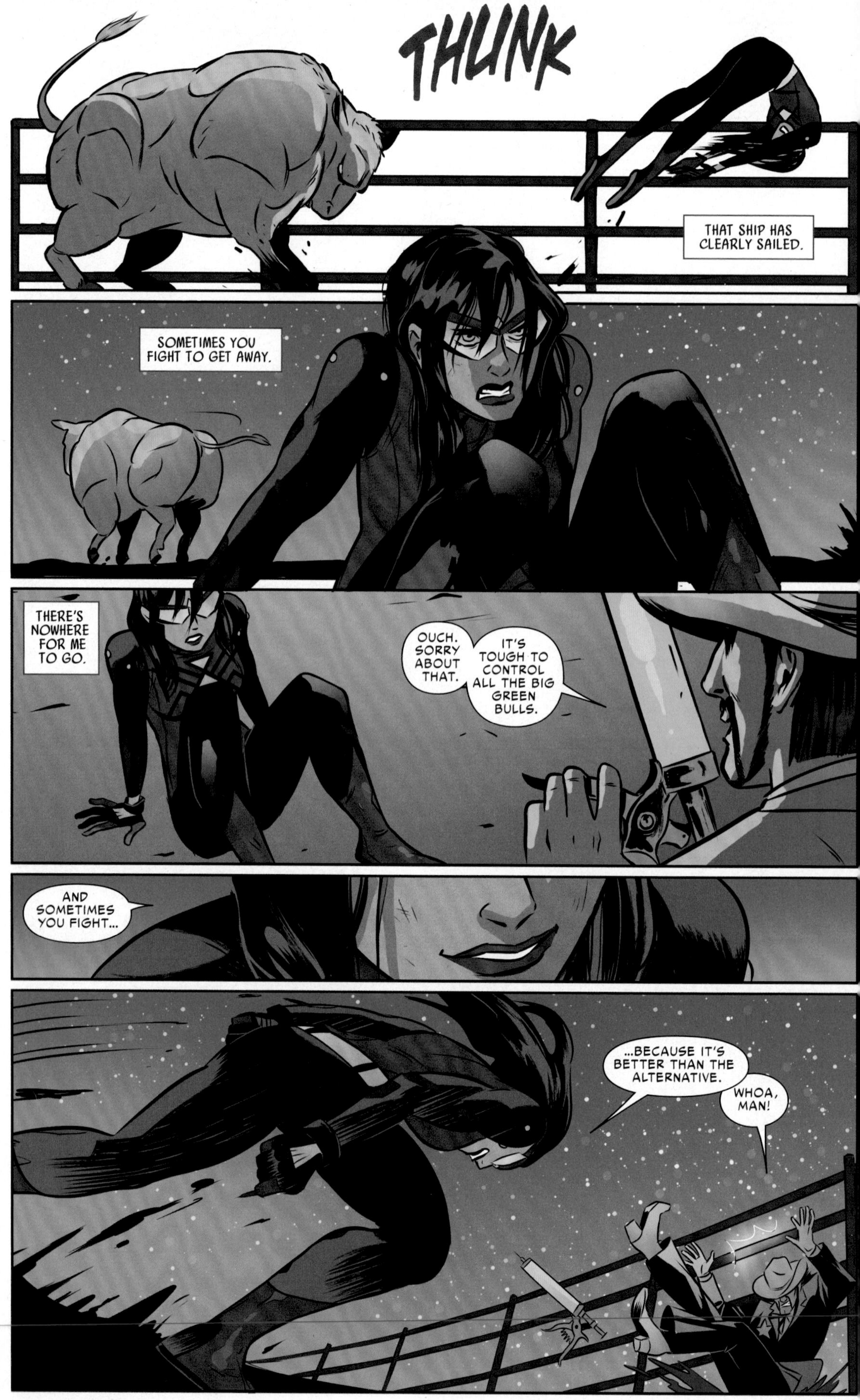
THUNK
THAT SHIP HAS CLEARLY SAILED.
SOMETIMES YOU FIGHT TO GET AWAY.
THERE'S NOWHERE FOR ME TO GO.
OUCH. SORRY ABOUT THAT.
IT'S TOUGH TO CONTROL ALL THE BIG GREEN BULLS.
AND SOMETIMES YOU FIGHT...
...BECAUSE IT'S BETTER THAN THE ALTERNATIVE.
WHOA, MAN!

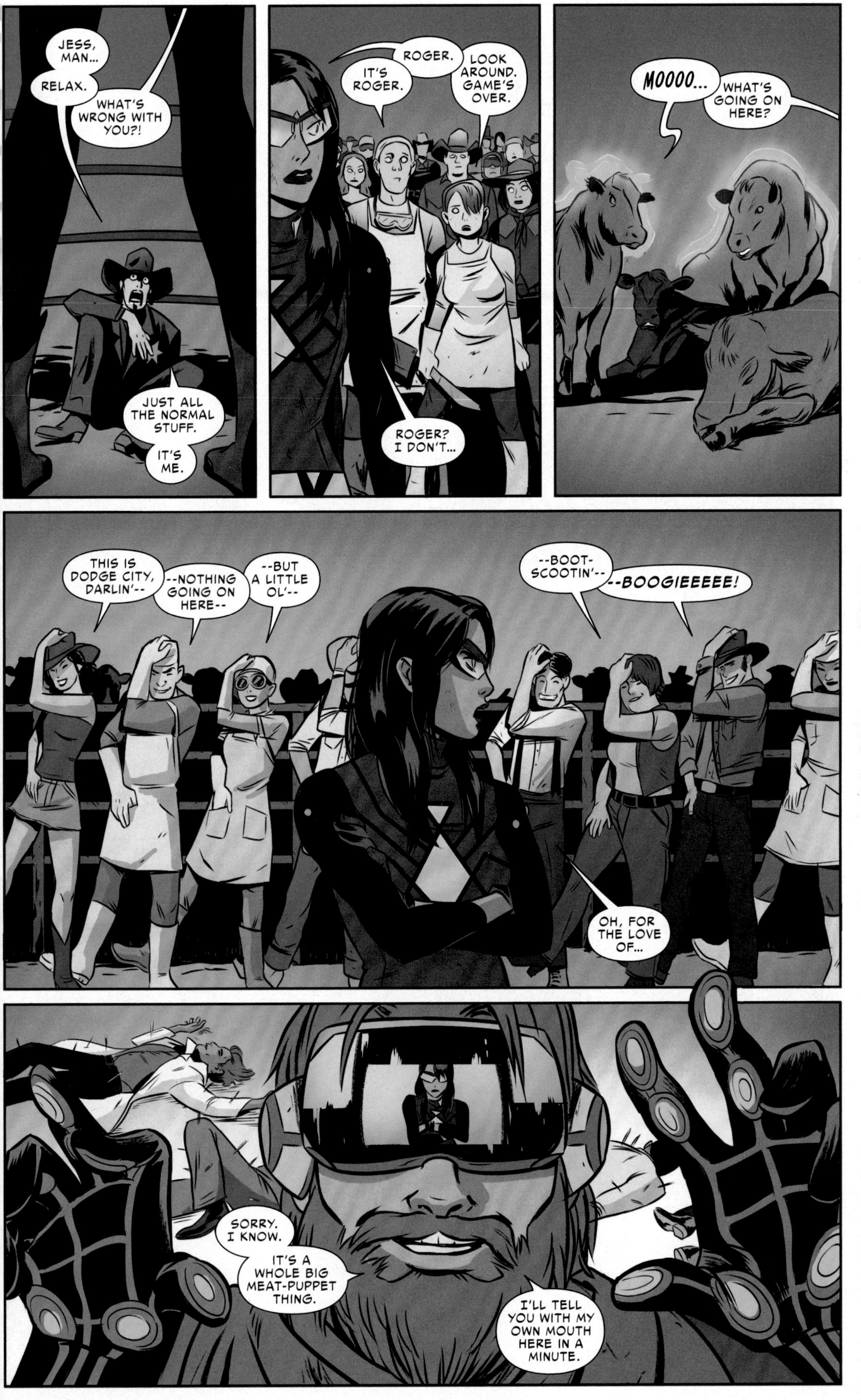
JESS, MAN...
RELAX.
WHAT'S WRONG WITH YOU?!
JUST ALL THE NORMAL STUFF.
IT'S ME.
ROGER.
IT'S ROGER.
LOOK AROUND. GAME'S OVER.
ROGER? I DON'T...
MOOOO...
WHAT'S GOING ON HERE?
THIS IS DODGE CITY, DARLIN'--
--NOTHING GOING ON HERE--
--BUT A LITTLE OL'--
--BOOT-SCOOTIN'--
--BOOGIEEEEE!
OH, FOR THE LOVE OF...
SORRY. I KNOW.
IT'S A WHOLE BIG MEAT-PUPPET THING.
I'LL TELL YOU WITH MY OWN MOUTH HERE IN A MINUTE.

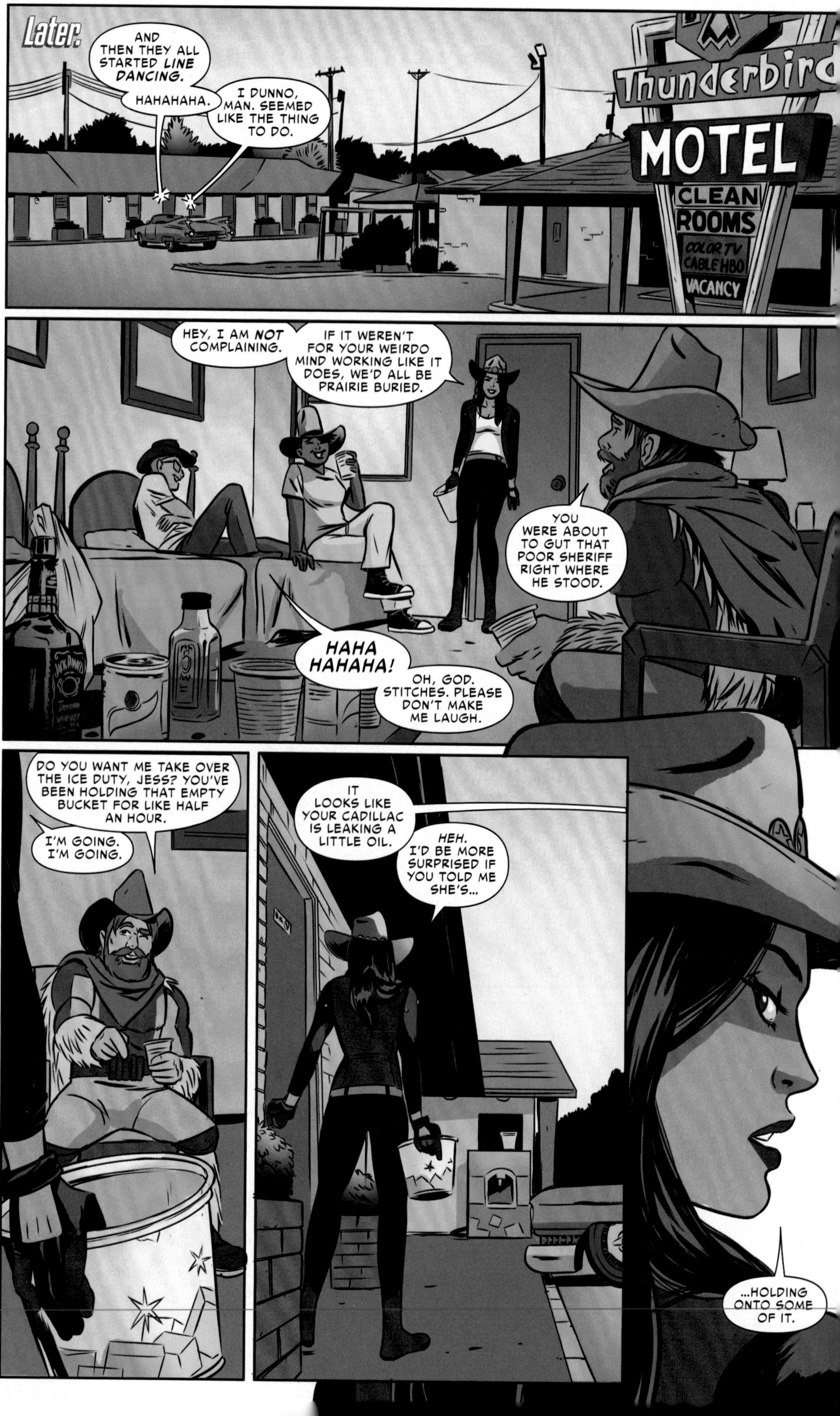
Later.
AND THEN THEY ALL STARTED LINE DANCING.
HAHAHAHA.
I DUNNO, MAN. SEEMED LIKE THE THING TO DO.
Thunderbird
MOTEL
CLEAN ROOMS
COLOR TV CABLE HBO
VACANCY
HEY, I AM NOT COMPLAINING.
IF IT WEREN'T FOR YOUR WEIRDO MIND WORKING LIKE IT DOES, WE'D ALL BE PRAIRIE BURIED.
YOU WERE ABOUT TO GUT THAT POOR SHERIFF RIGHT WHERE HE STOOD.
HAHA HAHAHA!
OH, GOD. STITCHES. PLEASE DON'T MAKE ME LAUGH.
DO YOU WANT ME TAKE OVER THE ICE DUTY, JESS? YOU'VE BEEN HOLDING THAT EMPTY BUCKET FOR LIKE HALF AN HOUR.
I'M GOING. I'M GOING.
IT LOOKS LIKE YOUR CADILLAC IS LEAKING A LITTLE OIL.
HEH. I'D BE MORE SURPRISED IF YOU TOLD ME SHE'S...
...HOLDING ONTO SOME OF IT.

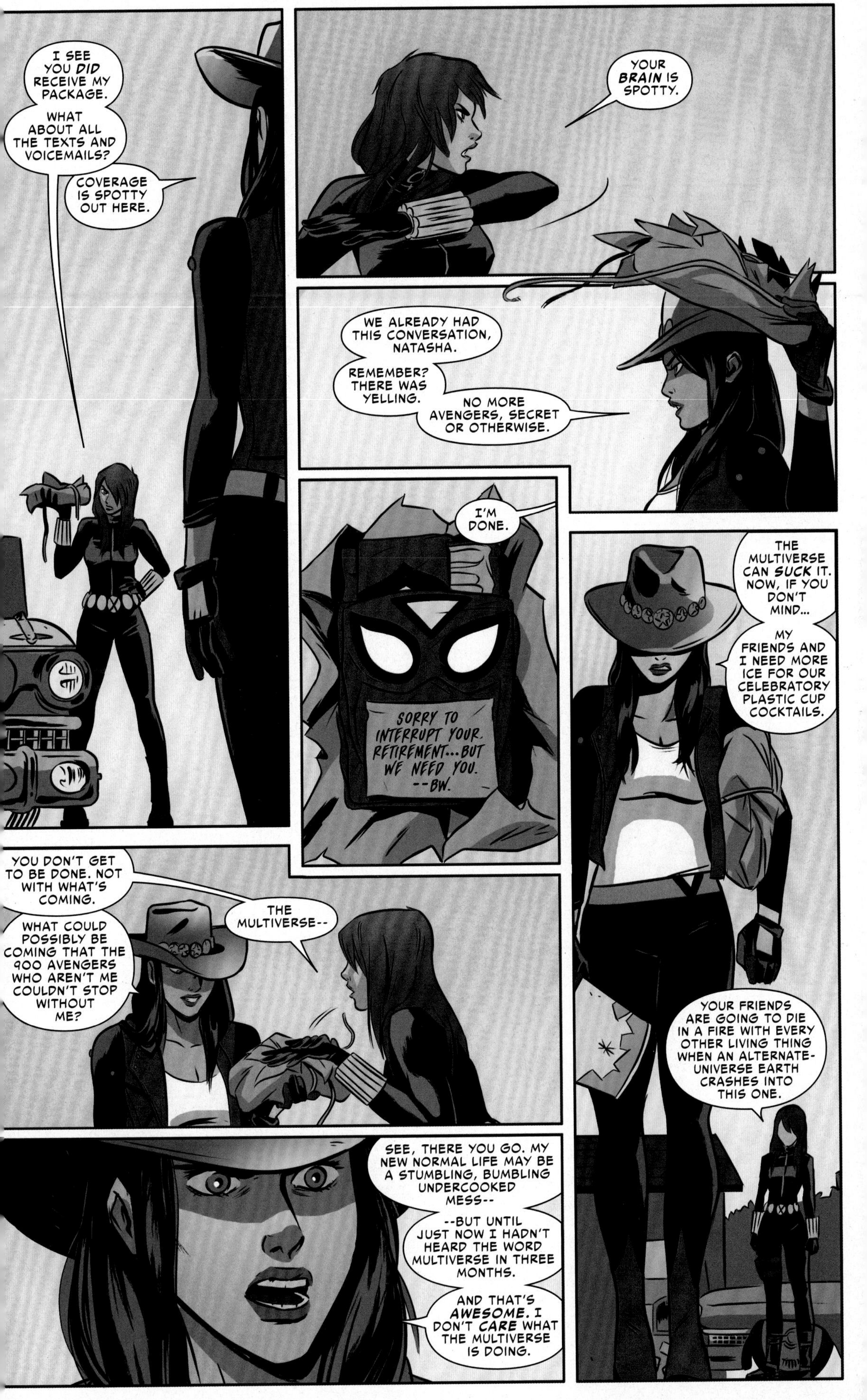
I SEE YOU *DID* RECEIVE MY PACKAGE.
WHAT ABOUT ALL THE TEXTS AND VOICEMAILS?
COVERAGE IS SPOTTY OUT HERE.
YOUR *BRAIN* IS SPOTTY.
WE ALREADY HAD THIS CONVERSATION, NATASHA.
REMEMBER? THERE WAS YELLING.
NO MORE AVENGERS, SECRET OR OTHERWISE.
I'M DONE.
SORRY TO INTERRUPT YOUR RETIREMENT...BUT WE NEED YOU. --BW.
THE MULTIVERSE CAN *SUCK* IT. NOW, IF YOU DON'T MIND...
MY FRIENDS AND I NEED MORE ICE FOR OUR CELEBRATORY PLASTIC CUP COCKTAILS.
YOU DON'T GET TO BE DONE. NOT WITH WHAT'S COMING.
WHAT COULD POSSIBLY BE COMING THAT THE 900 AVENGERS WHO AREN'T ME COULDN'T STOP WITHOUT ME?
THE MULTIVERSE--
YOUR FRIENDS ARE GOING TO DIE IN A FIRE WITH EVERY OTHER LIVING THING WHEN AN ALTERNATE-UNIVERSE EARTH CRASHES INTO THIS ONE.
SEE, THERE YOU GO. MY NEW NORMAL LIFE MAY BE A STUMBLING, BUMBLING UNDERCOOKED MESS--
--BUT UNTIL JUST NOW I HADN'T HEARD THE WORD MULTIVERSE IN THREE MONTHS.
AND THAT'S *AWESOME*. I DON'T *CARE* WHAT THE MULTIVERSE IS DOING.

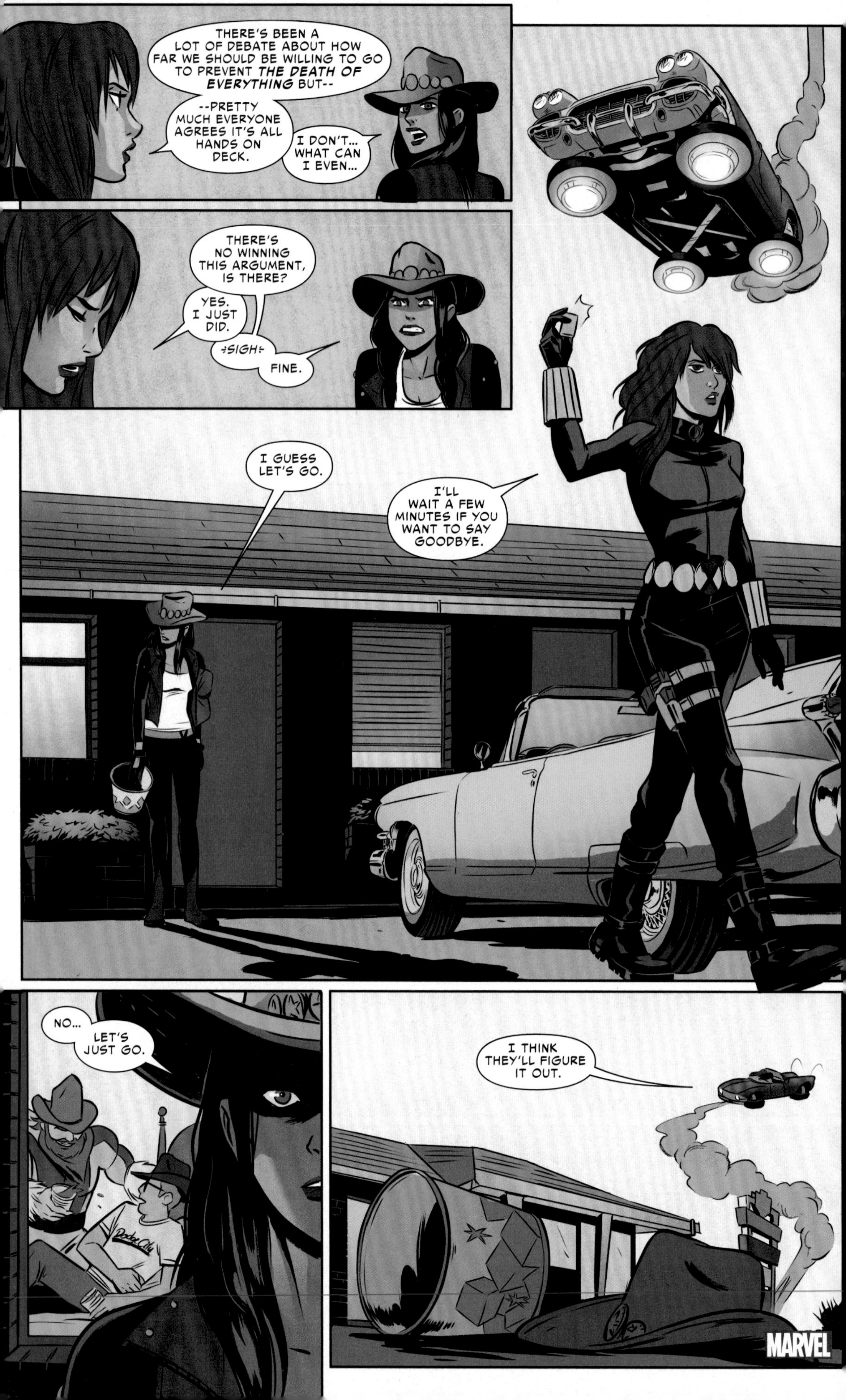
THERE'S BEEN A LOT OF DEBATE ABOUT HOW FAR WE SHOULD BE WILLING TO GO TO PREVENT *THE DEATH OF EVERYTHING* BUT--
--PRETTY MUCH EVERYONE AGREES IT'S ALL HANDS ON DECK.
I DON'T... WHAT CAN I EVEN...
THERE'S NO WINNING THIS ARGUMENT, IS THERE?
YES. I JUST DID.
SIGH
FINE.
I GUESS LET'S GO.
I'LL WAIT A FEW MINUTES IF YOU WANT TO SAY GOODBYE.
NO... LET'S JUST GO.
Dodge City
I THINK THEY'LL FIGURE IT OUT.
MARVEL

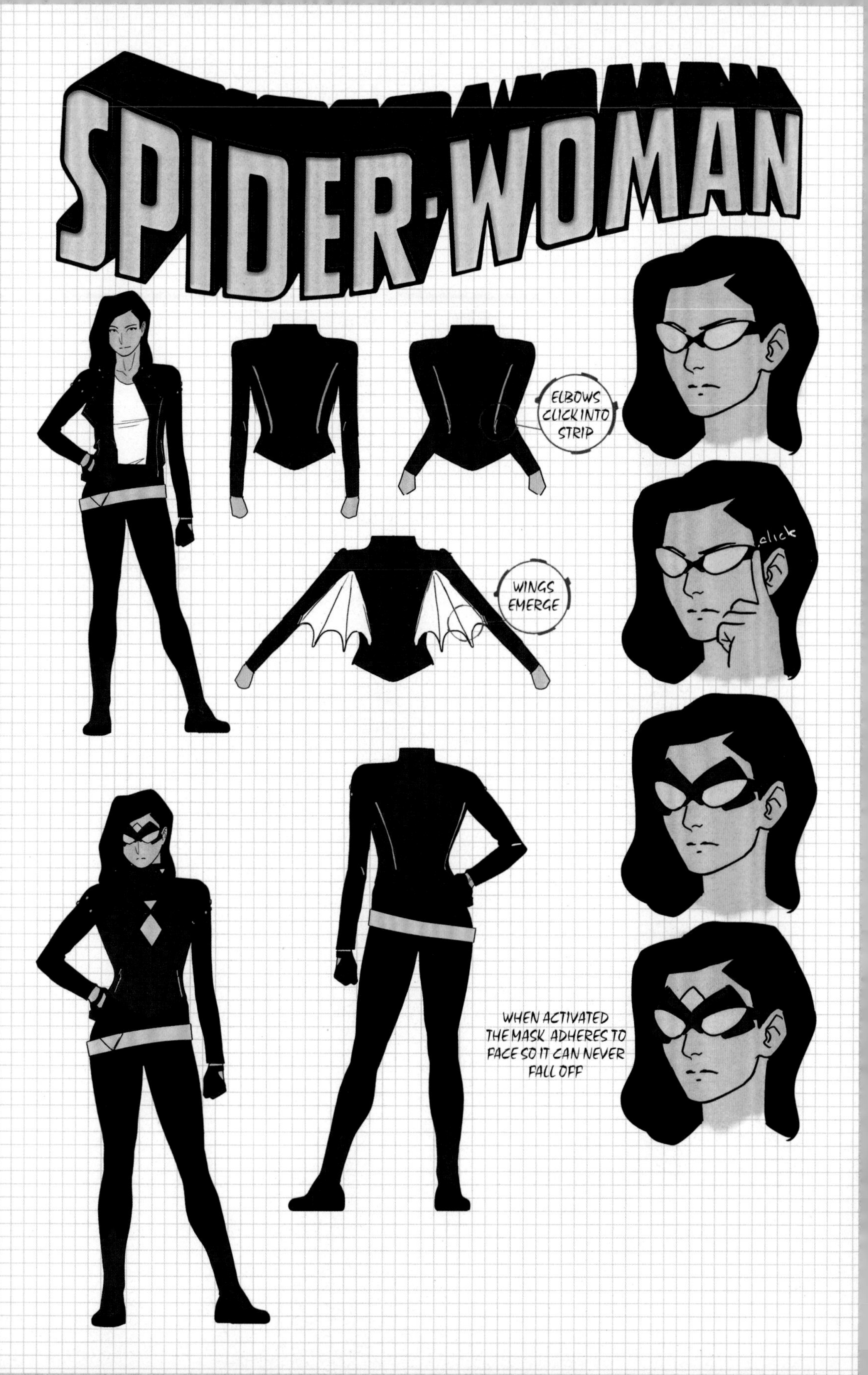
SPIDER-WOMAN
ELBOWS CLICK INTO STRIP
click
WINGS EMERGE
WHEN ACTIVATED THE MASK ADHERES TO FACE SO IT CAN NEVER FALL OFF

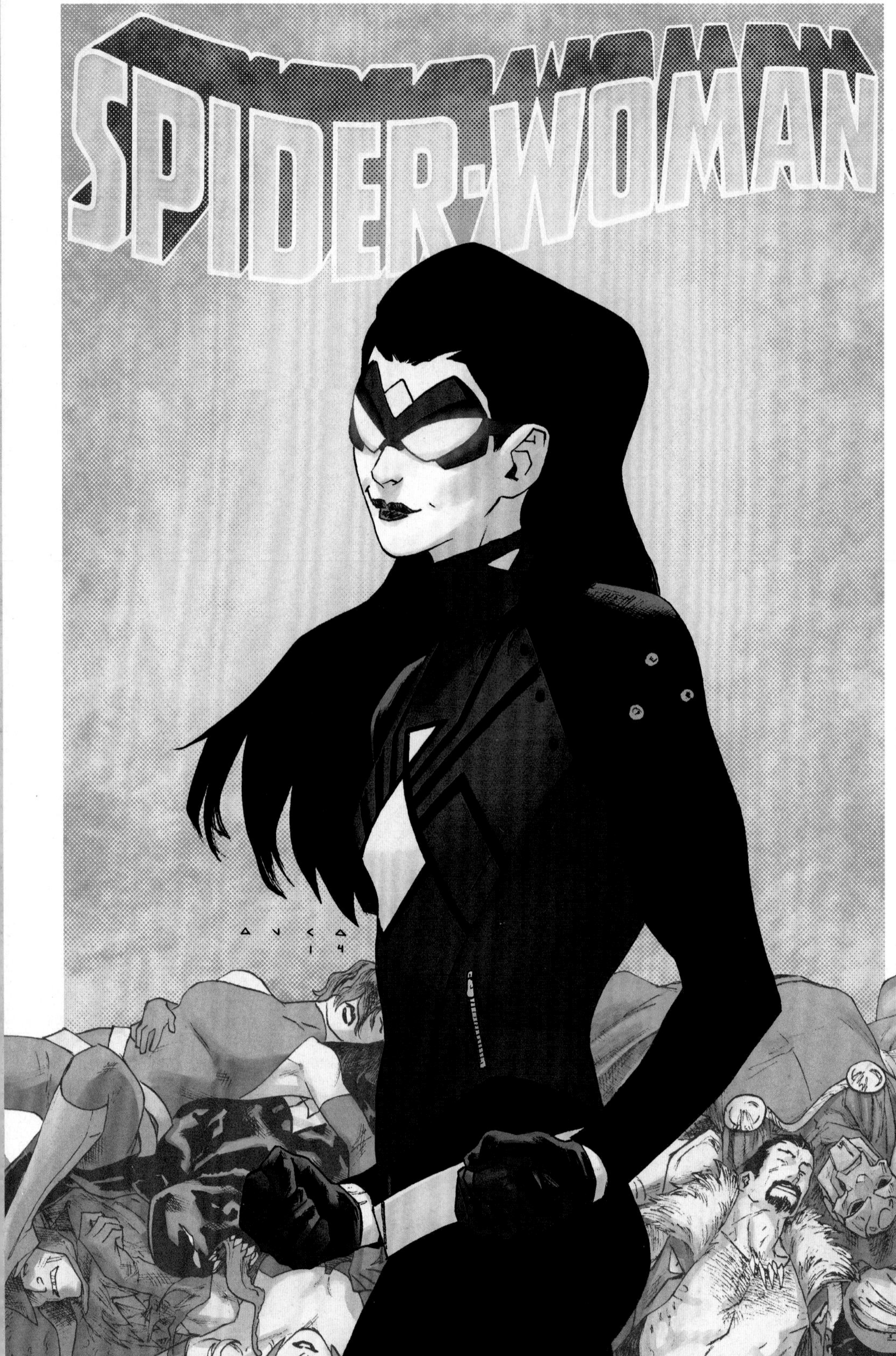
SPIDER-WOMAN
ANKA 14

#5 VARIANT COVER BY KRIS ANKA

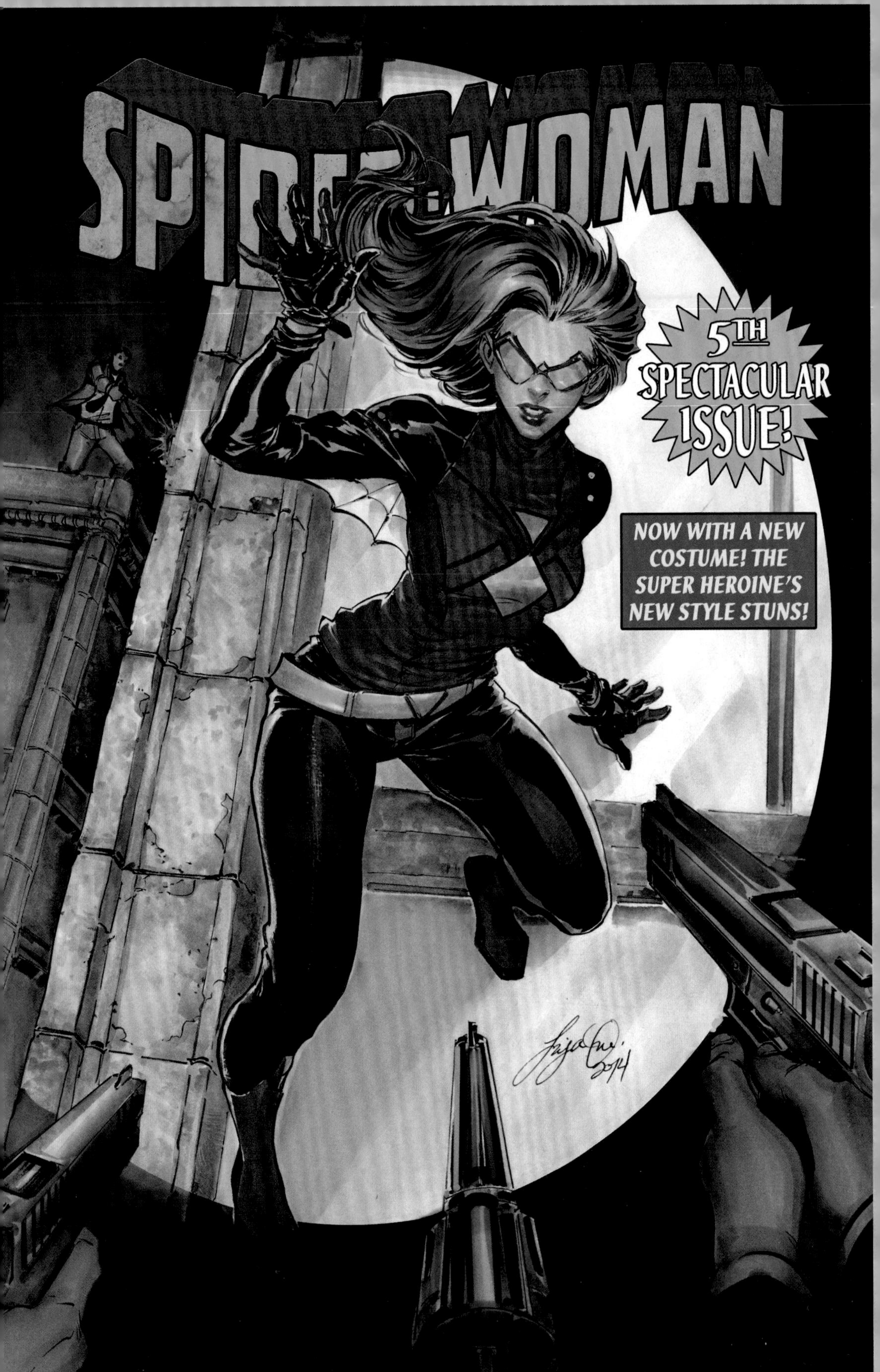

5TH SPECTACULAR ISSUE!
NOW WITH A NEW COSTUME! THE SUPER HEROINE'S NEW STYLE STUNS!